The Letters of John

9 STUDIES FOR INDIVIDUALS AND GROUPS

N. T. Wright

with Dale and Sandy Larsen

An imprint of InterVarsity Press
Downers Grove, Illinois

InterVarsity Press
P.O. Box 1400, Downers Grove, IL 60515-1426
World Wide Web: www.ivpress.com
E-mail: email@ivpress.com

InterVarsity Press® is the book-publishing division of InterVarsity Christian Fellowship/USA®, a movement of students and faculty active on campus at hundreds of universities, colleges and schools of nursing in the United States of America, and a member movement of the International Fellowship of Evangelical Students. For information about local and regional activities, write Public Relations Dept., InterVarsity Christian Fellowship/USA, 6400 Schroeder Rd., P.O. Box 7895, Madison, WI 53707-7895, or visit the IVCF website at <www.intervarsity.org>.

Design: Cindy Kiple
Cover image: Lynn Koenig/Getty Images

ISBN 978-0-8308-2198-3

Printed in the United States of America ∞

InterVarsity Press is committed to protecting the environment and to the responsible use of natural resources. As a member of Green Press Initiative we use recycled paper whenever possible. To learn more about the Green Press Initiative, visit <www.greenpressinitiative.org>.

P 20 19 18 17 16 15 14 13 12 11 10 9 8 7
Y 29 28 27 26 25 24 23 22 21 20

CONTENTS

Getting the Most Out of the Letters of John

"I have seen the future; and it works." That notorious statement was made by an American journalist, Lincoln Steffens, in 1919. He had just returned from a visit to the recently established Soviet Union, formed on Marxist principles after the Russian Revolution had swept away the old aristocracy and its method of government. Steffens echoed the hopes of millions in Europe and America. Perhaps this entirely new ideal, this new way of ordering human society, was the answer to all the old problems of tyranny and oppression. Perhaps this was indeed *the future,* the thing that would come to the rest of humanity as a great revelation, a great display of enlightened progress. We would all catch up one day; but for the moment Steffens, at least, had had a glimpse into that future and declared that it worked.

Subsequent history has revealed, of course, that Soviet Marxism only "worked" in the sense of achieving certain ends at the enormous cost of human lives. The Soviet system, like other revolutionary regimes, found it necessary to imprison or kill millions of its own subjects, as well as enslave several adjacent nations. When it finally came crashing down under its own dead weight in the late 1980s, it became apparent that it had been rotten and hollow inside for many years, perhaps all along.

But that sense Lincoln Steffens had of a glimpse of the future, of an advance display of the new world waiting to be born, is exactly the picture the apostle John offers in his short but glowing letter we call

1 John. The ancient Jews believed that world history was divided into two periods or ages. There was the *present age,* which was full of misery and suffering, injustice and oppression; and there was the *age to come,* the time when God would sort it all out, would put everything right and would in particular rescue his people from the evil they had suffered.

Now, John says, God has provided an advance display of this future! God has kept the age to come under wraps, waiting to reveal it at the right time. But the secret at the heart of the early Christian movement was that the age to come had already been revealed. The future had burst into the present, even though the present time wasn't ready for it. The word for that future was Life: Life as it was meant to be; Life in its full, vibrant meaning; a Life which death tried to corrupt, thwart and kill but a Life which had overcome death itself and was now on offer to anyone who wanted to come and take it. Life itself had come to life, had taken the form of a human being, coming into the present from God's future, coming to display God's coming age. And the name of that Life-in-person is of course Jesus.

John, the author of this and two other letters we will study in this guide (prepared with the help of Dale and Sandy Larsen, for which I am grateful), is most likely the same John who wrote the Gospel that bears his name. This would be the same John who was one of original twelve apostles. (For more on all these letters, also see my *The Early Christian Letters for Everyone* published by SPCK and Westminster John Knox, on which this guide is based. New Testament quotations in this guide are from my own translation, published as *The Kingdom New Testament* by HarperOne in the United States and published as *The New Testament for Everyone* by SPCK in England.)

In the first two letters, John writes against deceivers, false prophets, antimessiahs. We can't be sure exactly who these people were that John was challenging because there were so many religious movements, as well as political ones, in the first century. It's quite possible the false prophets John has in mind didn't belong to any particular group that we know of from elsewhere. But in several places John emphasizes the physicality of Jesus—that he had a body—and warns his readers to reject those who say Jesus did not come in the flesh. Such a belief looks suspiciously like one religious movement that came to be known as Gnosticism—a kind of religion that specialized in secret knowledge (from the Greek word *gnosis*), a knowledge revealed to the elect. According to this system of belief, by gaining this knowledge one might escape entirely from the physical world, and enter a realm of pure spirit.

Gnostics claimed there was some kind of manifestation of a "Jesus" who seemed to be human, even if he was not fully so. But they couldn't allow that this "Jesus" would actually die, be really dead. And because they claimed he didn't die, they also denied his bodily resurrection. For them the resurrection would have only had a spiritual dimension. Yet to deny his death and bodily resurrection was not just to deny something about Jesus. It was denying something about God. No other god, no other power, no other being in all the world loved like this, gave like this, died like this. All others win victories by fighting; this one, by suffering. All other gods exercise power by killing; this one, by dying.

John emphasizes that the Spirit enables us to bear witness to what the Father has done in sending the Son. He reminds us forcefully that such witness must of course come not in word only but also in deed, as we read in 1 John 3:18. Our love must come in the flesh, just as God's love did in Jesus.

SUGGESTIONS FOR INDIVIDUAL STUDY

1. As you begin each study, pray that God will speak to you through his Word.

2. Read the introduction to the study and respond to the "Open" question that follows it. This is designed to help you get into the theme of the study.

3. Read and reread the Bible passage to be studied. Each study is designed to help you consider the meaning of the passage in its context. The commentary and questions in this guide are based on my own translation of each passage found in the companion volume to

this guide in the For Everyone series on the New Testament (published by SPCK and Westminster John Knox).

4. Write your answers to the questions in the spaces provided or in a personal journal. Each study includes three types of questions: observation questions, which ask about the basic facts in the passage; interpretation questions, which delve into the meaning of the passage; and application questions, which help you discover the implications of the text for growing in Christ. Writing out your responses can bring clarity and deeper understanding of yourself and of God's Word.

5. Each session features selected comments from the For Everyone series. These notes provide further biblical and cultural background and contextual information. They are designed not to answer the questions for you but to help you along as you study the Bible for yourself. For even more reflections on each passage, you may wish to have on hand a copy of the companion volume from the For Everyone series as you work through this study guide.

6. Use the guidelines in the "Pray" section to focus on God, thanking him for what you have learned and praying about the applications that have come to mind.

SUGGESTIONS FOR GROUP MEMBERS

1. Come to the study prepared. Follow the suggestions for individual study mentioned above. You will find that careful preparation will greatly enrich your time spent in group discussion.

2. Be willing to participate in the discussion. The leader of your group will not be lecturing. Instead, she or he will be asking the questions found in this guide and encouraging the members of the group to discuss what they have learned.

3. Stick to the topic being discussed. These studies focus on a particular passage of Scripture. Only rarely should you refer to other portions of the Bible or outside sources. This allows for everyone to participate on equal ground and for in-depth study.

4. Be sensitive to the other members of the group. Listen attentively when they describe what they have learned. You may be surprised by their insights! Each question assumes a variety of answers. Many questions do not have "right" answers, particularly questions that aim at meaning or application. Instead the questions push us to explore the passage more thoroughly.

   When possible, link what you say to the comments of others. Also, be affirming whenever you can. This will encourage some of the more hesitant members of the group to participate.

5. Be careful not to dominate the discussion. We are sometimes so eager to express our thoughts that we leave too little opportunity for others to respond. By all means participate! But allow others to also.

6. Expect God to teach you through the passage being discussed and through the other members of the group. Pray that you will have an enjoyable and profitable time together, but also that as a result of the study you will find ways that you can take action individually and/or as a group.

7. It will be helpful for groups to follow a few basic guidelines. These guidelines, which you may wish to adapt to your situation, should be read at the beginning of the first session.

   - Anything said in the group is considered confidential and will not be discussed outside the group unless specific permission is given to do so.
   - We will provide time for each person present to talk if he or she feels comfortable doing so.
   - We will talk about ourselves and our own situations, avoiding conversation about other people.
   - We will listen attentively to each other.
   - We will be very cautious about giving advice.

Additional suggestions for the group leader can be found at the back of the guide.

The Word of Life

1 John 1:1–2:2

The very idea of God's new Life becoming a person and stepping forward out of the future into the present is so enormous, so breathtaking, that a tone of wonder, of hushed awe and reverence, becomes appropriate. That is what we find in the opening verses of 1 John. *That which was from the beginning* . . . pause and think about that for a moment . . . *which we have heard, which we have seen with our eyes, which we have gazed at* . . . pause again . . . your own eyes? You didn't just glimpse it, you gazed at it? Yes, says John, and what's more *our hands have handled* . . . you touched it, this Life? You touched *him*? You *handled* him? Yes, repeats John; we heard, saw and touched this from-the-beginning Life. We knew him. We were his friends.

And we still *are* his friends. Once the future has come into the present, the present is transformed forever. When you reflect on what it means, then you have to say this: we have seen the future, and it is full of light and life and joy and hope.

OPEN

Think of an unusual experience you have had—an amazing place you visited, an incredible meal you ate, a remarkable person you met. How would you go about explaining it to people who have not had the same experience?

STUDY

1. *Read 1 John 1:1-4.* How are the opening verses of this letter reminiscent of Genesis 1?

2. What is John trying to communicate by this similarity?

3. What does John declare as his reasons for writing this letter?

In verse 2 John writes, "We announce to you the life of God's coming age, which was with the father and was displayed to us." Unfortunately the word for "age" in 1:2 has often been translated as "eternal" or "eternity," which gives modern readers the idea that John and other early Christian writers who refer to God's new age were thinking of something "eternal" in the sense of "purely spiritual," something that had nothing to do with the world of space, time and matter. That's what people often hear when they read the phrase "eternal life," which is what most translations have at 1:2. But this is mistaken. John, like Paul, and indeed like Jesus himself, is thinking of the new age, the age to come, which God has promised.

They were in line with what ancient Jews believed—that world history, as mentioned at the beginning of this guide, was divided into two periods or ages. The present age was full of injustice and oppression, whereas in the age to come God would put everything right—in particular rescuing his people from the evil they had suffered.

4. Consider what you think of when you hear the word *fellowship* in Christian circles. How do your impressions compare with John's usage of the word *fellowship* in 1:3?

5. *Read 1 John 1:5–2:2.* What contrasts does John draw between darkness and light?

6. What deceptions does John warn against?

7. What are some ways we deceive ourelves about sin?

It's all very well for John to say that we have fellowship with God himself. But what if we have already ruined our lives by carelessness, stupidity or downright wickedness? We are—or ought to be—ashamed. If only we could hide or God would give us a chance to clean up! But that's not how it works. God is light, and in him is no darkness at all. The darkness which encroaches upon our messy, rebellious, unbelieving lives cannot survive in his sight. If we pretend to be in fellowship with him while walking in the dark (behaving in the less-than-human way we often choose), it's like telling lies.

8. What does John mean by the phrase "walk in the light" (1:7)?

Follow Christ

9. How does confession of sin bring an end to deception (1:6-9)?

We are forgiven

10. Throughout this passage what do we see that Jesus Christ does to resolve our dilemma?

11. How is having Jesus Christ pleading your cause before God radically different from pleading your own cause (2:1-2)?

From the very earliest days of Christian faith, Jesus' followers believed that his death had been the very thing the world had been waiting for. It was the ultimate sacrifice. The blood that flowed from Jesus' body as he hung on the cross was the very lifeblood of God himself, poured out to deal with sins in the way that all the animal sacrifices in the world could never do. That blood, that sacrificial death, that God-life given on our behalf and in our place, is available for all who "walk in the light." That doesn't mean we have to get our act together, morally speaking, before God can do anything. It means that when we consciously turn to the light—when we face up to what's gone wrong in the past and don't try to hide it, and when we are determined to live that way from now on—two things happen. First, we find ourselves sharing that intimate God-life, not only with God himself but with one another. Second, we find that Jesus' blood somehow makes us clean, pure and fresh inside.

12. In 1:1–2:2, John offers a sharp dose of reality and extraordinary good news. How are both a comfort?

PRAY

Reread 1:8-9, and ask God to show you which description fits you in his eyes.

Offer prayers of confession of sin, then prayers of gratitude to the One who pleads your cause before the Father—the Righteous One, Jesus the Messiah.

NOTE ON 1 JOHN 2:2

This verse is very near the heart of it all. It seems that John is writing to Jewish Christians who might have been tempted to suppose that Jesus, as Israel's Messiah, was the remedy for their problems, for their sins, and for them alone. Not a bit of it, says John. Jesus' sacrifice atones for our sins, "and not ours only, but those of the whole world." Just as God didn't remain content to be in fellowship only with his own son, but wanted to extend that fellowship to all those who met and followed Jesus; and just as John is writing this letter so that its readers may come to share in that same divine fellowship; so now all who know themselves to be forgiven through Jesus' death must look, not at their own privilege, but at the wider task. God intends to call more and more people into this fellowship.

2

THE NEW OLD COMMAND

1 John 2:3-14

If someone (like myself) has spent a long time studying Paul and then suddenly moves across to John, and particularly to 1 John, one is tempted to be a bit frustrated. Surely John should get on with it, say what he means and move on to the next point. But that isn't John's style. He is mulling it all over and wants his hearers to do so too. John's whole letter is repetitive, and yet it is also on the move. He keeps coming back to very nearly the same point, but at the same time he is moving forward. There is some kind of an ongoing narrative, but it isn't the type that moves from A to B to C to D in strict order. It's A with a bit of B, then A and B with a bit of C, then A, B and C with a bit of D and so on. So we shouldn't be surprised if we think we've heard it before. We probably have. The question is, what is the particular point that John is making this time?

OPEN

What stories or sayings do you find yourself repeating often? Why do you repeat them?

STUDY

1. *Read 1 John 2:3-11.* Obeying or disobeying God's commandments would appear to be a matter of externals—what we do or refrain from doing. How does John explain obedience as a matter of the heart (vv. 3-6)?

2. Why does obedience to God give us assurance that we know him?

3. John does not overtly state the "old command" (vv. 7-8). From the context, what is this command?

4. John says the old command is also the new command. But while there is similarity and continuity between the two, in what way is the new command actually new?

5. In verses 3-6 John writes that if we say we know God but don't keep his commands, we're liars. How does verse 9 offer a similar thought but in a different way?

6. John writes serious warnings about hating a family member in Christ (vv. 9-11). How are conflicts destructive for those on both sides of a dispute as well as for the church as a whole?

For John, as for Paul, and above all as for Jesus, the commandments are all summed up in one word: Love. The Life of God's New Age is revealed as the Love of God's New Age. All other commandments—the detail of what to do and not to do—are the outflowing of this love, the love which has been newly revealed in Jesus, the love which God now intends should be revealed in and through all those who follow Jesus.

7. Given John's warnings about hating a fellow believer, how should we respond instead when we find ourselves in deep disagreement with people in our fellowship or the church broadly?

8. *Read 1 John 2:12-14.* How does John's style of writing change from the preceding passage?

9. John addresses several groups of people. What does he say each group has known or experienced?

10. Following his stern warnings in 2:3-9, how are these words now an encouragement?

11. Sometimes when we sing hymns, the hymns tell a story. There is something satisfying about this. We feel we have been on a journey and have arrived somewhere. But in some traditions the songs we sing in church are deliberately repetitive. We use them as a way of meditation, of stopping on one point and mulling it over, of allowing something which is very deep and important to make an impact on us. Repetition can touch, deep down inside us, parts that other kinds of hymns cannot reach, or do not very often. In verses 12-14, John breaks into a sing-song, repetitive formula. Perhaps we shouldn't try to analyze it in strict terms but rather appreciate it as a meditation, a long, lingering gaze at his audience and what they need, at the way God works in people's lives. Perhaps it's only as we give ourselves to the strange, haunting repetition that the meaning will begin to sink down into us.

    As you let the repetition of these verses sink in, what effect does it have on you?

12. How do the themes in 2:12-14 offer a summary of what John has written about so far?

"You have conquered the evil one" (vv. 13-14). John will have more to say about this. But we note this element just in case God's love is starting to sound cozy or easy. Love demands a victory over the old enemy who does his best work through human hatred.

PRAY

Pray that God will shine his light into every corner of your life, revealing sin and cleansing you of it so that you will walk in light rather than darkness.

Pray that more and more you will obey the new command which is also the old command: to love people as God loves them.

As mentioned above, verses 12-14 are a kind of hymn. Sing hymns or spiritual songs that pick up one of the themes from these verses you mentioned in answer to question 12.

3

You Have the Anointing

1 John 2:15-29

In his book *People of the Lie,* the late psychotherapist M. Scott Peck described some cases of extreme dysfunctional behavior. In much of his work he could track the causes of unhappiness in the people who came to consult him, but there were other cases where something much more sinister seemed to be at work. Peck was not prepared for this. All his training in secular psychiatry and psychotherapy had ruled out the word *evil* from his vocabulary. These unusual cases convinced Peck that he was wrong. The people he wrote about had taken a few more steps than most of us down a particular road. They had lied to themselves; they had lied to others; they had started believing and living by their lies. They had thereby invoked a kind of anti-power, the power of the Lie, an evil which was more than the sum total of their own deceits.

It is "people of the lie" that John now warns against. He isn't a psychotherapist, but he puts his finger on one great Lie above all and warns that those who accept this lie and live by it are a corrupting and dangerous influence. Those who do not believe the lie must learn to trust God's work in them, the work because of which they believe the truth.

OPEN

What damage have you seen a lie cause?

STUDY

1. *Read 1 John 2:15-29.* Generations of Western Christians have supposed that Christians are meant to renounce "the world" in any and every sense: natural enjoyments, the pleasures of food and drink, the created order itself. Perhaps, they think, "the world"—this world of space, time and matter—is actually evil! Perhaps we should try to live as though we were pure spirits? No: that's not what John has in mind. As in some other early Christian writings, "the world" here, like the word *flesh* when Paul uses it, means "the world as it places itself over against God." The world remains God's good creation, and as such is to be enjoyed with thanksgiving, as Paul says (1 Timothy 4:4-5).

   The command "Do not love the world, or the things that are in the world" (v. 15) refers not to the physical stuff of this world but to "the world" as it is in rebellion against God: "the world" as the combination of things that draw us away from God. The flesh, the eyes, life itself—all can become idols. Like all idols they demand more and more from those who worship them. All idolatry draws us into the lie, or if we're not careful, into the Lie. We must celebrate all the goodness of the world, all God's goodness to us within his creation. But we must not worship it.

   What are some present-day examples of the values of "the world" which John denounces?

2. What are practical things we can do to receive everything with thanksgiving but still not come under the control of "the world"?

3. In verses 18-19 John tells us how to recognize an *antimessiah* (which is the translation of a Hebrew word we know better in its Greek form *antichrist*). Jesus had warned that "false messiahs" would arise after him and deceive many people, perhaps even some from among his own followers. The complex world of first-century Judaism, particularly in Palestine, was full of people and movements claiming that God was acting at last in *this* way, in *that* way, through *this* movement, through *that* person. Many of the early Christians must have wondered, as they heard about a new movement in a neighboring town: *Can this be Jesus, back again?* Or even: *Perhaps this is the real thing, and all that extraordinary business about Jesus was just a preliminary, a warm-up act?* Some of those who had been with Jesus' followers did go off after these new movements. John says that these movements are antimessianic movements! They may have started out within our fellowship, but they left, because the heart of the matter was not in them.

   What, according to John in verses 18-23, characterizes antimessiahs?

4. How does John encourage his readers to protect themselves from antimessiahs?

5. What does it look like, practically speaking, for us to abide in the ways John mentions?

6. How can abiding in this way offer protection from the deceptions of the antimessiahs?

7. Why do you think "new" versions of Christianity are appealing to people?

8. The true follower of Jesus the Messiah has been anointed by his Holy Spirit (vv. 20-21, 26-27) so that a real change of heart and character has happened. One of the key symptoms of that change is the recognition that Jesus is indeed the Messiah. He truly is the Son of God. The antimessianic movements are bound to deny this. If they don't, they have no reason to set up a new movement in the first place! The greatest lie of all is to deny the Father and the Son (v. 22). To deny that Jesus really is God's son is to cut off access to the Father as well, since we truly know the Father only through the Son. Don't do it, says John. These people are deceiving you (v. 26). You know this deep down, because that "anointing" remains within you. Without anyone teaching you from the outside, you know the truth deep within.

   In the Greek, the word for *anointing* is the same root word as *Messiah*. The Messiah is, literally translated, "the anointed one," God's anointed king, his one and only "son." You have been *Messiah-ed,* you have been *anointed,* so you must not be deceived by their denials. They are not only denying that Jesus is the Messiah; they are denying everything that makes you, now, who you truly are. This is the lie that will, if given its head, eat its way like rust into the imagination and heart of a Christian, or a church.

How then does being anointed by the Holy Spirit help us recognize false claims about God and Christ?

9. No doubt many different people have taught you the Word of God: your parents, Sunday school teachers, pastors, Bible study leaders, authors and others. We all appreciate those people and have benefited from their teaching. John himself is teaching his readers through this letter. Then how do you explain his statement that "you do not need to have anyone teach you" (v. 27)?

10. In verse 28 John calls on his readers to abide in Christ "so that when he is revealed we may have boldness and may not be put to shame before him at his royal appearing." What are your feelings about the prospect of Christ's return: apprehension, joy, confidence, uncertainty or something else?

11. What is the promise for those who are still on earth at Christ's appearing (vv. 28-29)?

12. What does it mean emotionally and spiritually that we won't be put to shame but can count God as our father?

PRAY

Pray for wisdom and discernment to not be taken in by antimessiahs who deny that Jesus is God's anointed one. Thank God for the Holy Spirit who teaches you the truth.

Pray that you will think and live differently from those who are in love with "the world."

NOTE ON 1 JOHN 2:28

The whole passage, with these stark warnings, is framed within two short paragraphs which set the discussion in its proper context. This is the expectation of Jesus' return, his "royal appearing" (v. 28). Think of his appearing as his "coming," if you like, but don't be misled by that into imagining that he is at present far away from you; rather, he is very near, but hidden. When he "appears," then he will utterly transform the whole creation. And when that happens, the way of the present world will disappear (v. 17). That is why we are commanded "not to love the world" (v. 15).

God's Children Now

1 John 3

Not long ago I heard of a man who had gone blind in early adult life. He had subsequently got married and had children. They could all see him, but he had never set eyes on them. Then one day the medical breakthrough came, the operation was a success, and he could see at last. What an amazing moment—to come face to face, eye to eye, with the people he had loved but never seen.

There is something transformative about eye contact. People who spend a lot of time looking at one another sometimes come to resemble each other. Perhaps this is because they are instinctively copying one another's facial expressions until their muscles and tissue begin to be reshaped in that way. Imagine beginning that process at last after years of love which had been expressed through words and touch but never before through sight.

If we have any love for Jesus right now, our deepest longing ought to be that we would come face to face with him at last, to see his smile, to catch his facial expression, to begin to know him in a whole new way.

OPEN

Whose face would you like to see again, and why?

STUDY

1. *Read 1 John 3:1-10.* What does John say are characteristics (present and future) of God's children?

2. John says, "When he is revealed we shall be like him" (v. 2). In what ways do you think we will be like Jesus?

3. What is the benefit for us today in being reminded of the glorious future that is ahead?

Thinking about our glorious future and our resurrection, or about God's whole new world in which our resurrection will take place, is very difficult. Because the present world is God's good creation, we know it will be *like this, only more so:* without corruption, decay, death, injustice, illness, sorrow and shame. But what will *we* be like? Perhaps we should say *like we are, only much more so.* More gloriously physical, not less. With resurrected bodies, but not ones that are subject to sickness or death. Able to celebrate the joys of God's world but no longer lured or seduced into abusing them, lusting after them or worshiping them. Most important of all, we will be like Jesus. Think of the risen Jesus: the same, yet strangely different. He had gone through death and still bore the marks of the nails, yet he was never going to die again. He seemed to belong in both worlds, heaven and earth, at once—and that will be appropriate for the new world, since heaven and earth will have come together completely and forever.

4. What does John tell us in this passage about the person who "goes on sinning"?

5. In verse 7 John says, "Don't let anyone deceive you." What deceptive things is John referring to?

6. What deceptive things are said today about sin and righteousness?

7. *Read 1 John 3:11-24.* Cain—one of the sorriest and saddest cases in the Bible, I think—makes a cameo appearance here in verse 12, as the example of a hatred which led all the way to murder. For Cain (Genesis 4), that hatred took the form of jealousy. He brought an offering to God: nothing special, just what came to hand. Abel, however, brought an offering of the very best. God, not surprisingly, was pleased with Abel, not with Cain. (We're not told exactly how God made that clear.) And Cain, equally unsurprisingly, was angry. He'd been shown up, and by his younger brother at that! So, despite further warning, he killed him.

   The people to whom John writes are probably not in the habit of murdering other people. What is the point John is making so forcefully here (vv. 12-15)?

8. As mentioned, Cain's hatred took the form of jealousy. What are other ways hatred can be shown?

9. John says the opposite of hatred and murder is showing love by saving the life of another (v. 16). What is one practical way that you can lay down your life for a neighbor, stranger, family member or coworker this week?

10. Think of times that people have shown love to you not only "in word, or in speech, but in deed and in truth" (v. 18). How did their actions affect you?

We are who we are as Christians simply and solely because of God's love, because Jesus, out of love, laid down his life for us. Love is not something extra tacked on to the gospel. Love *is* the gospel. Of course it's possible to water the whole thing down into a vague, fuzzy benevolence. But it's equally possible to think of "the gospel" in mechanistic terms, as a system of salvation that people plug into by learning certain doctrines and saying certain words, and to think of love—actual kindness, generosity of spirit, going-the-second-mile kind of love for friend and foe alike—as an optional extra, a secondary hobby for when you've got some spare time. Not so. Love is at the very center. Not to love, both when obvious opportunity offers and when it doesn't, is to show that God's love is not, after all, abiding in you.

11. We might expect John to write something like, "If our hearts condemn us, they are accurate because we are all sinners." Instead he writes, "If our hearts condemn us, God is greater than our hearts" (v. 20). What is John communicating then by that statement?

12. What is the connection between prayer and the assurance of God's forgiveness (vv. 20-22)?

All Christians will sometimes wonder whether they have let God and other Christians down so badly that they no longer belong. This is what John calls "having your heart condemn you." When we realize the utter and absolute demand of love, we may well find that our hearts do condemn us. We simply haven't lived like that. But here is the mercy of God (v. 20): when that happens, "God is greater than our hearts. He knows everything." We can relax. He's in control, and we wouldn't even be experiencing this inner condemnation unless there was the work of God's Spirit (v. 24), stirring us up to glimpse the life of love, even if that glimpse shows us how far we have fallen short.

PRAY

We know that God is living, abiding in us, because he has given us his Spirit (v. 24). God's own Spirit; Jesus' own Spirit; living *in us*. This is breathtaking, but without it there is no true Christianity. Actually, we should say that it's breath*giving*. Perhaps those of us who have been Christians a long time should pause and reflect on what it might be like if we simply didn't have that gentle but powerful breath, that still, small voice, checking us as we are about to do something wrong, encouraging us in doing what is right, nudging us toward someone who needs help, reminding us it's time to pray, helping us to be patient in difficult circumstances, and above all holding Jesus regularly and gloriously before our eyes.

Give thanks for the Spirit abiding in us.

Since you can approach God boldly and with complete confidence, what would you ask him to do for you and for others? Consider 1 John 3:21-22 and pray accordingly.

God Is Love

1 John 4

One of my favorite stories from the Old Testament is found in 2 Kings 6. The context is one of continual hostilities and sometimes warfare between Israel and Syria. The Syrian king has discovered that all his plans and deliberations are being revealed to the king of Israel by Elisha. So the king of Syria sends his army to take Elisha captive. The next day Elisha's servant discovers that all around their city is an army with horses and chariots. He runs back to Elisha in a panic. What are they going to do? Elisha replies, "Don't be afraid; there are more with us than there are with them." Then Elisha prays that God would open the young man's eyes, and the lad sees the reality: the mountain is full of horses and chariots of fire all around Elisha.

The people to whom John is writing are in danger of being confused or even blown off course by all the different ideas, claims and would-be prophets swirling around them. From the hints in this passage and elsewhere, we can figure out enough to see what John's readers might see as they, like Elisha's servant, come out of the house in the morning and stare in dismay at the forces ranged against them.

OPEN

When have you felt overwhelmed and yet sensed God's reassurance that he is with you?

STUDY

1. *Read 1 John 4:1-6.* John instructs his readers to "test the spirits to see whether they are from God" (v. 1). How are they to discern the difference between true and false spirits?

2. Where do we find "the spirit of the antimessiah" today (v. 3)?

3. Why is it so important for Christians to "test the spirits"?

4. John writes that "the one who is in you is greater than the one who is in the world" (v. 4). Why do you think believers so often forget about that reality?

5. How would you suggest that a believer keep the truth of verse 4 in mind?

The problem with false prophets is that you can't tell them apart from the true ones at first sight. They seem devout; they seem reasonable; they claim to have a word from God; so who are we to disagree? But not everyone who claims to be a prophet is a prophet in fact. You need to listen carefully and sift and weigh what you hear. Such people are unlikely to come out directly with curses or obviously absurd teaching. But gradually, as you listen, you may discern a fatal flaw. *They don't really believe that Jesus the Messiah has come in the flesh.* Agreeing that Jesus the Messiah has come in the flesh is the crucial test. It is not an extra bit added on to the Christian message. As John wrote in his Gospel, it is the vital, central point: "The Word became flesh, and lived among us" (John 1:14). Take that away, and true Christian faith crashes to the ground. That's why any spirit that makes someone deny that Jesus has come in the flesh is the spirit of the antimessiah.

6. *Read 1 John 4:7-21.* The word *love* or some form of it occurs no fewer than twenty-seven times in these fifteen verses. What is the connection between human love and God's love?

7. John's statement "God is love" (vv. 8 and 16) could be taken as an abstract philosophical statement. What takes his statement out of the abstract (vv. 9-11)?

8. What can our love—or lack of love—be taken as evidence of, and why (vv. 13-21)?

The Christian faith grows directly out of, and must directly express, the belief that in Jesus the Messiah, the one true God has revealed himself to be love incarnate. Those who hold this faith and embrace it as the means of their own hope and life must themselves reveal the selfsame fact before the watching world. Love incarnate must be the badge that the Christian community wears, the sign not only of who they are but of who their God is.

9. John says we should not look to the day of judgment with fear. How does love drive out fear (vv. 16-18)?

10. "We love, because he first loved us" is one of the most well-known verses in this letter. How has experiencing God's love for you given you the motivation and ability to love God and others in turn?

Our love must "come in the flesh" just as God's love did. If you say you love God, but don't love your brother or sister (a fellow member of the Christian community), you are quite simply telling lies. The same door that opens to let out your love to God is the door that opens to let out love to your neighbor. If you're not doing the latter, you're not doing the former. Who can live up to this?

But in verses 17 and 18 John moves into almost lyrical mode as he talks, not about the fear of being found out, of failing to come up to the mark, but of the boldness and confidence that we shall have on the day of judgment. He does not say that we have this boldness and confidence because we look away from ourselves and simply trust in God's all-powerful, all-conquering love. No. He says that "just as he is, so are we within this world." He means that if God revealed himself in the world by turning his love into flesh and blood, when we do the same we should realize that we are "completing" God's love. What operates through us will be the true love of the true God. Love that has been made complete in this way leaves no room for fear. Once you learn to give yourself to others as God gave himself to us, there is nothing to be afraid of any more, just a completed circle of love.

11. In verses 20-21, John sounds a note he has intoned before—we can't claim to love God if we hate our brothers and sisters in Christ. Recently someone I was talking to, commenting gloomily on various experiences of actual church life, suggested that churches should have a "danger" sign outside, warning people to expect nasty, gossipy, snide conversation and behavior if they came in. Why are Christian groups, ironically, so often breeding grounds for such problematic conduct?

12. This week, how can you show love to others even when there are tensions or problems?

PRAY

Pray that the reality of God's life in you will be more and more evident to the people around you.

Make the effort to turn your prayers away from the abstract and think of specific people you have trouble loving. Pray for those people and for yourself, that relationships will be built or rebuilt.

NOTE ON 1 JOHN 4:2

As mentioned at the beginning of this guide in "Getting the Most Out of the Letters of John," to say that Jesus had not come in the flesh looks suspiciously like one branch at least of what came to be known as Gnosticism—a kind of religion that specialized in secret "knowledge" (*gnosis*). By gaining this knowledge it is thought that one might escape entirely from the physical world, and enter a realm of pure spirit.

For people who embraced this teaching—and it can be made to sound, for a while at least, quite like some bits of the genuine Christian message—it was out of the question that Jesus, the Messiah, should really have come "in the flesh." He was surely, they thought, a spiritual being. He couldn't have compromised that spiritual identity by having anything to do with "flesh," the sordid, dirty, physical stuff, that needed to eat and drink, to urinate and defecate, to sleep and even—horror of all horrors!—to die.

And so, when they talked about Jesus, it wasn't the real Jesus Gnostics were referring to. It was someone who only seemed to be a human like the rest of us. They made up stories about how he hadn't really died, because he hadn't really been a genuine, fleshly human all along.

For Gnostics, Jesus was a spiritual being who came to teach that things are not what they seem, that the world as we see it is deceptive, and that there's a conspiracy going on. The powers that are in control are actually very dark, covering up the truth. Gnostics claim Jesus taught that if you look within yourself you will see that there is a divine spark which your outward trappings of culture and upbringing have probably squashed. By following this you can escape this world altogether.

The four Gospels (which have every historical reason to claim that they go back to Jesus himself—in contrast to the Gnostic documents) are instead about a very Jewish first-century movement. The actual Jesus movement was not about God telling us to forget this world and discover your inner reality instead. Rather God says he is reclaiming this world, that it is a good and wonderful place. And God calls us, as part of this creation, as people made in his image, to be reborn and to discover redemption. Gnosticism is not about forgiveness or redemption but self-discovery. It says we are actually okay just as we are.

Gnosticism is still alive and well in many forms today. While *The Da Vinci Code* might be an obvious cultural example of putting forth conspiracy theories and a hidden history of Christianity (with flimsy historical underpinnings), there are others. Too many Christians downplay or denigrate the importance of our physical existence and that of God's creation. Heaven is the really important place, not this earth. As the old song says, "This world is not my home. I'm just a-passin' through."

In contrast, Jesus taught the very Jewish idea of the kingdom of God coming on earth as in heaven, that God has a love for the creation and that bodily resurrection is real. Loving God matters, but so does loving our physical neighbors. God came in the flesh in Jesus. We are also to come to our needy, broken world in the flesh as God's redeemed creatures.

Faith Conquers

1 John 5:1-12

The first time I went snorkeling on a tropical reef, I was overwhelmed by the sight. All around me were hundreds of fish of all shapes and sizes and particularly colors. It was like a kaleidoscope. Electric blues, vivid yellows, bright reds and many, many more. The fish were up to all kinds of tricks, too, in ways characteristic of their particular species. After a few minutes of having my mind blown by the sight, I thought: *I must go back to the boat, get a notebook and write down what I've just seen.* And then I thought: *typical scholar, wanting to record everything. Just relax and enjoy the show.*

By this stage of the first letter of John, the reader may be starting to feel as I did snorkeling on the Great Barrier Reef. So many points are coming and going that it is hard to keep track of where we are. John is producing variations on what he's already said, and then variations on the variations. Why not just sit back and enjoy what is now familiar music? But just when we might be in danger of thinking, *Yes, yes, you've said this before,* a striking new idea emerges. *Everything fathered by God conquers the world.* What is this about? Why should we want not just to resist the blandishments of the world but to overcome it?

OPEN

What do you wish you could overcome?

STUDY

1. *Read 1 John 5:1-12.* What does John say is true of those who believe that Jesus is the Messiah, the Son of God?

2. John writes that loving God means keeping his commandments and that God's commandments "are no trouble" (v. 3). What does he mean by that?

3. Most of us would say we find it difficult to keep God's commandments. How do verses 4-5 enlarge John's meaning?

4. As mentioned before, when John says "the world" he does not mean the physical stuff of our existence. It is instead the source of temptation; it distracts us from God. But in addition, it is an active power for evil. The world resents the arrival of its own creator who claims his rightful lordship over it. In what sense, then, does our faith overcome the world?

5. What are the most troubling manifestations of the world (in John's sense) in our own everyday world?

6. How can our faith then overcome these influences and forces around us?

While many translations render verse 4 as "everyone" born of God conquers the world, it is more literally "everything fathered by God conquers the world." What does that mean, and how does it happen? To begin with, why does John say "everything" rather than "everyone"? My guess is that he is referring not only to the human beings who have been fathered by God (v. 1) but to that which results from their life and work: the things they do, as well as the people they are.

So what is this conquest and how does it come about? In John's Gospel, Jesus speaks of "the world's ruler" being "thrown out" (John 12:31), and after warning the disciples that they will face persecution in the world, he concludes, "But cheer up; I have conquered the world!" (John 16:33). Jesus' crucifixion and death are the means by which he is conquering the world, even though it looks for the moment as though the world is conquering him. *The victory that conquers the world is the saving death of Jesus.* And those who by faith cling to the God who is made known personally in and as the Jesus who died on the cross—they share that victory, that conquest of the world.

7. Think of a situation right now in which it looks like good is losing. How does this portion of John's letter speak to that situation?

8. How has God borne witness to his Son (vv. 6-11)?

In John's Gospel, the writer emphasizes that when the centurion pierced Jesus' side with his spear, water and blood came out (John 19:34). The writer says this is something he can personally vouch for. His witness is true. The death of Jesus, with the water and the blood already separated, shows beyond doubt that his death was real. It gives the lie to any who say that he didn't really die or that he wasn't really fully human, "come in the flesh." John is now coming back to his controversy with the antimessianic teachers, who denied that Jesus had truly come "in the flesh." They were prepared to acknowledge a figure called "Jesus" who seemed to be human, but they couldn't allow that this "Jesus" would actually die, be really dead. That is the point to which the Spirit bears witness, through the testimony in the Gospel narrative and in the work of the Spirit in the individual hearts and minds of believers.

9. John keeps emphasizing that Jesus came in the flesh. Why would it not have been adequate for Jesus to have simply been a pure spirit as some claimed? Why does this make a difference for us that he came in a physical body?

10. What is the "life" that marks the differences between those who have the Son and those who do not (vv. 10-12)?

11. What evidence do you see and experience that you have "the life of the age to come" (v. 11)?

PRAY

Pray about the ways you desire to overcome the influences of the world on you. Thank Jesus for his death and resurrection that have overcome the world, and for the help and hope available to you in him today.

Give thanks for "the life of the age to come" that is within you now.

NOTE ON 1 JOHN 5:7

The Authorized (King James) Version translated from a manuscript in which someone had added, in verse 7, words which are found nowhere else, introducing the "trinitarian" formula: "there are three that bear witness in heaven, the father, the word and the holy spirit; and these three are one." It is important to say both that these words form no part of the original letter and that John would undoubtedly have agreed with them.

NOTE ON 1 JOHN 5:11

I mentioned the following in regard to 1 John 1:2, and it bears repeating here. The Greek word for "age" found in 5:11 has often been translated as "eternal" or "eternity." Thus 5:11 should be translated, "This is the witness: God has given us the life of the age to come, and this life is in his son." Without this, modern readers have the misimpression that John and other early Christian writers who refer to God's new age were thinking of something "eternal" in the sense of "purely spiritual," rather than something concerning the world of space, time and matter. That's what people often hear when they read the phrase "eternal life," which is what many translations have in 5:11. But this is mistaken. John has in mind a new life we live now, not in some non-material existence in "heaven."

John, Paul and Jesus were in line with what ancient Jews believed—that world history was divided into two periods or ages. There was the present age which was full of misery and suffering, injustice and oppression; and there was the age to come, the time when God would sort it all out, would put everything right and would in particular rescue his people from the evil they had suffered.

The True God

1 John 5:13-21

The Creator has brought his future purposes up into the present. That is why something radically new has been launched upon the world, even at the drastic cost of God's own Son. That is why sharp conflict has come into being between those who represent this new life and those who are desperately trying to contain the new wine in old bottles, to insist that nothing quite so drastic has actually happened. What then for those who find themselves caught up in this extraordinary and unprecedented overlap of the two ages? John amplifies what he said earlier and he echoes promises made by Jesus. Those who believe in Jesus, those who abide in God, can pray with a new, bold confidence.

OPEN

What do you pray for with confidence?

When do your prayers lack confidence, and why?

STUDY

1. *Read 1 John 5:13-21.* Why does John say we can have confidence in our prayers (vv. 13-15)?

2. Why might a Christian doubt that he or she has "the life of the age to come" (v. 13)?

3. How do you discern whether you are praying "according to his will" (v. 14)?

4. Most of our prayers concern the future, what we want to see happen or what we want God to do for us or for someone else. When we pray to God about the future, in what sense do we "already possess the requests we have asked from him" (v. 15)?

   Those who believe in Jesus, who abide in God, stand at the place where heaven and earth meet. They are encouraged to draw down the blessings of heaven into the life of earth, and to know as they make their requests that they have already been granted—even though, as Scripture itself and Christian experience both teach, they may be granted in ways one had not expected.

5. How is verse 16 an encouragement to keep praying even when we see people going in a wrong direction?

It's hard to know exactly where John draws the line between sin which is "deadly" and sin which is "not deadly" (vv. 16-17). Perhaps he means that those who deny that Jesus has come in the flesh have committed a sin which puts them beyond the reach of redemption, since they have cut off the branch from which the fresh shoots of rescue-promises are growing.

6. One of the comforting things about verses 16-17 is the light they shed on verse 18. Without this, we might suppose that John thinks all Christians have stopped sinning altogether; with it, it is clear that he means, as I translate it, "everyone fathered by God *does not go on sinning.*" It is the continuous habit of life that concerns John. Clearly he would rather one did not sin at all; but occasional sins, a blip on the chart, can be prayed for, can be confessed and forgiven. They are quite different from the hard-hearted sin which carries on regardless, and which, as in Romans 1:32, even comes to see the action in question as not sinful at all.

   In verse 18 John twice uses the phrase "fathered by God." Who is he referring to in each case, and what is the connection between the two halves of the verse?

7. As he draws his letter to a close, John writes that "the whole world is under the power of the evil one" (v. 19). It doesn't sound like he is going to wrap things up in a positive or hopeful way; but as you consider his letter as a whole, what gives you hope for continuing to live in such a world?

Believers are "everyone fathered by God," but Jesus is "The One *par excellence* who is Fathered by God." Jesus will keep believers under his protection, so that the evil one, who for the moment retains power over the world, cannot do them harm. It may not always feel like that. But part of the victory of faith (1 John 5:4) is believing that Jesus has in fact defeated all the powers that might endanger us, and that we are "in him" and so "in the truth," as opposed to being "in the lie," the lie of which the world has done its best to persuade us.

8. Sometimes a short story writer tells a story cleverly so as to lead us in one direction, and then, with the last sentence, reveals something which changes everything. I don't think John intends to play a trick on his readers, but the final sentence of this remarkable little letter causes us to think back through what he has written to see where this apparently new idea comes from.

   Why do you think John concludes his letter with the admonition "Children, guard yourselves against idols" (v. 21)?

9. What are the most troublesome or persistent idols which we must guard against?

10. What are some marks of "the life of the age to come" (v. 20) which you most admire in other Christians?

11. What marks of "the life of the age to come" do you hope other people see in you?

PRAY

Taking 1 John 5:13-15 for a model, pray confidently and boldly for other people, especially for anyone you know under the sway of sin.

Pray confidently and boldly for yourself, that you will be guarded against the idolatry of false ideas about God.

Pray confidently and boldly that the "life of the age to come" will be obvious to those who meet you, here and now

NOTE ON 1 JOHN 5:21

Certainly John would not want his readers to have anything to do with pagan worship. But by "idols" he means something more subtle than that, more in keeping with what he has been saying all through. The point of insisting on God's love, on the vital importance of loving one another and above all on Jesus the Messiah having come in the flesh, is that this isn't just one necessary truth among many. It is the sign that we are actually worshiping the true God *rather than some manmade idol*. The idol in question would not be carved and placed in a temple. The idol in question would be called "God" and might be worshiped by some people who called themselves "Christians." But it would actually be a different god, not the true one at all. The true God is known by the fact that he sent his Son to come into the world in human flesh to die a genuine human death. Deny that, and you're not just denying something about Jesus. You're denying something about God. This, then, is "the true God," and this life which we have in him is indeed "the life of the age to come" (v. 20).

The Sign of Life

2 John

I was going to quote a Beatles song, but then I remembered that you have to pay a lot of money even to quote a single line. But the song is well enough known, declaring that the only thing one might require in life is love. It's ironic, of course, that you have to pay through the nose to quote a song whose whole message is that love matters and money doesn't.

Just about the time the Beatles were making their song popular, another slogan, "Make love, not war," rang from those protesting against the war in Vietnam. The trouble is, of course, that "love" covers far too many things in our language today. Throughout the whole New Testament, not least in the teaching of Jesus himself, "love" was never meant to mean one of the main things which, sadly, it has come to mean today—tolerance. You should never say that anything is actually wrong: that's "unloving." You should never say, either, that one way of doing things is right; that is "arrogant." Here, then, is another irony: such a position is in fact extremely intolerant of people who take a more definite stance—which includes the mainstream adherents of many traditional faiths.

OPEN

How would you define *love*?

STUDY

1. *Read 2 John 1-6.* John the Elder—which seems to have been a title given to the aging apostle—is writing to another church, addressing it cryptically as the Chosen Lady. At the end of the letter he refers to the church where he himself is based as the Chosen Sister. We have no idea which churches these were or why he referred to them in this way. Perhaps danger was at hand, and the more he could make the letter look like an ordinary message within a family, the safer he and his readers would be. The point of what John says in this first part of the letter is that he has seen the signs of life in some members of this other church.

   What is John's apparent attitude toward the recipients of his letter?

2. In verses 1-3, John mentions *truth* no fewer than four times. What are the different dimensions of truth that John refers to?

3. John equates love with behaving in accordance with God's commandments (vv. 4-6). How is that similar to or different than your definition of love?

The great truth which is unveiled in the gospel of Jesus is that the powerful, redeeming love of God is the motor that drives the cosmos, and that those who are discovering the truth, or rather being discovered by it, must learn to let that love flow through them to their fellow Christians and to the world around. This is the commandment above all others, emphasized by Jesus himself and by one early Christian writer after another. Love is what matters. Love is not the optional extra to be added when everything else is sorted out. It is the thing that goes on round and round, like blood circulating in a healthy living body, or to and fro, like good strong breathing.

4. *Read 2 John 7-13.* John has already commended his readers for "walking in the truth" (v. 4). Still he urges them to watch out for themselves concerning the deceivers (v. 8). If they are walking in the truth, why would they still need to be warned against deception?

5. The deception John warns against is that Jesus has not come in the flesh. What variations of this and other deceptive views of Jesus are being presented today?

6. What is the most appropriate way to respond to these viewpoints?

7. In verse 9, what do you think is the significance of John's phrase "anyone who goes out on their own"?

8. In verses 10-11 John issues harsh warnings. How do you reconcile his earlier words about love (vv. 5-6) with his directive to refuse to welcome or even greet false teachers?

9. As he concludes, John brings his letter back to the warm mood with which it opened (vv. 12-13). What is the value of face-to-face communication over the written word?

10. Taking this letter as a whole, what are John's hopes for "the Chosen Lady and her children"?

11. What hopes do you have for your Christian community?

PRAY

Pray that you and your Christian community will continue to walk in the truth and love.

Pray for discernment, that you will detect false teachings about Jesus, no matter how attractive.

Pray for people who are spiritually deceived, that they would see and submit to the truth in Christ.

Welcome the Family

3 John

Apart from the journeys of Paul, we know very little of the movements of Christian leaders, teachers and missionaries in the first two or three generations of the church. Yet from the evidence we have, such people were numerous, and often on the move. The cheerful courage and faith of such first-century missionaries and of those who gave them hospitality (perhaps arousing suspicious questions from neighbors) ought to remind us that following Jesus is expected to be an adventure. New things will happen. New people will come into our lives, and even though they were strangers a moment before, suddenly we realize we are part of the same family. At the heart of the New Testament vision of the church is that sense of *family,* of being brothers and sisters.

OPEN

When have you been especially grateful for Christian hospitality?

When have you been especially glad that you extended Christian hospitality to someone?

STUDY

1. *Read 3 John 1-8.* Based on verses 1-4, what does John mean when he prays for Gaius that "all is going well with you"?

2. Think of people you know who are "walking in the truth" (vv. 3-4). What qualities in their lives are evidence of that?

3. How had Gaius's collaboration with truth benefited the church in practical ways (vv. 5-8)?

4. Why was it commendable that the traveling missionaries had not accepted help from outsiders (v. 7)?

Love for the early Christians was not primarily something you did with your heart and emotions. It was something you did with your whole life, not least your money and your home. So it had been with Gaius. Those from John's church who had visited Gaius had come back with a glowing report, and part of the reason for this letter seems to be to thank him. The traveling missionaries had gone out "for the sake of the Name," the great and powerful name of Jesus himself. This would put them at risk, and partly for that reason, they had determined not to receive help from non-Christians. We are meant to be "fellow-workers with the truth." This collaboration in the work of the Truth comes right down to the practical details of a meal, a bed for the night and a good start in the morning.

5. *Read 3 John 9-14.* As with so much else in the early church, we don't know anything about Diotrephes except what we read here. How was Diotrephes suppressing rather than walking in the truth (vv. 9-10)?

6. What difficult job lay ahead of John when he came to visit the Christian assembly of which Gaius was a part?

7. Like Moses, who was also accused of high-handedness, John is actually a very meek person. That is the secret of his pastoral strength; you can feel it between every line in these three letters. He has to say what he has to say, even though some independent-minded leaders in some of the local churches may not like being reminded either of the message or of the fact that John was chosen and equipped for a unique and vital ministry. So John has to warn Gaius about Diotrephes. There are some churches where people are too "nice" (in other words, nervous or embarrassed) to confront problems, with the result that the problems get worse and worse until people leave in disgust. John is not going to go that cowardly route. He is determined, if he can, to nip this problem in the bud.

Why is it so difficult to balance truth and love when confronting a problem in a Christian community?

8. How does verse 11 express that knowing God is more than just feelings or emotions?

9. Demetrius is almost certainly carrying this letter to Gaius and so needs a formal introduction. He stands in sharp contrast to Diotrephes. What does John mean by his statement that even the truth itself attests to Demetrius's character (v. 12)?

10. In the first part of his letter John emphasizes welcoming the family of God, yet he does not sound very welcoming toward Diotrephes. How do you reconcile the two tones in his letter?

11. Despite indications of conflict, John concludes with "Peace be with you." When have you most strongly experienced peace within yourself and within a church fellowship?

12. How do you account for the prevalence of peace in those situations?

Even though it's the shortest document in the Bible, and even though, remarkably, the name *Jesus* is nowhere in it (though John does refer to "the Name" in verse 7), 3 John breathes the spirit of Jesus just as strongly as its much longer cousins. It speaks, as in the closing verse, of peace, not the easy peace that comes from ignoring the problems, but the deeper peace that comes from confronting them in the knowledge that truth and love are the two arms with which God in Jesus now enfolds both church and world in one embrace.

PRAY

Pray that you will extend a warm welcome to other believers in the spirit of Gaius, in whatever form the opportunities arise for you.

Pray that you will never be guilty of any of Diotrephes's harmful attitudes and behavior.

Ask God for boldness and compassion in any situations where you are called to confront others.

Pray for the peace of Christ in yourself, in your Christian community and in the world.

Guidelines for Leaders

My grace is sufficient for you.
(2 Corinthians 12:9)

If leading a small group is something new for you, don't worry. These sessions are designed to flow naturally and be led easily. You may even find that the studies seem to lead themselves!

This study guide is flexible. You can use it with a variety of groups—students, professionals, coworkers, friends, neighborhood or church groups. Each study takes forty-five to sixty minutes in a group setting.

You don't need to be an expert on the Bible or a trained teacher to lead a small group. These guides are designed to facilitate a group's discussion, not a leader's presentation. Guiding group members to discover together what the Bible has to say and to listen together for God's guidance will help them remember much more than a lecture would.

There are some important facts to know about group dynamics and encouraging discussion. The suggestions listed below should equip you to effectively and enjoyably fulfill your role as leader.

PREPARING FOR THE STUDY

1. Ask God to help you understand and apply the passage in your own life. Unless this happens, you will not be prepared to lead others. Pray too for the various members of the group. Ask God to open your hearts to the message of his Word and motivate you to action.

2. Read the introduction to the entire guide to get an overview of the topics that will be explored.
3. As you begin each study, read and reread the assigned Bible passage to familiarize yourself with it. This study guide is based on the For Everyone series on the New Testament (published by SPCK and Westminster John Knox). It will help you and the group if you have on hand a copy of the companion volume from the For Everyone series both for the translation of the passage found there and for further insight into the passage.
4. Carefully work through each question in the study. Spend time in meditation and reflection as you consider how to respond.
5. Write your thoughts and responses in the space provided in the study guide. This will help you to express your understanding of the passage clearly.
6. It may help to have a Bible dictionary handy. Use it to look up any unfamiliar words, names or places. The glossary at the end of each New Testament for Everyone commentary may likewise be helpful for keeping discussion moving.
7. Reflect seriously on how you need to apply the Scripture to your life. Remember that the group members will follow your lead in responding to the studies. They will not go any deeper than you do.

LEADING THE STUDY

1. At the beginning of your first time together, explain that these studies are meant to be discussions, not lectures. Encourage the members of the group to participate. However, do not put pressure on those who may be hesitant to speak—especially during the first few sessions.
2. Be sure that everyone in your group has a study guide. Encourage the group to prepare beforehand for each discussion by reading the introduction to the guide and by working through the questions in each study.
3. Begin each study on time. Open with prayer, asking God to help the group to understand and apply the passage.

4. Have a group member read aloud the introduction at the beginning of the discussion.
5. Discuss the "Open" question before the Bible passage is read. The "Open" question introduces the theme of the study and helps group members to begin to open up, and can reveal where our thoughts and feelings need to be transformed by Scripture. Reading the passage first will tend to color the honest reactions people would otherwise give—because they are, of course, supposed to think the way the Bible does. Encourage as many members as possible to respond to the "Open" question, and be ready to get the discussion going with your own response.
6. Have a group member read aloud the passage to be studied as indicated in the guide.
7. The study questions are designed to be read aloud just as they are written. You may, however, prefer to express them in your own words.

   There may be times when it is appropriate to deviate from the study guide. For example, a question may have already been answered. If so, move on to the next question. Or someone may raise an important question not covered in the guide. Take time to discuss it, but try to keep the group from going off on tangents.
8. Avoid answering your own questions. An eager group quickly becomes passive and silent if members think the leader will do most of the talking. If necessary repeat or rephrase the question until it is clearly understood, or refer to the commentary woven into the guide to clarify the context or meaning.
9. Don't be afraid of silence in response to the discussion questions. People may need time to think about the question before formulating their answers.
10. Don't be content with just one answer. Ask, "What do the rest of you think?" or "Anything else?" until several people have given answers to the question.
11. Try to be affirming whenever possible. Affirm participation. Never reject an answer; if it is clearly off-base, ask, "Which verse led you to that conclusion?" or again, "What do the rest of you think?"

12. Don't expect every answer to be addressed to you, even though this will probably happen at first. As group members become more at ease, they will begin to truly interact with each other. This is one sign of healthy discussion.
13. Don't be afraid of controversy. It can be very stimulating. If you don't resolve an issue completely, don't be frustrated. Explain that the group will move on and God may enlighten all of you in later sessions.
14. Periodically summarize what the group has said about the passage. This helps to draw together the various ideas mentioned and gives continuity to the study. But don't preach.
15. Conclude your time together with the prayer suggestion at the end of the study, adapting it to your group's particular needs as appropriate. Ask for God's help in following through on the applications you've identified.
16. End on time.

Many more suggestions and helps for studying a passage or guiding discussion can be found in *How to Lead a LifeGuide Bible Study* and *The Big Book on Small Groups* (both from InterVarsity Press/USA).

Other InterVarsity Press Resources from N. T. Wright

The Challenge of Jesus
N. T. Wright offers clarity and a full accounting of the facts of the life and teachings of Jesus, revealing how the Son of God was also solidly planted in first-century Palestine. *978-0-8308-2200-3, 202 pages, hardcover*

The Challenge of Easter
The meaning of Easter seems lost among the colored eggs and chocolate candies. In this excerpt from *The Challenge of Jesus*, N. T. Wright explains Easter's bold, almost unbelievable claim: Jesus has risen from the dead. Here is God's announcement of an invitation to live as though God is among us, making everything new. *978-0-8308-3848-6, 64 pages, paperback*

Resurrection
This 50-minute DVD confronts the most startling claim of Christianity—that Jesus rose from the dead. Shot on location in Israel, Greece and England, N. T. Wright presents the political, historical and theological issues of Jesus' day and today regarding this claim. Wright brings clarity and insight to one of the most profound mysteries in human history. Study guide included. *978-0-8308-3435-8, DVD*

Evil and the Justice of God
N. T. Wright explores all aspects of evil and how it presents itself in society today. Fully grounded in the story of the Old and New Testaments, this presentation is provocative and hopeful; a fascinating analysis of and response to the fundamental question of evil and justice that faces believers. *978-0-8308-3398-6, 176 pages, hardcover*

Evil
Filmed in Israel, South Africa and England, this 50-minute DVD confronts some of the major "evil" issues of our time—from tsunamis to AIDS—and puts them under the biblical spotlight. N. T. Wright says there is a solution to the problem of evil, if only we have the honesty and courage to name it and understand it for what it is. Study guide included. *978-0-8308-3434-1, DVD*

Small Faith—Great God
N. T. Wright reminds us that what matters is not how much faith we have but Who our faith is in. Wright looks at the character of the faith God calls us to. He unfolds how dependence, humility and mystery all have a role to play. But the author doesn't ignore the messiness and difficulties of life, when hard times come and the unexpected knocks us down. He opens to us what faith means in times of trial and even in the face of death. Through it all he reminds

us, it's not great faith we need: it is faith in a great God. *978-0-8308-3833-2, 176 pages, hardcover*

Justification: God's Plan and Paul's Vision
In this comprehensive account and defense of the crucial doctrine of justification, Wright also responds to critics who have challenged what has come to be called the New Perspective. Ultimately, he provides a chance for those in the middle of and on both sides of the debate to interact directly with his views and form their own conclusions. *978-0-8308-3863-9, 279 pages, hardcover*

Colossians and Philemon
In Colossians, Paul presents Christ as "the firstborn over all creation," and appeals to his readers to seek a maturity found only in Christ. In Philemon, Paul appeals to a fellow believer to receive a runaway slave in love and forgiveness. In this volume N. T. Wright offers comment on both of these important books. *978-0-8308-4242-1, 199 pages, paperback*

FORREST CHURCH

A SPIRITUAL
GUIDEBOOK
FOR THE
JOURNEY OF
YOUR LIFE

Bringing God Home

ST. MARTIN'S GRIFFIN
NEW YORK

www.stmartins.com

Permissions on page 244

ISBN 0-312-28218-4 (hc)
ISBN 0-312-31602-X (pbk)

First St. Martin's Griffin Edition: May 2003

10 9 8 7 6 5 4 3 2 1

CONTENTS

There is something that comes
home to one now and perpetually,

It is not to be put in a book. . . . it is not
in this book,
It is for you whoever you are. . . . it is no
farther from you than your hearing
and sight are from you,
It is hinted by nearest and commonest
and readiest. . . . it is not them,
though it is endlessly provoked by
them. . . . What is there ready and
near you now?

—Walt Whitman, *Leaves of Grass*

Bringing God Home

Embarking

When I was a child, God watched over me, especially at night. My mother tucked me into bed, I said my evening prayers, and God was with me, right there in my room. Half a century later, how clearly I remember:

Now I lay me down to sleep
I pray the Lord my soul to keep.
And if I die before I wake,
I pray the Lord my soul to take.

Following this incantation came my roll of blessings. "God bless Mommy. God bless Daddy." "God bless Mom-mom and Pop-pop" (my grandparents). "God bless Jimmy" (my best friend). "God bless Smokey" (my cocker spaniel). After ticking off the names of everyone I could think of—prompted by my mother should I forget someone important—I would go on to bless the sun, moon, and stars, stretching my bid for wakefulness and her companionship as long as possible.

Chanted nightly, these simple prayers made up part of my earliest remembered set of rituals. I took my bath, slipped into my pajamas, and brushed my teeth. My mother read to me, we said "our prayers," then off went the light, followed by the words "Night night, sleep tight, don't let the bedbugs bite." Because I felt so safe tucked snugly under the covers, so secure and unquestionably loved, the nightly reminders of bedbugs and death rarely penetrated my consciousness. Apart from the occasional visitation by a midnight monster, death and bedbugs number among my grown-up concerns. Back then they simply rang like chimes beckoning me to close my eyes and drift off into gentle sleep.

My first home was a tiny house in Boise, Idaho. Until I was six years old, we lived on Logan Street, a one-block cul-de-sac of only eight residences. My parents' best friends had the house behind ours; Jimmy and his family lived right next door. We shared the same backyard. If this much of my early geography remains fixed, I remember little else from early childhood. For instance, I have no idea what our house looked like, save that it was tiny, which must have been true, given that everything seems larger than life to a child. I can't remember my father coming home from work, though he did so almost nightly. I can barely recall our family vacations (a four-story Paul Bunyan and his Blue Ox somewhere in California is the one vivid exception to this rule). Our car, a two-toned red and white '52 Kaiser with plastic straw upholstery, was unforgettable, though we had it until I was twelve and my memories of it may not be early ones.

Some of the things I've forgotten amaze me. I can't call to mind either my parents' room, which my mother tells me was painted, by accident, a color she describes as "electric pink," or (save through photos in the family album) her surely fashionable rhinestone-studded glasses. Yet, among the things I do remember, I am blessed: most of them are happy memories. How vividly I recall the canary yellow walls of my room, and the phosphorescent moon, planets, and stars appliquéd to my ceiling. Every night when the lights went off, the stars in my room came out. I can picture a handful of backyard birthday parties, my swing set and wading pool, popping tar bubbles in our driveway on hot summer afternoons, roughhousing with Smokey, and my bedtime prayers.

I also know by heart the grace we said at table before dinner. We would close our eyes, pitch our hands into tents, and say:

God is great, God is good,
And we thank Him for our food;
By His hand our mouths are fed;
Thank you, Lord, (for) our daily bread.

We didn't ever include the last *for,* I suppose because the prayer sounded better without it, but that scarcely mattered. If one didn't think about it—which almost surely was true in my case—"Thank you, Lord, our daily bread" made perfect sense. Like my bedtime prayers, this grace was not a lesson but a mantra. Its moment lay in the event it signaled much more than in the meaning of the words. Nonetheless, however slightly the meaning registered, however unthinking I may have been when reciting my prayers or saying grace, my bedtime prayers and mealtime blessing remain with me. I remember them so clearly and unquestioningly that I am certain these daily rituals offered little Forrest Church the assurance he needed to feel that God was in His Heaven and all was right with the world.

I have no memory of when or why my family stopped saying grace at table or when I started going to bed on my own, without benefit of a story or of saying my prayers. I know only this. Decades later—and after years in the parish ministry—I gradually awakened to the fact that God had slipped away without my noticing. Nor was I at home within myself. Somewhere along the line, I had lost my way, and with it all sense of direction. My search for meaning had led to a dead end. But also to a turnabout. Seeking to recover my life before it became too late, I set out on this pilgrimage.

My quest was not for the God of my childhood. Losing such a God was no more tragic than losing a favorite toy that one has outgrown. Nonetheless, I longed for the sense of place I had known as a little boy, both within myself and within my world. In his essay "The Unseen Wilderness," Wendell Berry writes, "The world cannot be discovered by a journey of miles, no matter how long, but only by a spiritual journey, a journey of one inch, very arduous and humbling and joyful, by which we arrive at the ground of our feet, and learn to be at home." From the moment of my awakening, the question I found myself asking is this: If a journey of a thousand miles begins with a single step, how do we embark on a journey that requires us to move only one inch and yet commences in a place where we don't want to be?

By way of an answer, I offer this traveler's guide. It is a map, reflecting my experience but also drawing freely upon the insights of others who preceded me and helped me on my way. Drawing illustrations from each decade of my life, I include my own story in passing, but the closer I feel to God, the less unique I find it to be. It is not my central concern here. Our story is.

Spiritual autobiography can be helpful. Awareness of another's struggle lessens our sense of isolation. Putting aside the New Testament and the Qu'ran, one could make a claim for St. Augustine's *Confessions* as the most influential religious book of the past two millennia. Though tricky, the open sharing of our personal struggles certainly beats the pretense that all is well when it's not. How readily we forget that the cover of another's life may be far more alluring than its contents. For instance, those of you who don't happen to be parish ministers might presume that we have a built-in advantage in the God department. This is not necessarily the case. Our studies and even our weekly pronouncements make us, or should make us, all the more conscious of our spiritual failings. This may—and, again, should—engender feelings of insufficiency, hypocrisy, or both. In my own case, I tried to mute such feelings for years. This came naturally to me. Not only have I run from uncomfortable feelings since childhood but also my initial interest in religion had little to do with God, not in a personal sense anyway. What drew me to religion was instead a deep fascination with the "idea" of God and with questions of meaning, especially as manifested in the lives and writings of idiosyncratic souls. It was Kierkegaard and Nietzsche, not St. Augustine, who drew me toward divinity school.

At Harvard, where—this will not surprise you—knowledge is honored more highly than piety, I continued to be attracted by spiritual renegades, particularly heretics. I wrote a doctoral dissertation on the Gnostic Gospel of Thomas, which captured my interest precisely because it *didn't* make it into the Bible. At the outset of my ministry, realizing how spare my personal experience of God actually was, I did everything I could to avoid preaching on the subject. In a Unitarian Universalist church, this is not difficult. I'm not sure that anyone noticed.

But eventually *I* began to notice. My career was proceeding quite well; yet, when drawn into self-examination, I reached into pockets of emptiness. At first I did this only when I had to, escaping as quickly as I could. But flight from my feelings had its price. My first marriage died. I drank too much. I was looking both too high and too low for a fulfillment that continued to elude me. For years I inhabited this Limbo. I performed my tasks, helped build my church, and wrote my books, but the satisfaction I once had derived from such accomplishments had an ever-shorter shelf life. My wife recognized this before I did; my children may have suspected it; but few other people, even my closest friends, seemed to sense that anything major was wrong with me. My career continued to thrive. By outward appearances, my life prospered. But it was hollow at the core.

Delving into this hollowness taught me (as I had heard somewhere once) that when we don't believe in God, it's not that we believe in nothing; rather we believe in almost anything. Having outgrown my childhood God, I awakened to the realization that for years I had persisted in worshiping a string of much smaller gods, all of which failed me. As they did, I failed others, especially the people I loved best. I was lost in the desert of self. Had I known enough to ask, Augustine's question to God would have echoed in my emptiness: "Where was I when I was seeking for You? You were there before me, but I had departed from myself. I could not even find myself, much less You."

My subsequent journey, which took place over the course of a decade, is not punctuated by a dramatic conversion like Paul's on the road to Damascus. I look back on it more as a gradual awakening, interrupted and delayed by the constant temptation to drift back to sleep. My flight from the God who now beckoned to me was still spurred by long-standing fears of vulnerability. Afraid of what I might discover if I delved too deeply into myself, I continued to find ways to subdue my consciousness. I accomplished this feat most effectively through the expedient of alcohol, which for years had served me as a kind of God substitute. As long as another power greater than myself presided over me, I could not bring God into my life. Because my wife wouldn't look the other way, and because I had grown bone weary of my penchant for evasion, I couldn't live like this much longer. All my excuses and rationalizations had far outrun their expiration date. After several aborted attempts and long experimentation with variously successful half measures, one year ago I quit drinking.

This is not a book about freeing oneself from an addiction to alcohol. If that happens to be your goal, other books will prove of greater use to you. Alcohol may have conspired with my inner demons to distract me from my spiritual quest, but that in no way suggests that God was my prize for getting sober. In fact, getting high is but another chapter (if a long and broken one) in my search for spiritual fulfillment. I was losing myself to be found. Filling myself with spirits, spiritually I became more and more empty, but this too led me to realize that I could be filled only by self-emptying. Tentatively at first, and then with growing faith and confidence, I surrendered my willfulness and reached out for God. What I mean by God I shall try to explain in the pages to follow. The simple truth remains, without the aid of a power greater than my own, I would still be languishing.

Over the years my journey has taken me on many other detours, but it has also blessed me along the way with travel companions, whose travails and triumphs struck an inner chord. People's experiences of God are as varied as God's mystery is deep. Yet patterns emerge, archetypes of journey and discovery that manifest themselves in literature and life from age to age. Poets and storytellers touch me more deeply than theologians do, myths and parables more than philosophy or doctrine. As for my orthodox religious guides, their teachings draw my attention, but their doubts and struggles rivet it. I treasure especially their moments of awakening. In such good company, I am less the author of a spiritual manual than the editor of a storybook, each story as unique and as familiar as are fingerprints. I dust them for clues to life's mystery.

Should you discover something new between these covers, I assure you it is not original. Finding God has nothing to do with either individual or collective knowledge (both of which are ever changing). It springs from wisdom (which changes but slightly from one generation to the next). What wisdom I have garnered during the course of my journey dwells latent within each of us. Spiritual insight opens the doors of perception, it does not construct them.

Neither do I pretend to be an authoritative guide. Although I think I know now how and where to look for it, life's meaning springs more surely from following a direction than from arriving at a destination. Its goal may be veiled, but the journey itself is part of our destination. However faltering our steps, God approaches us whenever we walk toward God. This is the essence of grace—never deserved, always present, and accessible only to those whose hearts are open to receive it. There is only one prerequisite to bringing God home: we must be prepared to find God there.

There is a Hasidic story about a certain Rabbi Isaac of Cracow. One night Rabbi Isaac has a dream. In it, God tells him to leave his home and travel to Prague. There, beneath the bridge, he will find a great treasure. Isaac is far from superstitious, but this is the third time the dream has recurred. So Isaac sets out on the long journey to Prague. Exhausted, he finally arrives at the bridge underneath which the promised treasure purportedly is buried. But soldiers guard the bridge day and night, and Isaac cannot dig for the treasure without attracting their attention. Hours pass and then days. At last, abandoning all hope, he turns to leave, empty-handed. As he walks away, a soldier calls out to him, "Old man, for the longest time you've been hanging about, and now you're leaving. What strange quest brought you here, and why do you now go?"

"I had a dream," Isaac confesses. "God told me to go to Prague, where I would find a great treasure buried beneath the bridge."

"Fool," the soldier replies. "I once had such a dream. God told me that if I went to Cracow and looked up Rabbi Isaac, I too would find a great treasure, buried beneath his stove."

Thanking the soldier, Rabbi Isaac returns home to find his promised treasure where it always was, hidden under his own hearth. In the words of T. S. Eliot,

> *. . . the end of all our exploring*
> *Will be to arrive where we started*
> *And know the place for the first time.*

Over the pages to follow, you will hear this story many times, expressed in various ways and in differing voices: however circuitous and arduous our journey, the key to spiritual fulfillment is always in our pocket. By no accident, this same key unlocks our hearts.

1 *The Shortest Way Home*

At length I got unto the gladsome hill,
Where lay my hope,
Where lay my heart; and climbing still,
When I had gained the brow and top,
A lake of brackish waters on the ground
Was all I found.

George Herbert, "The Pilgrimage"

In pilgrimage stories, searchers often embark on a lengthy journey only to discover what they are seeking when they return to the place they began. "The longest way round is the shortest way home," one proverb puts it. And it is true. To find the most important things in life, we almost *have* to look too high for things close by.

The greatest travelogue of the soul in English literature is John Bunyan's *Pilgrim's Progress.* Bunyan's pilgrim is named Christian. His quest is for salvation, to flee worldly snares and fleshly distractions and secure eternal bliss in the great Hereafter. Christian makes it to Heaven, but not without many adventures along the way. He struggles through the famous (if unpronounceable) Slough of Despond; ascends the Hill of Difficulty; traverses the Valley of Humiliation; battles with pagan, pope, and demon; plucks up his courage in crossing the Valley of the Shadow of Death; and survives, most notably and memorably, the many attractions of that great city Vanity, with its unsurpassed fair. If you don't mind happy or predictable endings, it's not a bad story. But let me bring to your attention a little-known tale published two centuries later and inspired directly by it, Nathaniel Hawthorne's "The Celestial Railroad."

Something extraordinary transpired over the intervening centuries. The enterprising citizens of the City of Destruction constructed a railroad between this flourishing town and the Celestial City. Think of the advantages. First, one doesn't have to shoulder one's burden; it can be placed in the baggage compartment. And they built a bridge over the Slough of Despond. Hawthorne's guide ("Mr. Smooth-it-away") describes how they turned this slough, a disgrace to all the neighborhood, into a foundation sufficient for the bridge's pylons: "by throwing into the slough some editions of books of morality, volumes of French philosophy and German rationalism, tracts, sermons, and essays of modern clergymen, extracts from Plato, Confucius, and various Hindu sages, together with a few ingenious commentaries upon texts of Scripture—all of which, by some scientific process, have been converted into a mass like granite."

This is just one of the wonderful things they did to streamline the modern pilgrim's trek to the Celestial City. For instance, they cut a tunnel through the Hill of Difficulty and used the excavated dirt as landfill for the Valley of Humiliation. Later in the journey, another troublesome valley, the Valley of the Shadow of Death, is blocked from view by a quadruple row of klieg lights lining each side of the tracks. These lamps cast a somewhat eerie glow but keep passengers diverted from having to contemplate the stark reminders of mortality that litter the valley below.

Most marked of all, at least in Hawthorne's view, are the pilgrims themselves.

> By the aspect and demeanor of these persons it was easy to judge that the feeling of the community had undergone a very favorable change in reference to the Celestial pilgrimage. It would have done Bunyan's heart good to see it. Instead of a lonely and ragged man with a huge burden on his back, plodding along sorrowfully on foot while the whole city hooted after him, here were parties of the first gentry and most respectable people in the neighborhood setting forth towards the Celestial City as cheerfully as if the pilgrimage were merely a summer tour. Among the gentlemen were characters of deserved eminence, magistrates, politicians, and men of wealth, by whose example religion could not but be greatly recommended to their meaner brethren. . . . There was much pleasant conversation about the news of the day, topics of business, politics, or the lighter matters of amusement; while religion, though indubitably the main thing at heart, was thrown tastefully into the background.

There was only one downside to this wonderful railroad. Though it simplified the religious journey in oh so many ways—offering shortcuts and sparing travelers the giddy heights and echoing depths of experience and consciousness, as well as all troublesome pangs of conscience—one problem remained. Its final stop was not Heaven, as promised. It was Hell.

When the seventeenth-century English poet Francis Quarles wrote, "The next way home's the farthest way about," I doubt that he had Hell in mind. Yet, for pilgrims fated to travel the farthest way about, Hell may be as good a stop as any. In fact, we can't help stopping there. Whether courtesy of a drunk driver or one drink too many, delivered via pink slip or telegram, packaged in a doctor's diagnosis or a Dear John letter, or gradually building in our subconscious until one day it breaks forth into full-scale depression or uncontrolled anxiety, Hell will surely invite us to pay many visits during the course of a lifetime. The problem with Hawthorne's pilgrims is precisely their obliviousness to this reality. Self-entitled, hell-bent to follow the easiest path to their appointed destination, and pleased with themselves for having found a means to accomplish this goal, they streamline their journey in so many ways that they can't possibly experience Christian's triumph.

I know the temptation. Being well-versed in shortcuts, sunny-side-up liberalism, and feel-good philosophy, I would feel right at home shooting the breeze with Hawthorne's pilgrims in the club car on its way to Hell. Nathaniel Hawthorne was, as I am, a Unitarian, but his consciousness was tangled deep in Puritan loam, which most of his liberal religious contemporaries found too mealy for their mental cultivation. "The Celestial Rail-road" is clearly a satire on the high Unitarian fashions of Hawthorne's day.

I am not dismissive of my faith's virtues. I treasure my freedom of belief and subscribe to our emphasis on "deeds not creeds," holding with Thomas Jefferson that "it is in our lives and not our words that our religion must be read." I quote Plato in my sermons, ponder Hindu scriptures, and seek insight from contemporary biblical criticism. I would be a hypocrite to disdain essays written by members of the modern clergy. And I remain a humanist to the extent that I believe all meaning to be a product of human experience not divine revelation. But I have long since become disenchanted with the tiny gods of our modern age, including, but not limited to, materialism, success, knowledge, and, if we worship them, both health and happiness.

Every religion has its idols. When we grow too comfortable in our faith, there is always the danger that the God we believe in is too small. Yet nonbelievers fare no better. When we accustom ourselves to disbelief, the God we disbelieve is someone else's little God. In either instance, tripping along unmindfully from one day to the next, we need a prison breaker: rock over scissors, scissors over paper, paper over rock.

The British orthodox Christian polemicist and philosophical gadfly G. K. Chesterton tells of a story he always wanted to write about a yachtsman who slightly miscalculated his course and discovered England under the mistaken impression that it was a new island in the South Seas. "One might imagine that the man who landed, armed to the teeth and talking by signs, to plant the British flag on that barbaric temple which turned out to be the Pavilion at Brighton, felt rather a fool," Chesterton observes. However, when you think about it, unlike that of Hawthorne's pilgrims, his mistake was rather an enviable one. Chesterton goes on to ask, "What could be more delightful than to have in the same few minutes all the fascinating terrors of going abroad combined with all the humane security of coming home again? . . . What could be more glorious than to brace oneself up to discover New South Wales and then realize, with a gush of happy tears, that it was really old South Wales?" Pointing the moral to his imagined tale, Chesterton poses an additional series of questions that are well worth pondering: "How can we contrive to be at once astonished at the world and yet at home in it? How can this queer cosmic town, with its many-legged citizens, with its monstrous and ancient lamps, how can this world give us at once the fascination of a strange town and the comfort and honor of being our own town, . . . our own cottage, to which we can safely return at evening?"

Similar questions present themselves on our own spiritual travels. In his book *The Snow Leopard,* Peter Matthiessen writes, "The search may begin with a restless feeling, yet one senses that there is a source for this deep restlessness, and the path that leads there is not a path to a strange place, but the path home." This restlessness is an expression of spiritual longing. Carl Jung observed of his patients over thirty-five that, though we may not recognize it as such, looming at the heart of midlife discontent is the need for a religious outlook. Orthodox travelers can experience this as well. Dante opens his *Divine Comedy* (the greatest pilgrimage story in the Western canon) by telling us that, halfway through his life's journey, he too found himself lost in the middle of a dark wood.

One can set out on a spiritual pilgrimage without passing through the gates of organized religion. Hidebound institutions are as likely to thwart our progress as to advance it. Though his father served as a pastor in the Swiss Reformed Church, Jung himself was not religious in the conventional sense. But he did recognize how ancient religious stories might relate to our broader experience. From what his patients told him, Jung sums up his understanding of successful therapy in a single formulation that certainly conforms with my own journey home: "They came to themselves, they could accept themselves, they were able to become reconciled to themselves, and thus were reconciled to adverse circumstances and events." Jung concludes, "This is almost like what used to be expressed by saying: He has made his peace with God, he has sacrificed his own will, he has submitted himself to the will of God."

Describing his patients' need to develop a religious outlook in order successfully to negotiate their midlife passage, Jung speaks of religion not as a formal set of rules and rites established for the worship of a particular deity, but rather as a universal impulse. I, too, define religion broadly. For me, *religion is our human response to the dual reality of being alive and having to die.* We are not the animal with tools or the animal with advanced language; we are the religious animal. In addition to an intellectual desire for knowledge, we possess an existential need for meaning. In fact, knowing that we are going to die, we cannot help but wonder what life means. Death can throw life's meaning into question, rendering it moot for some people. But knowing that we must die inspires most of us to search for answers that will justify our days.

That this search should become more urgent in midlife makes perfect sense to me. In young adulthood, life seems long and childhood distant, strangely more distant than it feels as one grows older. As we enter our middle years, life shortens and its moment intensifies. A heightened sense of immediacy impels our quest for faith. To know what we need and to find it are two different things, however. Complicating matters further, the road to God is poorly marked. Signs are prominently posted, but they point in several directions at once—beckoning us down both forks of almost every beaten and newfound path. Not only do differing road maps perplex the pilgrim's progress but the destination itself is in question. No word is more mysteriously freighted or admits to a wider range of meanings than the word God.

For this very reason, both to avoid being misunderstood and also to keep from fooling myself, for years I skirted God language whenever possible. When I employed it in my writings, more often than not I spoke "about" not "of" the subject, keeping God at a distant and thus comfortable remove. Though I had formed an image of God that my intellect could countenance, I truly believed only in what I could demonstrate by proof, in things I could count and touch and see. The problem was, as with Hawthorne's pilgrims, this knowledge got me nowhere.

Over time, my attitude has changed. Today, in a sense, I believe only in God. Only something as large as God encompasses the mystery and wonder of my being. To do justice to life as I experience it, everything else is far too small. Yet because this single word embraces so many contradictions, and since I invoke it here so lovingly and often, before continuing let me try to explain what I mean when I say "God."

⁂

Truth in religion is like truth in poetry, our common text being the creation. Though limited by the depth and field of our vision, we are driven to interpret this text as best we can. So we tell stories, formulate hypotheses, develop schools of thought and worship, and pass our partial wisdom down from generation to generation. Not only every faith but every philosophy, ideology, and scientific worldview uses the creation as its text. By whatever name we call its author, we are all interpreters of the poetry of God.

Compare this approach with literary criticism. How various are the ways in which we read a masterpiece, such as *Hamlet, Crime and Punishment*, or the Book of Job. A great piece of literature admits to many levels of interpretation: literal, metaphorical, symbolic, political, structural, moral. Two critics may arrive at radically different interpretations of the same passage, both founding their views on carefully reasoned logic and demonstrating impressive erudition in the course of their proof. Within and between schools of criticism, a continuing discussion takes place, sharpening perspectives and issuing in new and relevant discoveries, all of which help to illuminate the nature of the masterpiece.

The same dynamic holds for competing theologies, except

that here the text we are interpreting is the greatest masterpiece of them all—the creation itself. With differing approaches, methodologies, and tools, each of us struggles to discover who we are, where we have come from, how we got here, where we are heading, and why and how. All work from a set of basic presuppositions. Each school of interpretation has its trusted tools, ranging from the Bible to the Hubble telescope. As among literary critics, there is an ongoing discussion within each school and occasional dialogue between schools. Theologians incorporate new discoveries in science. Scientists sometimes reach the point of furthest penetration and turn to the mystical language of reverence and adoration. (Einstein said that the greatest thing we can experience is the mysterious.) The stakes are high. Of all intellectual contests, none is more charged or dangerous. Each side reckons the score in a different fashion, and there is no mutually accepted guideline for who is winning, not to mention how to play. Viewed as competition, the only way to secure a final theological victory is to discredit or eliminate one's opponents.

And yet, if there can be many compelling and competing interpretations of a literary masterpiece, what should this tell us about the cosmos itself? Nothing is more mysterious or veiled than the creation. No dogma can begin to comprehend it. Even as a scientific investigator cannot measure the velocity and position of a particle at the same time, the moment we begin to parse the creation we change its apparent nature. Gestalt psychology suggests a like point in object-and-field studies such as that well-known optical illusion of two faces in profile that also outline the shape of a vase. It is possible to go back and forth from one focus to the other, but—though both are before our eyes—we can't see the faces and the vase at once. In each instance the investigator becomes part of the experiment, affecting the very data he or she is attempting objectively to collect. Not only are we the interpreters of God's poetry but we are at least one stanza of the poem itself.

When people boast to me that they don't believe in God, I ask them therefore to tell me a little about the God they don't believe in. Almost surely, I don't believe in "him" either. The ancient Hebrews recognized that "God" is not even God's name. By my own definition, *God is our name for a power that is greater than all and yet present in each*: the life force; the Holy; Being itself. God doesn't exist only because we need God; we exist because the universe was pregnant with us when it was born. In miracle and fact, our gestation traces to the beginning of time. Accidents abound—one amino lapse or missed coupling and we would not be in the position to wonder why we are here. Yet, in my experience, only by positing the existence of a power beyond our comprehension can we begin to account for the miracle of being with an appropriate measure of humility and awe.

I recognize that for many people the word God has shrunk from repeated use. But we can always restretch it. If you can't manage to do this—if the "G word" fits your mind more like a straitjacket than like a divine garment—substitute another. Spirit may work for you, or the Sacred or Higher Power. So long as the scope of your reverence is large enough, it doesn't really matter, not at all. There is nothing novel, and certainly nothing blasphemous, about redesigning or renaming God. Responding to life-and-death questions, we have reinvented and thereby rediscovered the Holy throughout the centuries.

Consider our ancestors, the searchers who came before us. Begin with cave dwellers—hunters and gatherers—for whom the greatest imaginable powers were forces of nature. "God" was manifest in fire, therefore, in lightning and in thunder, perhaps even in the game they hunted for sustenance. When agriculture replaced hunting and gathering, these gods turned into goddesses. Power now lay in reaping and sowing, in the turning of the seasons. Fecundity determined survival, "God" became "Goddess"; procreation, creation; birth, life.

Later, with the city-state, power was invested in the robes of authority. "God" was now Lord or King, protector, enforcer, and judge. A breakthrough in this view of the divine nature occurred with the Hebrews, who believed that their God and King was the only God and King. Less an imperialistic than an ethical development, this belief led them to attribute their failures not to another stronger God but to their own shortcomings. With Jesus, God became Father (in fact, Daddy or "Abba"), a far more intimate authority figure.

In Western society the God most unbelievers reject is the traditional Judeo-Christian God: loving, just, demanding, capricious on occasion, sometimes cruel. Yet, aided by the Copernican revolution, for many thoughtful people this God was overthrown centuries ago. As has happened many times before, God was not therefore dead; "God" was reimagined. When Copernicus displaced us from the center of the universe, in reimagining God one group of scientists and theologians seized upon a metaphor better suited to their new worldview. Enter God the Watchmaker, who created the world, set it ticking, and then withdrew to another corner of the cosmos. This is the God of the Deists, icy and remote, still transcendent but no longer personal.

Today we are witness to a further revolution, one as profound as that initiated by Copernicus and Galileo half a millennium ago. From quantum physics to cosmology, scientific studies of the creation are riddled by paradox. Postmodern philosophers contemplate the dynamic relationship between how we say something and what we mean. Political theorists speak of a global empire whose emperor, though virtual not factual, is no less powerful and real. And theologians entertain notions of divinity no longer encumbered by static concepts such as omniscience and omnipotence. Having moved from one transcendent God to another (first Lord and Judge, then absentee landlord), we are beginning to encounter what might best be called a reflexive God, co-creator with us in an unfolding, intricate drama of hitherto unimaginable complexity. This God is not immutable but ever-changing, reaching, and growing, even as we change, reach, and grow. No longer merely actors on God's stage, we may also be participants in the scripting of God's drama.

As for the discovery of God, we find evidence for the divine first within ordinary things and in daily encounters. The surest way to find God (the Sacred or the Holy) is to share our deepest experiences, not only of joy but also of sorrow. Everyone suffers. We are all broken and in need of healing. We struggle to accept ourselves and forgive others. To adopt the old language, we are all sinners. Aware of our imperfections, we seek more perfect faith, hope, and justice. At our best, we see our tears in one another's eyes and rise together in answer to the urgings of conscience. We discover the Holy—its healing and saving power—within the commonplace. Anyone who embraces the familiar definition that "God is love" discovers God's nature in his or her own experience of love. This may not mean that God actually is love, but it certainly suggests that love is divine.

Since truth in religion is like truth in poetry, by its very nature the language of religion is poetic language: words like *God, soul, angels, spirit; Heaven, Hell,* and *Purgatory; salvation* and *sin*. Because such words are imprecise, many thoughtful people shy away from them. I can understand that. Even as a divinity student I avoided traditional religious language whenever possible. Today, however, I need such words. Rather than abandon it, I do my best therefore to rescue the old language from captivity by literalists, who strip it of all poetry, diminishing its symbolic nuance and vitality. Though easily reduced to an idol, God is still the biggest word I know. It points toward a power beyond our own yet mysteriously present within us. Stretching here the metaphorical possibilities of both God and home, I am no longer ashamed to mine the poetry of my forebears in search of touchstones for my faith.

If reimagining God necessarily involves a degree of poetic license, by taking such license we quickly discover that the spiritual quest is filled with poetic possibility. Traveling far from our point of embarkation only to find God on our return is itself a recurring theme in the literature of pilgrimage.

One modern mythmaker, the Roman Catholic theologian John S. Dunne, recasts this archetype of the journey in his book *The Way of All the Earth*. He calls his pilgrimage tale "The Parable of the Mountain." One day a group of seekers begins to climb a mountain. Having been told that God lives at the top of it, they jettison their daily cares and leave them in the valley below. Climbing into the clouds on a quest for perfect wisdom, they follow the official signs that point to God: transcendent, all-knowing, all-powerful.

Finally, they reach the mountaintop. From the crest they can see farther than they have ever seen before. And the air is thin at the top of the mountain. This atmosphere promotes abstract and disembodied reflection on the eternal verities, which are confounded and veiled by the grossness, busyness, and squalor of life below. There is only one problem. God is not there. It seems that while they were climbing up the mountain in search of God, God was climbing down the mountain into the valley.

How can this be? Perhaps because God seeks us as eagerly as we seek God. In the words of the poet Gwendolyn Brooks:

Perhaps—who knows?—He tires of looking down.
Those eyes are never lifted. Never straight.
Perhaps sometimes He tires of being great
In solitude. Without a hand to hold.

As earthbound pilgrims dream to escape their human lot, desiring transfiguration into something immortal and divine, perhaps God hopes to embrace humanity, to become incarnate in mortal flesh and thus escape the everlasting emptiness of eternity.

If we climb up as God comes down, each to the other is like a vanishing pot of gold at the opposite end of a rainbow. The mystery is, by reaching for God—for a divine hand that turns out not to be there—we may in fact be changed, even saved. And in seeking us out, who knows? Perhaps God too is changed. Humbled. Spun into webs of passion and stung with pain. Brought to life.

The notion that God lives on a mountain dates back to the ancient Greeks and beyond. One can easily understand why. If I were God, I would want a lofty perch with an expansive view, particularly if it were relatively inaccessible. After all, part of my power would have to do with the awe in which mortals held me. The only problem with living on a mountaintop—especially when one is immortal—is that every now and then one gets terribly, terribly lonely. To abate such loneliness (as myth tells), the Greek god Zeus would disguise himself as a bull or swan, descend into the valley below, and father a child.

A like intersection of human and divine is manifest in parables, most notably in the New Testament. Of Jesus' parables of the Kingdom, such as the parable of the sower or the parable of the woman at the well, the symbols pointing to God's presence on earth (in each case similes or metaphors drawn from common experience) are reflexive symbols. They participate in the very reality to which they refer. In part because these parables are unpretentious, they invite us to look again at commonplace things, beckoning us to view them not as they appear but as signs of something more essential and abiding. "The Kingdom of heaven is like yeast" one such parable begins; or "The Kingdom of heaven is like a mustard seed." In each instance the divine is manifest within the ordinary. Such "cleansing of the doors of perception," to borrow the poet William Blake's phrase, permits one (as he did):

To see a world in a grain of sand,
And a heaven in a wild flower,
Hold infinity in the palm of your hand,
And eternity in an hour.

Though mystical in nature, this is not otherworldly thinking. On the contrary, Jesus' parables invite us to ponder the world with new eyes. Beckoning us not to experience the supernatural but to awaken to the "super" in the "natural," they haunt our workaday lives with questions that cast all we take for granted into divine relief. Jesus' parables constitute a frontal assault upon the dogma of the apparent. They remind us where Heaven really is.

When asked by the Pharisees when the Kingdom is coming, Jesus himself says, "The Kingdom is not coming with signs to be observed; nor will they say, 'Lo, here it is!' or 'There!' for behold, the Kingdom of God is within you." And in another version of this same saying, recorded in the Gospel of Thomas (the second-century collection of the sayings of Jesus on which I wrote my dissertation), Jesus tells his disciples, "What you expect has come, but you know it not."

It doesn't really matter whether we are searching for God or simply seeking some divine characteristic attributed to God. Nor does it matter if we find exactly what we seek. Likely we will not. By its very nature, the spiritual quest is destined to disappoint. But also to surprise. Native Americans speak of the coyote, Buddhists of the monkey, each a divine trickster who brings new insight to seekers by confounding their expectations. Jesus' parables and the Taoist scriptures as well (which teach that we must bend in order to become straight) challenge us with like paradox. They turn our accustomed ways of thinking upside down and inside out. In Ralph Waldo Emerson's words, they alter our "angle of vision."

Viewed from a new angle, should its goal elude us, our search for God may yet surprise and reward us with something very like old-fashioned redemption. Though what we seek abides within ordinary experience, not beyond it, from the top of the mountain we gain new perspective on our lives. We awaken to heady and mysterious things. However quickly we discover that we can no longer breathe such thin air and must therefore return to the valley, not only does our journey continue but we are closer to our ultimate goal. When we look carefully with newly opened eyes, we find that in our absence God has paid a visit. Loved ones become more precious. Work is suddenly an honor to perform. Daily tasks sparkle with new luster. Before we were half asleep, our lives living us, the sand unwatched running out of our glass. Now we awaken to the unaccountable miracles of life and love.

⁂

Francesco Petrarch had his most memorable spiritual awakening on a mountaintop. For years Petrarch (a fourteenth-century Italian poet and philosopher) had determined one day to climb the Windy Mountain, a great peak overlooking not only his immediate neighborhood but out across the mountains of Lyons from the Aegean to the Adriatic, encompassing everything from Marseilles to Aigues-Mortes. In a letter to his spiritual adviser, Petrarch reports that the journey, which he undertook with his brother, proved more arduous than he imagined. His brother climbed straight up the ridge toward the top. Petrarch followed an easier, if longer, route up the mountain. At intervals he would encounter his well-rested brother, who had arrived at each outlook long before him. But he persisted in seeking switchbacks for the next stage of his ascent. Reflecting on his folly, Petrarch writes, "I wandered through the valleys, looking for the longer and easier path and stumbling only into longer difficulties. Thus I indeed put off the disagreeable strain of climbing. But nature is not overcome by man's devices; a corporeal thing cannot reach the heights by descending."

Both climbers finally conquered the windswept peak. The sun was setting, the mountain's shadow lengthening over the valley below. Having attained his longtime goal, Petrarch pondered his life. Soon to reach the age of forty, he wondered what he could claim to have learned during this span of years. He opened his knapsack and took out the book he had specially selected to read on the mountaintop—Augustine's *Confessions.* Opening it at random, he put his finger on a passage and read these words: "Men go to admire the high mountains, the vast floods of the sea, the huge streams of the rivers, the circumference of the ocean, and the revolutions of the stars—and desert themselves." Petrarch had journeyed for years on his search—he even climbed to the mountaintop—but these words of St. Augustine finally awakened him: he had been looking too high for things close by.

L. Frank Baum draws a similar lesson in his well-known fantasy of a little girl swept away on an adventure and trying to return home. When I read *The Wizard of Oz* as a child (perhaps because of expectations fostered by the wonderful Judy Garland movie), I took it at face value. I wouldn't wish to ruin its fun by taking it too seriously, or to suggest it posseses the weight of Augustine's *Confessions* or Bunyan's *Pilgrim's Progress,* but there is more here than meets the eye.

In the movie Dorothy's song "Somewhere over the Rainbow" is a lament. Her life is as flat as Kansas, bound by limitations and riddled with longing. Dorothy also has true grievances. A nasty neighbor threatens to take away her dog, Toto, who means everything to her (the name Toto in fact means "everything"). Dorothy dreams of escape. "Birds fly over the rainbow," she sings, "why, then, oh why can't I?" As long as Dorothy imagines her treasure to lie beyond the rainbow, her heart is unfulfilled. Only when she returns from her Technicolor adventures does everything (though cast again in shades of gray) appear in a new, more gracious light. Dorothy's dream does come true, but not in a way that she could possibly have imagined. What she was searching for beyond the rainbow had been at her very doorstep.

The same lesson holds for Dorothy's travel companions (something the book makes particularly clear). Begin with the Tin Woodman. He pines for a heart and is willing to risk everything, even life itself, to possess one. Yet time and again he proves himself to be remarkably tender, compassionate, and sensitive. When the Lion proposes to go out and kill a deer for food, the Tin Woodman pleads, "Don't! Please don't. I should certainly weep if you killed a poor deer, and then my jaws would rust again." The Tin Woodman has a heart, a wonderful heart. He simply does not know it.

On one occasion the Woodman crushes a beetle that is crawling across his path. He weeps. Tears roll down his face into the hinges of his jaw, and it rusts shut. Dorothy is beside herself, but the Scarecrow opens her basket, takes out an oil-can, and lubricates the Woodman's jaw; in moments he is good as new again.

Remember, the Scarecrow is the one without brains. He too is searching for what he already has. In fact, whenever smarts are called for, the Scarecrow saves the day. For instance, when the four travelers happen upon a deep, impassable ravine blocking their path toward the Emerald City, it is the Scarecrow who comes up with a solution to their dilemma. The Lion can jump across, carrying them over one by one on his back.

The Lion, you recall, is the one seeking courage. Though frightened to death, he promptly does the courageous thing. He agrees to the Scarecrow's brilliant plan, makes the attempt, and succeeds. Not that the Lion thereby proves himself courageous (at least not in his own eyes). After all, he is afraid. This deepens his belief that he is cowardly. But courage has nothing to do with fearlessness. In fact, courage is possible only where fear is present. Courage is not the elimination of fear; it is the mastery of fear. By mastering his fear, the Lion manifests as much courage as he could possibly dream of possessing.

Adventure by adventure Baum's parable unfolds, with the Lion demonstrating courage, the Scarecrow using his brains, and the Woodman opening his heart. Finally, they arrive at the gates of the Emerald City and ask to see the great Wizard of Oz. Oz, of course, turns out to be a humbug. Though he knows he lacks the power to make good on his promise, he pledges to fulfill their wishes. He asks only that they kill the Wicked Witch of the West, which—to his great surprise—they do. When they return to the Wizard's throne room and he attempts to avoid discovery by tabling their petition yet again, the Cowardly Lion roars, a great screen falls down, and behind it a cowering little man appears.

Dorothy tells the not-so-great Oz that he is a very bad man. "Oh no, my dear," he replies. "I'm really a very good man; but I'm a very bad Wizard, I must admit." This turns out not to matter, for even after confessing that he has no special powers, this very bad Wizard fulfills the seekers' dreams. The Scarecrow gets his brain, the Woodman his heart, and the Lion his courage. All three are delighted and completely satisfied. It is yet another paradox. Each is saved by the grace of a wizard who does not exist; yet all would have remained lost had the Wizard not saved them.

As for Dorothy, she must continue on her journey for a time. But she, too, finally receives a gift that was already hers. The Good Witch Glinda tells Dorothy that to return home all she has to do is click her heels together three times. Dorothy realizes then that all along she had held the power to escape the perils she encountered in Oz.

"But then I should not have had my wonderful brains!" the Scarecrow cries.

"And I should not have had my lovely heart," adds the Tin Woodman.

"And I should have lived a coward forever," the Lion declares.

This is the final lesson in Baum's enchanting book. On our journeys in search of things that really matter, in finding what is already ours we can help others find what is already theirs.

Legend promises a pot of gold at the end of every rainbow. When dreamers embark on a spiritual pilgrimage, they set out, in part at least, on a quest for gold. However vain, such a journey is both predictable and necessary. All of us dream; we should dare to dream more often than we do. But we will be saved—and then but one moment at a time—only when we awaken to the ribbon of gold within the rainbow's compass. Back from beyond the rainbow, Dorothy perceives in the linings of her everyday existence a beauty that before had eluded her. Discovering through experience that there is no treasure beyond the rainbow, she arrives at an awareness that her heart's treasure was at home all along. Only then does she abandon wishful thinking in exchange for what might be called "thoughtful wishing." Dorothy thinks to wish for what she already has. Of all of our wishes, this wish alone will surely come true. Remember also, the rainbow could not exist without the rain. These are simple but elusive truths, as fleeting as the rainbow itself is. And yet, like Noah's rainbow in the Book of Genesis, they represent the promise of "a lasting covenant between God and every living creature of all flesh that is upon the earth," a holy sign arching across the sky "that we may look on it and remember."

Success on our journey has nothing to do with domesticating spirituality by making religion safe. Settling for too easy a faith or too small a God diminishes the creative, powerful, and inevitable restiveness that infuses both our lives and our spiritual quests with depth and meaning. George Moore, the Irish playwright, was right when he said that "a man travels the world over in search of what he needs and then returns home to find it," but this admission takes nothing away from the journey's purpose. Without searching the world over, we might well not discover what we need on our return. We therefore can be said to "bring God home," even though God never left us. We bring God home by returning with new eyes.

As for the difficulty, it too comes with the territory. In T. S. Eliot's words, to arrive where we are, to get from where we are not, we "must go by a way wherein there is no ecstasy." That the path to meaning is marked with switchbacks and surprises should not depress, only humble us. Since all manner of impediment frustrates our attempts at enlightenment, humility attends every sacred journey. And yet, on the Hill of Difficulty, in the Slough of Despond, even in the Valley of the Shadow of Death, there are opportunities for awakening. Besides—though fairgoers in the city of Vanity might not appreciate this—since pride is the greatest sin, humility must be the highest virtue.

As for having to turn things upside down and inside out in order to see them rightly, this too can prove a blessing. Like those rainbow-enchanted days when the sky is laced with blue as the rain comes pouring down, such experiments help us to discover that things are not always what they seem. Searching for ourselves, we remember that until we are lost we cannot be found. Struggling for meaning, we recognize that until we are empty we cannot be filled. Seeking something in our lives that will abide, we awaken to the astonishing fact that only those things we have given away can ever truly be ours. We look out our window into the sun-drenched rain and say, "Even if God does not exist, we are here only by the grace of God."

Think of little things. Reaching out for the touch of a loved one's hand. Shared laughter. A letter to a lost friend. An undistracted hour of silence, alone, together with our thoughts until there are no thoughts, only the pulse of life itself. Imagine an afternoon spent free from worry about the things we have to do, or an afternoon tackling tasks we have avoided. Both may be somehow easier now, for we have been to the mountain. Though God was not there, upon returning home, if we look very closely, we too may discover that all has been touched by grace. God has returned to the mountaintop, but here in the valley below we follow for a blessed time in God's footsteps. The very ground we walk is holy land. We may not understand any better than before who we are or why we are here. But for this fleeting moment—the one moment we can bank on—our life becomes a sacrament of praise.

2 *Running Away*

I fled thee, down the nights and down the days;
I fled thee, down the arches of the years;
I fled thee, down the labyrinthine ways
Of my own mind . . .

Francis Thompson, "The Hound of Heaven"

Etched in my soul, and by far the most haunting memory of my childhood, is a fantasy of death. I date it to sometime after my family moved to Washington, D.C., when I was eight years old. I can't remember how often I succumbed to this fantasy, but I do recall what prompted it (a brutal argument with my mother), the time of day when these battles took place (right before bed), and the thing that triggered them (always a lie). When my mother caught me lying, not content to leave bad enough alone, I would fabricate more lies to cover up the first one. What finally piqued her anger into fury, whether my transparent mendacity or my panic-driven tears, I'm not certain. Given the premium placed on cheerfulness in our household, probably the latter. In either case, possessed by my favored demon (naked fear), I spun out of control, my mother's anger intensifying until it reached a fevered pitch. Invariably, the battle ended with me in total humiliation and banished to my room.

More vivid in my memory than the struggle itself is its

aftermath. After sobbing uncontrollably for a few minutes, I would launch my mind into a sea of self-pity. Into this wine-red sea sailed my fantasy of death.

Running away from home, I crawl out my bedroom window into the snowy night. Wearing only my pajamas, I wander in the bitter cold through the woods between our house and my elementary school. I fall into a snowdrift. Never have I felt so alone. And then I die. The snow stops and morning dawns. A schoolmate finds me lifeless in the snow, bursts into tears, and rushes off to tell my parents. "Come quickly. Forrest is dead." My parents hadn't missed me. They didn't even notice I had run away. Hastening to my side and falling to their knees to embrace my body, they beg me to awaken. My father becomes distant. My mother moans in disbelief. Through tears of self-recrimination and overcome by grief, she pities me with all her heart.

At this moment in my imagined melodrama, the floodgate opens once again, my self-pity magnified by the specter of me dead, my mother's lamentations almost too poignant to bear. But not quite, for with this I rewind my fantasy and play it back again, embellishing it yet further with loving detail: ripped pajamas, my beloved sock monkey frozen to my breast, my mother's raven hair blowing in the wind, the dark sun, the snow on my forehead.

And then, interrupting my fantasy, the bedroom door opened. A crack of light pierced the darkness, and in slipped my mother. Sitting down on the bed, she leaned over and hugged me, saying that she was sorry, confessing how very much she loved me. We cried together. She cradled me in her arms, my tears subsiding. An inexpressible calm settled over me. I shut my eyes. My mother rocked me gently until I drifted off to sleep. When I awakened in the morning, my fantasy of death was but a distant dream.

Tortured by addiction yet prescient of God's grace, the Victorian Roman Catholic poet Francis Thompson prayed for the same happy ending to his own flight. In Thompson's pilgrimage poem, "The Hound of Heaven," God reminds the fleeing seeker,

> *All which thy child's mistake*
> *Fancies as lost, I have stored for thee at home:*
> *Rise, clasp my hand, and come!*

When I was a child, my parents were more godlike than was the little God I prayed to at suppertime and before bed. Recalling this nightmare reminds me of how absolute my need for their love must have been. My childhood could hardly have been less traumatic, yet a single fight and its aftermath could plunge me into the depths of absolute abandonment. At times such as these, just how hopeless I must have felt is mirrored in the desperate measures—running away and dying alone—my mind concocted to reclaim my mother's affection.

Death is the ultimate escape fantasy. As anyone who has flirted with suicide knows, killing oneself not only represents the most perfect act of revenge but also guarantees an end to pain. As a painkiller, and as a curtain call as well, the idea of suicide can be incredibly seductive. Moving to the center of attention, we treat ourselves to a luxury that life heretofore has denied us. To fantasize about our own death and other people's shocked remorse over it permits us to cry at our own funeral. In addition, such a fantasy offers the bittersweet pleasure of imagining others crying for us, shedding the very tears for which we had longed unrequitedly during our lifetime.

Feeling underappreciated or misunderstood may stir similar reflections among people who have never toyed with suicidal thoughts. This phenomenon could explain the pleasure so many of us take from the funeral scene in Mark Twain's *Adventures of Tom Sawyer.* Presumed dead, Tom, Huck, and Joe walk down the church's center aisle at the end of the preacher's eulogy for them. Tears of sorrow turn into tears of joy as the entire congregation launches into the Old One Hundredth, praising God "from whom all blessings flow." Instead of being in the doghouse for misbehaving, Tom and his friends get high fives all around, simply for being alive. "Tom got more cuffs and kisses that day . . . than he had earned before in a year."

Our bemusement over Tom's vindication is innocent enough. But to fantasize provoking such grief drives logic to an illogical conclusion. My boyhood living nightmare is a case in point. To recapture (if only in imagination) my mother's love and pity, by fantasizing my death I removed myself from love's field of possibility. More than a matter of "looking for love in all the wrong places," this is a perfect example of hiding from the very thing one seeks.

My waking nightmare and its aftermath also reflect the basic elements of a familiar tale of sin and redemption. First, I abandon love in a search for love, flee home to find the comforts of home, destroy myself in order to be saved. Then, through no act of my own, I receive love, find home, and experience salvation. My mother knew nothing of my fantasy. It was not by willfulness or self-pity that I found fulfillment. It entered my room uncoerced and undeserved, like grace. All I contributed to my own redemption was to long for it and to be willing to receive it when it came.

In this childhood drama my mother assumes the role of a traditional Judeo-Christian God. She punishes me for my wrongdoing and then forgives me, each an act of love. I play the part of a two-bit Jonah. I sin, run away from God, cast myself into the deep, and—at the moment when everything seems lost—am saved. The story of Jonah is more nuanced, of course. For one thing, Jonah knows what is happening to him (at least until the very end he does). Beyond this, he takes flight for a nobler reason than that which prompted me to fantasize my death. Nonetheless, this well-known tale from the Hebrew scriptures fits the same archetype. Jonah jumps from God's arms only to have God catch him.

Jonah didn't want to be a prophet. As so often is the case, where there are many openings few apply. And it's hard to blame him. A true prophet must suffer. So when God calls Jonah and says to him, "Arise and go to the great city of Nineveh, go now and denounce it, for its wickedness stares me in the face," Jonah runs away. He books passage on the next ship out, not to Nineveh but in precisely the opposite direction. Almost at once Jonah's ship runs into high seas and then is hit by a mighty storm. White-capped waves crash over the bow. Should the storm continue, the ship will go down. Clearly the heavens are angry, and all eyes turn to Jonah. "Who are you?" the Phoenician sailors cry. "Where do you come from? What have you done wrong?"

"I am a Hebrew," Jonah replies. "And I worship the God of heaven, who made both sea and land. It is my fault that the sea has risen against you. God called upon me and I tried to flee from God. You must throw me overboard, and the sea will go down." Over Jonah goes; at once the sea grows calm, the ship is saved, and a great fish swallows Jonah.

For three days, deep within the belly of the fish, Jonah

prays to God, offering up his thanks and promising to do his duty should God give him a second chance. Jonah's prayers are answered. The fish spits him out onto the beach. Thankful and chastened, Jonah this time fulfills God's will, not his own. He travels straight to Nineveh and denounces its crimes, proclaiming that in forty days the city will be destroyed. But then something wonderful happens. The people listen, their king decrees a period of penitence, and God spares Nineveh.

Having followed God's orders, Jonah is furious. He did his duty, proclaiming God's vengeful justice, and nothing happened. Jonah feels a fool, his honor tarnished. He placed his reputation on the line, but God didn't deliver. Not to mention the fact that justice was not done. So what does Jonah do? He sits down east of the city and sulks. Displaying a divine sense of humor, God ordains that a climbing gourd should grow over Jonah's head to shade him from the sun. Jonah is grateful for the gourd, but at dawn the next day a worm attacks the gourd and it withers. As if to burn away his self-deceit, the sun beats down on Jonah's head. But Jonah will not abandon his newfound virtue. Growing faint, he offers up a final prayer to God, this time for death.

In the course of this brief story, Jonah fails twice—first on account of selfishness and, then, of self-righteousness. Yet, having saved the people of Nineveh despite their sins, God will not permit Jonah to destroy himself by self-pity. Instead God asks this leading question: "Are you so angry over the gourd?"

"Yes," Jonah answers, "mortally angry."

God suggests that Jonah consider things more carefully. "You are sorry to lose the gourd, though you did not have the trouble of growing it, a plant that came up in a night and withered in a night. How is it then that I should not be sorry for the great city of Nineveh, with its hundred and twenty thousand who cannot tell their right hand from their left, and cattle without number?" So ends the Book of Jonah. Everyone is saved: the sailors from the storm; Jonah from the sea; the people of Nineveh, themselves not Jews, by the God of the Jews; and Jonah once again, this time from himself.

The moral clarity of this tale springs in part from the first-name basis on which Jonah and God conduct their relationship. In our own stories God is more likely to be hidden than manifest. This fact complicates whatever personal seek-and-find or find-and-flee strategy we may employ in our relationship with God. But the question remains: What impels us to run away in the first place? In the search for an answer, consider the broader question: Why would we run away from anything we seek: success, companionship, community, health, freedom, responsibility, even love? What could drive us to subvert our most cherished aspirations?

Surely ignorance plays a role. We misread the map, choosing roads that lead away from our destination. In retrospect it is easy, perhaps too easy, to trace such mistakes. "I took the wrong job, married the wrong person, joined the wrong church, chose the wrong role models, picked the wrong friends, followed the wrong set of instructions." The problem is, such mistakes tend to repeat themselves. We jump from job to job, relationship to relationship, faith to faith.

Often our flight is spurred by disappointment. We know the nature of what we are fleeing better than we do the reality hidden beneath the promise of what we seek. At least we think we know it. We tend to forget that, wherever we go, we take ourselves with us. The trouble may not be in our stars after all, but in ourselves. In either case, whether we reach a dead end in life only to stay parked there or back into one cul-de-sac after another, when experience fails to teach us where to find what we are seeking, we remain in thralldom to ignorance.

Fear also spurs our flight from things we seek. For instance, when we approach a given goal, a fear of failure (or success) may kick in and send us packing in the opposite direction. An inner voice whispers that we are not worthy, or ready, or able to seize the very thing within our grasp. Then we rationalize backing away. We don't need the responsibility. Why court trouble or risk embarrassment? Having talked ourselves out of it, we take flight from our dreams in order to avoid judging ourselves for having failed to realize them. In this game of seek and hide, we shut down our dream works. Fearing the pain of an honest self-assessment, we distance ourselves from all reminders of our former aspirations by running, like Jonah, in the opposite direction. This avoidance lessens our fearfulness by muting our consciousness; it also completes the circle of our ignorance.

Fear, not hate, is love's true opposite. We can actually hate and love another person at one and the same time. In fact, we are more likely to hate people we care deeply about. But when fear takes possession of our hearts, no room remains for love. This is dramatically true of the most justifiable fear, when our lives are haunted by real not imagined monsters. Few horrors are more frightening than those inflicted by an abusive spouse or parent. When justifiable fear compels us to run away from home, we are far more likely to find God in a safe house than by cowering behind our own locked bathroom door.

More often, however, when fear spurs our flight we are running away not from another but from ourselves. Having many times been prompted to flight by inner demons—muting life or changing channels and turning up its volume—I know this pattern well. Turning to the comforts of the bottle was for me itself (at least in part) a fear-driven attempt to escape pain, especially that of worry or regret. Only after years of mistakenly self-serving resistance did I finally learn that suppressing pain strengthens its grip. Whether disguised through self-medication or by the distractions of work or some other all-consuming passion, hibernating pain gains in strength, securing—under cover of inattentiveness—its dominion over our lives. We may be chasing success, money, or security, only to discover ourselves more comfortable in the office than in our own living room. One can even run away from home at home itself, lost in the television or hiding under the bedcovers.

By contrast, though by definition a childish act, running away from home as a little boy might—not to die in the snow but on an adventure—break the spell of inertia. When our lives are languishing, it makes good sense to take a risk or two. Besides, fear will be as quick to dissuade us from embarking on a difficult, perhaps necessary, journey as it will to impel us on a foolish one. The same thing holds for ignorance. We may hate where we are in life, but at least we know what to expect when we get up in the morning. Wariness about unknown consequences can prevent us from doing anything of consequence to turn our life around. We may know enough to tinker with our lifeboats, but our backyard remains a dry dock, not a mooring, for them. By the time we finish all the repairs we deem necessary, it may be too late to sail.

To weigh the mixed advantages of running away, consider it in its safest and most familiar form. All of us run away when we travel on vacation. Why do people fortunate enough to exercise this option prefer to go away on vacation? Part of it has to do with escape. When we leave town, we break free from the grind of everyday routine, shelving in the backs of our minds those forever self-replenishing "to-do-today" lists, guilt-inducing reminders of unfulfilled good intentions and unfinished business.

Note that the words *routine* and *rut* share the same root. Daily routines invest our lives with coherence. To this extent, we should cherish them as hedges against chaos. Fulfilling everyday obligations invests our lives with purpose and gives them a recognizable shape. Just as it is sometimes easier to accomplish ten things in a day than to accomplish only one, the more organized our lives are, the more productive and predictably satisfying they are likely to be. Nonetheless, that which contains our lives can as easily constrain them. Apart from things such as daily devotions (for those who meditate or pray), repetition of most actions becomes stultifying; it numbs the mind. We can even get into a rut with our prayers. For all these reasons a vacation away can be liberating. When we stay in town instead, our week will not be free from household chores, e-mail, bills, phone calls, and appointments. Time off at home rarely constitutes a real vacation, one that disencumbers our lives by freeing them from familiar distractions.

Cynics may dispute this opinion. "What an odd thing tourism is," Bill Bryson observes. "You fly off to a strange land, eagerly abandoning all the comforts of home, and then expend vast quantities of time and money in a largely futile attempt to recapture the comforts that you wouldn't have lost if you hadn't left home in the first place." I admit, a few of my own vacations flirt with inclusion in this category. Happily, most do not. Simply by breaking our customary regimen, even frivolous vacations can serve a spiritual purpose, if only a modest one.

Besides, we don't go away on vacation merely to escape. We also travel in the hope of discovering something missing from our everyday lives. If shedding daily cares liberates us from routine fretfulness, traveling also expands our horizons. When motivated by a desire for significant experience, we journey in search of the eventful or extraordinary. For instance, I took my family on vacation to Egypt recently. As happy as I was to escape the responsibilities of home, far more enticing was the prospect of intellectual or, better, spiritual adventure. Putting aside such memorable moments as when a shopkeeper (in jest) offered me one hundred camels in exchange for my then sixteen-year-old daughter, everyone in the family discovered that it is almost impossible to visit the pyramids without coming away with a heightened sense of humility and awe. We embarked with the expectation of expanding our experience of human history and destiny. In neither case were we disappointed.

Should we expect too much from a vacation, however, our expectations will rarely be met. This outcome is particularly likely for ambitious travel, when a difficult journey is coupled with a lofty, life-transforming goal. The African explorer James Bruce offers evidence for this in his book *Travels to Discover the Source of the Nile,* published in 1790. In his own travels through Egypt, upon fulfilling his lifelong dream by discovering what he believed to be the fountainhead of the Nile River, Bruce was not elated but strangely depressed. "I was, at that very moment, in possession of what had, for many years, been the principal object of my ambition and wishes," he writes. "Indifference, which from the usual infirmity of human nature follows, at least for a time, complete enjoyment, had taken place of it. The marsh, and the fountains, upon comparison with the rise of many of our rivers, became now a trifling object in my sight." He thought back on the rivers of England—recollecting them as being in no way inferior to the Nile in beauty—and dismissed his quest as "a violent effort of a distempered fancy."

In his best-remembered admonition, Ralph Waldo Emerson warned us to be careful what we pray for, because we may get it. The human tendency is to want only what we do not have. When we get what we pray for, stripped of its mystery it may lose its allure. By the same token, whether with respect to vacations or spiritual quests, our risk of disappointment will bear a direct relationship to the misplacement of our expectations.

One who discovered his heart's desire near at hand after seeking "heaven" elsewhere was the English Romantic poet William Wordsworth. In his travelogue of the soul, *The Prelude,* Wordsworth blames unrealistically high expectations for his deflating experience upon reaching the Simplon Pass in the Swiss Alps, the ostensible "high point" of his 1790 tour through Europe. As for Bruce, the reality of Wordsworth's experience pales in contrast to his imagined vision, which "hides it like the overflowing Nile." Bruce's Nile is the goal that disappoints upon our attainment of it; Wordsworth's Nile is a perfect vision that floods reality once we actually experience it. It was only upon returning to his familiar haunts that Wordsworth

. . . shook the habit off
Entirely and for ever, and again

In Nature's presence stood, as now I stand,
A sensitive being, a creative soul.

As Wordsworth rediscovered, by expecting to find elsewhere what is missing from our daily lives, we overlook the divine within the familiar. Casting our hopes into the future, rather than being expectant of the present, we miss perceiving what he himself called "the kindred points of heaven and home."

If the repetitive nature of our everyday activities has placed us on automatic pilot, breaking this pattern can pay dividends. Nonetheless, despite the potential advantages of escape (getting out of our ruts) and adventure (discovering new things), the Nile—or whatever destination we set our hearts on—is no better a metaphor for success in the spiritual journey than is the proverbial pot of gold at the rainbow's end. Escape fantasies promote the mistaken belief that our dreams of fulfillment cannot be met right here and now. That we first must look elsewhere to discover this belief to be false makes it no more true.

For Wordsworth, imagination (not as fantasy but as insight) is the secret to spiritual fulfillment. Though our lives may be going smoothly, we may still dwell in disquietude, sensing the absence of what we have at our fingertips, not fulfilled by its presence. Whether seeking freedom, fleeing boredom, or both, we run away whenever our imaginations betray us.

Remember how as a child you would long for the coming of summer vacation? By February the very thought of summer was so sweet you could almost taste it. Summer meant freedom: freedom from school; freedom from indoors; in my case, even freedom from my parents for a few choice weeks. How I would pray for summer to come. I can recall many good things about summer, but I also remember the disappointment I felt while sitting with Jimmy on the stoop of my grandparents' house on Idaho Street in Boise almost any midsummer's day.

"Do you want to play baseball?"

"Nah, I'm tired of playing baseball."

"So am I."

"We could play soldiers, but we did that yesterday."

"How about Monopoly?"

"It takes too long."

And so we sat, plumped up in the very lap of summer, bored to tears. We were free as birds but with nowhere to fly, two little boys sighing on the stoop, budding existentialists weighed down by the burden of time on our hands and the luxury to do what we would with it. We could have done anything we wanted but couldn't find anything we wished to do. And then we grew up—still tempted to do only what we wanted to do, give just what we felt like giving, and go only where we cared to go. We called this freedom.

I continued my search for freedom throughout the years to follow. Not only by chasing rainbows but by seeking freedom from my feelings as well, I would purchase tickets to almost anywhere advertising itself to my fickle affections as a getaway from life's daily responsibilities. I lived *for* today, not *in* today. Finally, to myself I prayed, obliterate today. Crawl out the window. Lie down in the snow. Feel sorry for yourself and curse your mother. I spent years of my life either running away from home or burrowed deep in hiding there. I fled myself ostensibly to find myself; in search of God, I ran away from God.

Discontent stirs the imagination to range widely and sometimes wildly in the quest for inner peace. And yet, as Walt Whitman (the most present-minded of poets) is ever ready to remind us, everything we could possibly hope for in life is right before our eyes.

Will you seek afar off? You surely come back at last,
In things best known to you finding the best or as good as the best,
In folks nearest to you finding also the sweetest and strongest and lovingest,
Happiness not in another place, but this place... not for another hour, but this hour.

Though as simple a truth as any in life, this is one lesson I have to keep relearning. But I mustn't be too hard on myself. By one derivation, the word *experience* means "out of peril." What experience taught me is that sometimes the only way to ensure a safe homecoming is by submitting to the perils of running away.

3 *Home from the Sea*

I am here, more than that I do not know,
further than that
I cannot go. My ship has no rudder, and it is
driven by
the wind that blows in the undermost regions
of death.

Franz Kafka, "The Hunter Gracchus"

Fortune brings in some boats that are not steered.

William Shakespeare, Cymbeline

In a sense, we begin our life at sea. In our mother's womb we float untroubled by the dark, fed and warm within our amniotic sacs. Though memory is mute here, birth—to be thrust or wrenched into the piercing light of day—has got to be painful. Until we die, hard experience elaborates this pain, and the womb becomes a metaphor for refuge. This makes perfect sense to me. As grown-ups, when we find ourselves at sea, we are no longer safe there as we once were; we are lost and seek return to a secure mooring.

During my longest nights I find myself reflexively assuming the fetal position, curling my body into a ball, clutching a pillow for dear life. I am not ashamed of this. Whether it is driven by instinct, prenatal experience, or prehistoric memory coded in the cortex of our brain from the time of our ocean-dwelling ancestors, homing for the womb is a natural response to psychic overload. We reenact return passage to that tiny, heated domestic pool where life began.

With life comprising a succession of little deaths and births, in traditional religious terms, existential crisis offers the possibility of being born again. Think of it as the soul being in embryo. At times of trouble, fantasies of death may dance in our consciousness but new birth can follow. Rebirth can be painful too, but it is far preferable to the way we most ominously lose ourselves at sea, lulled into complacency, adrift and unaware of our peril.

Seafarers describe what happens to them after a few days away from land as a sea change. Even as they develop their sea legs, the grounding experience of home fades in memory. Sailors lose their grip on life-sustaining connections. We too suffer a sea change in the classic sense of the term when we forget our bearings, especially those that remind us of our responsibilities. Our affections wither; our lifelines to a saving, grounding reality fray. We can drift like this for years, oblivious to our soul's jeopardy, looking forward only to a numbing ration of rum and the sway of our hammock.

In every great sea story, from Herman Melville's South Sea adventures to Patrick O'Brian's Aubrey-Marturin chronicles, at some critical moment the fog lifts upon the specter of looming cliffs and hidden shoals. Only then does the captain realize how far his ship has strayed from where his calculations placed her. Until the advent of modern navigational devices, the most skilled seaman had to fix his sextant on the North Star. When clouds rendered this calculation impossible, the captain relied on rougher measures, including instinct, to negotiate safe passage. Without a star to guide us, we too may come to believe that we are heading toward a port of call while sailing in precisely the opposite direction. Just as perilously, should we grow accustomed to the fog banking our lives, we may forget the stars' very existence.

In these ways and many others, the sea constitutes a powerful metaphor for life's journey. It evokes both existential drift and essential awe. Whether it beckons us to contemplate eternity or we are lost there, it challenges our spiritual imagination. To pique our imaginations, the seventeenth-century English philosopher and scientist Francis Bacon reminds us, "They are ill discoverers who think there is no land, when they see nothing but sea."

The sea is not merely a solemn place, ever beckoning deep reflection. We are equally capable of domesticating the oceans for our enjoyment. Let me tell you a sea story about my mother and me, one that took place long after I had begun to bring God home and proof that perfection is not my journey's goal.

Two years ago, in the heart of winter, some agent of temptation invited me to be the speaker on a Caribbean cruise. I've been in the ministry long enough to know that to accept such an invitation—imagining myself basking in the sun while my congregants slogged through ice and snow—would be wrong. Clearly it would be wrong. "What week?" I asked.

And then I was saved. They wanted me to speak the first week of February, the week of my church's annual meeting. Deftly scrambling back to higher moral ground, I just said no.

Two days later they rang me up again. "How about the third week of January?" I should note that they called on a particularly frigid day, just the sort of day on which anyone, even a minister, might be tempted to sneak a look at his or her calendar. Mine, obviously doctored by the Devil, happened to be completely free. Not only did I fall, I leapt from grace.

Almost immediately I started feeling guilty. To begin with,

my wife had no interest whatsoever in wasting one of her vacation weeks on a cruise to almost nowhere, so I would have to go by myself. On reflection, I realized that this would not be particularly enjoyable. Since the only legitimate rationalization for doing something shamelessly self-indulgent is actually to indulge oneself, my sense of guilt was now compounded by a feeling of stupidity. And then it hit me. I could redeem myself. I could transfigure this dilemma into a moral triumph. I could take my mother.

I should say a bit about my mother. In a *New York* magazine article on Mrs. Bill Bradley written during the 2000 presidential primary campaign, the author described Bethine Church as the "godmother of Idaho politics." Not "fairy godmother," by the way, but a "grandmotherly figure with the soul of a cigar-chomping backroom pol." On this particular occasion, as the chair of the Gore campaign in Idaho, this seventy-seven-year-old "godmother" had managed to crash a large dinner party where Ernestine Bradley was slated to speak by bringing Tipper Gore along and insisting, in the spirit of fairness, that Mrs. Gore share the platform. My favorite depiction of my mother in the article reads as follows: "Bethine Church, a creaky granddam in a bright red blazer and a wild grin, escorted Tipper through the crowd, and . . . commandeered the best table, right in front of the lectern." (You should have seen her in a toga on our last evening at sea.)

In any event, with a clear conscience I devoted an entire week—as every son occasionally should—to caring for my poor, "creaky" mother. The weather wasn't perfect, but this didn't dampen my spirits. For one thing, an experience I recalled from the only other occasion when I lectured on a cruise ship had inoculated me against complaining. It was back in the late 1980s, and I was sailing on the *QE II* from Miami to Lima,

Peru. I remember waking early one morning and venturing out to greet the remnants of dawn. The sea air was brisk, the sky a canopy of clouds. Only one other passenger was with me on deck.

"Lousy day," he said.

"Not great," I replied.

And then a deckhand carrying a bucket and mop sashayed down the stairway singing a rousing, slightly off-color ballad. My fellow passenger took great offense. "Hasn't the idiot got eyes?" he muttered to me under his breath. And then, confronting the man directly, his voice dripping with sarcasm, he asked, "What do you sing on a good day, a dirge?"

"A good day?" the fellow questioned. "Why, this is a good day."

"You've got to be kidding," said the other. "I might as well have stayed home."

To which the deckhand replied, "My friend, there's many a blind man who would give his eyeteeth to look out on this day."

Thinking back on this little epiphany, I found myself a decade later somewhat perversely welcoming the occasional bout of misty weather. Consciously resisting any disappointment I might otherwise have felt presented me with an opportunity to give thanks instead for things that really mattered. I was alive. My mother was alive. We were together, and the day was young.

I grew up in the mountains of Idaho, but the ocean has always captured my imagination more than the mightiest peaks. The sea's horizon beckons me to contemplate eternity; its unfathomable depths, life's mystery. If I am paying attention, the humility I feel reminds me how tiny we are; the awe I experience fires me with an appreciation for the unsearchable expanse of the creation. Gazing over the ocean toward a distant horizon, I sense, with the poet Richard Wilbur, that "outside the open window/the morning air is all awash with angels." When it comes to miracles, far more persuasive than the stopping of the sun or the parting of the seas are the sun and sea themselves.

In reflecting on God's nature, the twentieth-century philosopher Karl Jaspers speaks of "the encompassing." This metaphor untethers the imagination. Poised halfway between infinitude and the infinitesimal—as much larger than our tiniest constituent part as we are smaller than the cosmos itself—our minds encompass the creation even as it encompasses us. Though dwarfed by the immensities of space, the mind that measures these immensities manifests its own true greatness. We are no less tremendous or fascinating than the universe we ponder.

Tremendous and *tremble* share the same root, as do *awesome* and *awful* and *terrific* and *terrifying.* In its haunting depths and darkness—together with the spell it holds over the lives of those who dare to challenge its power—the sea accordingly suggests a more forbidding set of images for life's journey. When lost we say, "I am at sea," when inundated, that we are drowning in whatever may be swamping us. We can drown in anything, even details. But most of the time when we feel lost at sea, it is because we are drifting through uncharted or turbulent waters.

Poets early seized on the ocean voyage as a template for life's journey. To reach home, sailors must navigate their vessels across treacherous seas, often with the shore nowhere in sight. By now the pattern should be familiar. We sail forth on an adventure, endure perfect storms, and are beached on distant islands, all in an attempt to return to safe harbor. Along the way—figuratively as well as literally—we are at sea. Beguiled by distant prospects or preoccupied by our daily struggles, we may even forget our ports of embarkation and final call. And when we do remember, we are less likely to be seasick than homesick.

Such is Homer's immortal tale of Odysseus, "the man of twists and turns driven time and again off course, . . . heartsick on the open sea, fighting to save his life and bring his comrades home." Everyone in ancient Greece knew the *Odyssey* by heart. Today it is a classic—that is to say, familiar more by name than by acquaintance. Yet, in its twists and turns, Odysseus's journey offers many telling metaphors for our own life voyage and longed-for homecoming.

Setting out from Troy for the isle of Ithaca (where his wife, Penelope, and son, Telemachus, await his return), Odysseus endures the hell and resists the seductions of a life lost at sea. The dramatic pitch may be higher in Odysseus's adventures than in our own, but over the course of a lifetime we too must resist the Sirens' song, navigate between shoals and monsters, disinter ourselves from the allures of false comfort, and remember who we are.

Odysseus's troubles begin when he purchases the ire of Poseidon by blinding one of the Sea God's sons in battle. Tossed off course by a great storm, Odysseus and his men finally happen upon the isle of the Lotus Eaters. Its amiable inhabitants can eat the delicious lotus leaves with more impunity than could the Greeks, many of whom lose all memory of home. Like the poppy fields in *The Wizard of Oz,* the lotus leaves induce a waking sleep that leads, if more subtly and slowly, just as surely to death.

After several more narrow escapes, Odysseus's fortunes brighten. Arriving at the island home of Aeolus, the king of the winds, Odysseus and his men enjoy a period of rest and hospitality. The king places all adverse winds that might blow their ships off course into a bag. Presenting this bag as a gift, he then charts for Odysseus the way back to Ithaca. Ten days later and in sight of their homeland, his sailors let the winds out of the bag.

Blown again off course, eventually Odysseus lands at Aeaea, isle of the Greek goddess Circe. Aeaea proves as dangerous as its temptations are enticing. Entering a pleasure palace filled with scores of beautiful women, Odysseus's men indulge their appetites. The women then cast a different spell, fittingly turning the revelers into pigs. In exchange for her lifting this curse, Odysseus consents to remain as Circe's consort. He might have lingered forever in the comfort of her arms, but this time his men save him, by urging Odysseus not to forget his quest.

The path home to Ithaca next passes through the Underworld, where Odysseus receives guidance from the blind prophet Teiresias, who reveals to him the dangers yet in store before he can regain Poseidon's favor. Even full knowledge of these dangers (including instructions on how to resist the Sirens' deadly song) offers insufficient protection to his crew. Odysseus secures a safeguard by chaining himself to his mast, but many others, though knowing they must plug their ears, nonetheless succumb to the Sirens' call. Enchanted, they dive into the reef and to their deaths.

Left with but a handful of companions, Odysseus next must navigate the narrow channel between the six-headed monster, Scylla, and the whirlpool of Charybdis. To avoid the whirlpool, Odysseus has to sacrifice six men to the monster. Finally, he washes ashore on a beach in Phaeacia. There he tells his story, wins Poseidon's forgiveness, and safely embarks on the last leg of his long journey homeward.

When Odysseus finally arrives in Ithaca, he doesn't recognize his homeland. Bereft of his last hope, he drags himself along the shoreline until he meets the goddess Athena disguised as a young shepherd. "Tell me where I am," Odysseus begs. "What is the country called and who live here?"

"Sir," replies the goddess of the gleaming eyes, "you must be a simpleton or have traveled very far from your home to ask me what this country is."

⁂

In *Returning,* his chronicle of redemption from a life of willfulness and addiction, Dan Wakefield observes that "following the spiritual thread of one's life sometimes seems like the plot of a science-fiction novel, one of those good ones like Isaac Asimov's 'Foundation' series, in which forces are at work moving people here and there in ways they don't themselves see and for purposes they don't yet even know about." Whether for good or ill, it does sometimes feel as if we are chance protagonists in someone else's story. Much theology is predicated on precisely the same caprice. If God is all-knowing and all-powerful, God knows the plot that our lives will take better than we do. We nod to this hypothesis whenever we try to explain the inexplicable by saying that it must be "God's will."

My own understanding of life and God leads me in a different direction. Though I may have little control over what will happen to me, I can choose how to respond. The choices I make affect both my character and the direction my life will take. Long before the Sirens beckoned them, both Odysseus and his crew knew exactly what they had to do to save themselves. Yet only Odysseus and a handful of others demonstrated the requisite discipline. The rest chose to tempt the fates, and perished.

Taken literally (in Hebrew and Greek as well as Latin), *conversion* is not "rebirth" but "turning." Once converted, we redirect our journey homeward. Conversion comes in many guises. For instance, the American short-story writer Raymond Carver turned his life around by a decision to stop drinking. From that point forward, he met life's trials with equinimity and grace. When dying of brain cancer at the age of forty-nine, Carver summed up the nine years of freedom he had enjoyed during what turned out to be the final decade of his life as "gravy."

For every Raymond Carver there is a Chris Antley, a convert who experiences the joy of homecoming only to drift back to sea to be lost forever. Tales of men and women who, longing for home, cannot manage to remain there once they find it, hold their own special power. Falling in this category, Antley's life story is both tragic and typical. He finds God, but even God cannot save him from himself.

Before dying of an overdose at the prime of his career, Antley was perhaps the greatest jockey of his generation. Newly married and a first-time father, he had long battled his addictions with the same passion that he contested races. The sportswriter Ed Fountaine calls Antley "the Joe DiMaggio of thoroughbred racing." At the apex of his reign, he crowned at least one winner for sixty-four straight days. In 1999—scarcely a year before he died—Antley won both the Kentucky Derby and the Preakness, a feat all the more impressive because, to do this, he overcame an eating disorder that had ballooned his weight by thirty pounds.

Fountaine assesses Antley's journey with the verve typical of great sportswriters: "The tale of his miraculous comeback from those dark days of despair made Antley an American hero. . . . How he vowed to his father he would ride again. How, like Forrest Gump, he ran through the countryside twenty-five miles a day to get back in fighting trim. How, at the last minute, he was handed the mount on Charismatic, then rode him to upset victories in the Derby and Preakness. And how, when the coppery chestnut colt broke his leg near the finish of the Belmont Stakes, costing him the Triple Crown, Antley jumped off and cradled the injured limb in his arms, saving Charismatic's life." To the untutored eye, not only these athletic and moral victories but his meteoric rise from petty thief and stable boy to champion represented the triumph of will over all manner of adversity. Chris Antley was the poster child for Horatio Alger's American dream.

Antley was brilliant, cocky, kind, and courageous. But he was something else as well. Chris Antley was powerless over drugs and alcohol. He disappeared for weeks immediately following his wedding, an event he called the happiest of his life. He returned to his wife, but in a deep depression. He couldn't shake drugs and appears to have run afoul of his dealers. Friends found him dead one day in the entryway of his home. They thought he had been beaten to death; toxicology results proved otherwise. Chris Antley was thirty-four years old.

After his first rehab, Antley told a friend about his newfound faith in God. "God is in every one of us," he said then. "You just have to find him. Something was growing inside of me without my realizing how powerful it was. Before I was blind to see that. I had a paranoia about sharing my feelings. I was hiding behind a wall. I don't have to live that way anymore. I wish you could jump inside my body right now to know how good I feel."

Shortly before his death, Antley scrawled on his living room wall a drawing of a crucifix together with this anguished prayer: "Jesus Please Save Me." You could take this as proof that God does not exist and Jesus cannot save. In fact, it demonstrates only that competing gods hold their own destructive and captivating power.

Describing his four-month residence in a rehabilitation facility in 1997, Antley spoke of having "dug deep into the depths of [his] soul and faced down some monsters." Yet, as anyone suffering from the disease of addiction knows full well, its monsters still beckon once one has escaped from them. Like Scylla, hidden in shadow, they can either seize you unawares or drive you into a whirlpool. The wonder is not that Chris Antley failed to negotiate the straits of addiction; it is that Raymond Carver and millions of others can look back from their deathbeds over their final years as a bonus, like pure gravy.

The literature of pilgrimage is rich with stories that weigh redemption against damnation, exploring how one person finds salvation while another succumbs to fate. In the early 1800s there lived a Dutch sea captain known for his devil-may-care pugnacity. Arrogant and audacious, he sailed routes no other captain would dare contemplate, braving the most vehement conditions—not to ensure swift passage but simply for the sport of it. One day the captain swore an oath that he would never balk at any wind or weather, should he have to sail all the way to Judgment Day. The Devil promptly cashed in on this golden opportunity, damning the captain to the high seas forever. Only one thing might rescue him from this fate—a woman's love.

This story held great sway over sailors' hearts. Terrified of the mortal consequences that might follow upon any encounter with the Flying Dutchman, they would hammer horseshoes to their masts. Legend has it that the ghost ship is sailing still on its never-ending voyage to Armageddon.

A classic tale of hubris and nemesis, the Flying Dutchman's story contains two lessons. Pride leads to a fall, and love can save a prideful heart. Whether the love of another or the love of God delivers us, once we lock our hearts, only a power beyond our own can spring them open. Even should we gain liberation, we must still bear the scars of punishment. Such scars have their purpose, however. They remind us of pride's cost and love's saving power.

Samuel Coleridge drives this message home in his parable "The Rime of the Ancient Mariner." Borne to the edge of Antarctica by a mighty storm and fated almost certainly to perish in an ocean of ice, Coleridge's mariner and his mates are rescued by an albatross who guides their ship's helmsman through the maze of icebergs back into the open sea. When first the bird arrives—"as if it had been a Christian soul"—they hail it in God's name. Yet on a whim, once rescued, the mariner cannot resist destroying the agent of their redemption. Lifting a crossbow to his shoulder, he shoots the albatross and with it their good fortune, as if through the heart. The wind dies; becalmed waters and a burning sun seal the ship's fate. Surrounded by water—"with not a drop to drink"—the irate crew drapes the albatross, a symbol of his impiety, around the mariner's neck. Parched and near death, they at last catch sight of a ship on the horizon. But it is a death ship (the Flying Dutchman?), and all but the mariner who damned them meet their doom.

He too is damned, "alone on a wide wide sea," with none to take pity on his soul's agony. Unable to pray to God, the mariner languishes without hope until one day he takes notice of a school of water snakes glistening athwart the bow of his ship.

O happy living things! No tongue
Their beauty might declare:
A spring of love gushed from my heart,
And I blessed them unaware.

With this the albatross falls from the mariner's neck, and his journey begins anew. His shipmates first return to life and are promptly and joyfully elevated to Heaven. Soon the mariner finds his way back home but with a charge to fulfill in order to expiate his sin. To the end of his days, he must share with others the lesson of love that saved him. Coleridge sums up this lesson in his best-remembered words:

He prayeth best, who loveth best
All things both great and small;
For the dear God who loveth us,
He made and loveth all.

Calling to mind the words of a well-known hymn, who once was lost now is found. "The Rime of the Ancient Mariner" is the story of a wretch saved by grace.

The sea captain John Newton wrote "Amazing Grace" to commemorate his conversion on that day in 1748 when, having survived a hurricane, he offered his life to God in thanks for his deliverance. Newton earned his living in the slave trade. Working his way up from impressed seaman to captain, he piloted ships filled with human chattel from Sierra Leone to the American South. It was on one such voyage, heading homeward to England, that this man, wholly lacking in religious convictions, threw himself on God's mercy as his ship appeared to be going down. He fell to his knees and prayed, confessing his sinfulness and begging God's forgiveness. Upon surviving the storm, he credited God for his salvation.

To those who knew Captain Newton, the change was evident. For one thing, he finally treated his cargo like human beings. Shortly thereafter he abandoned the slave trade entirely. Newton educated himself, then apprenticed under the Methodist evangelist George Whitefield and became a minister known throughout the world for his hymnody.

> *Thro' many dangers, toils, and snares,*
> *I have already come;*
> *'tis grace has bro't me safe thus far,*
> *and grace will lead me home.*

Only a heart open to grace can receive its gift. Odysseus's heart led him to continue homeward despite setbacks and temptations. Chris Antley could not resist temptation and lost first his heart and then his life to addiction. A woman's love could have saved the Dutchman. A spontaneous expression of praise for other creatures opened the ancient mariner's heart to God. And when John Newton felt that he could not save himself, he reached out to God—whom he may not actually have needed to keep his ship from going down but whom he did need to transform his wretched existence of shameless gain to a life of serving others.

When we don't feel lost, we must still pay heed. Sometimes the wreckage of a life is subtle. Our lives drift unconsciously from birth to death. Minding our own business, risking nothing, we drown slowly, keeping count of endless laps in far too small a pool. Until we know how lost we are, we will never be found. For this reason, life crises offer a promise that the peace of oblivion can't equal. To this extent, they serve us better. However trying the passage home may be, it is not to death alone, but to new life as well, that the sailor comes home from the sea.

4 *The Prison House*

. . . tear down
this house. A hundred thousand new houses
can be built from the transparent yellow
carnelian
buried beneath it. . . .

Rumi, "The Pickaxe"

The world is not a "prison-house" but a kind of spiritual kindergarten, where millions of bewildered infants are trying to spell God with the wrong blocks.

Edward Arlington Robinson

Right before finishing this book I flew in to New York City from the Dominican Republic on the very same plane that, on its return trip the next morning, mysteriously crashed, leaving 265 people dead on the sidewalks of Queens. Something that would have spooked me two months before—being one twist of wind, metal, or fate away from death—I took in stride. The terrorist attack on America didn't inure us to danger. But it did domesticate danger for us, bringing it—where it belongs—within the circle of everyday possibility. We need no further evidence of how fragile life is. Millions of tons of smoldering girders offer sufficient witness.

Yet few of us would wish to return to the way we were before September 11. More deeply aware of life's tenuousness, and more cognizant therefore of what really matters, many of us have become, at least for the moment, different people. Having been heartened, chastened, tempered, and challenged by the myriad witnesses to how magnificent the human spirit can be when called to rise to its true occasion, we have examined and questioned our own lives and priorities. And pondered our mortality. And wondered what we might do from this day forward to rescript our obituaries. The very stories that break our hearts make them beat faster. The emptiness we feel casts every selfish thought of petty fulfillment into question. These are good things. They save us from ourselves by saving us for others.

In my counseling over the few weeks following the September 11 tragedy, I talked to several people who finally, after months, even years of procrastination or rationalization, were ready to commit themselves to make something finer of their lives. "I've stopped drinking for good," one man told me. "I haven't been to church for twenty years," another confessed. "I've got to get my spiritual life in order." A third almost wept, "This has brought my husband and me back together. It's a miracle. I can't believe it. We've lost three friends. A dear cousin. And yet somehow in the midst of this tragedy we found one another."

Love's relationship to death is riddled with paradox. The more you love the more you risk to lose and therefore stand to fear. Yet love casts out all fear. The greater your love the deeper your grief at a time of loss. Therefore, grief is good.

The Chinese ideogram for the word *crisis* contains two ideographs, or word pictures. One represents danger, the other, opportunity. In a sense the extent of the danger in which we find ourselves is the measure of our opportunity for growth. One reason conversion stories can be so compelling is that they juxtapose the soul's preconversion bondage with its postconversion liberty. Before our redemption we hold ourselves captive. We remain prisoners until another turns the key that unlocks our hearts. Chinese finger puzzles—those little woven sheathes of bamboo grass—illustrate a like point. When we pull our fingers apart, the trap tightens; when we push them together, it loosens and we spring free. We needn't confront terror to observe this. We see it every day.

Some time ago a young man came to me for counseling concerning an unmade decision that had frozen his life. For a number of years he had been living with a woman who wanted to get married. He loved her deeply but was frightened of marriage. For months he had been going back and forth, paralyzed, unable to decide. Above all else he was worried about making the wrong decision, doing the wrong thing. And so he did nothing at all. In many ways he was a typical twenty-first-century, thirty-five-year-old, successful, unmarried man. That is to say, he was scared to death of commitment.

I met with him quite regularly. We made no progress. He simply couldn't decide. After eight months, not wanting to have him follow me to the grave with his problem, I said this to him: "There are only four options. You will get married and be thankful or get married and regret that you did; or not get married and be thankful or not get married and regret that you didn't." There was a long pause. He finally asked, "Well, what should I do?"

"Be thankful," I replied.

I told this story to my mother. She responded by asking me to remind her never to send anyone to me for counseling. Yet how often we find ourselves in a like predicament, living on the cusp, balancing past and future on the fulcrum of the present. At its worst, this balancing act suspends regret on one side of life's equation with fear on the other.

We can find ourselves trapped by inaction in many ways. First, when weighing a decision we need to make, we are on the cusp as this man was. On such occasions, however poignant our dilemma, it does have the decided advantage of being obvious. We have until Friday to make a decision, or—in the case of relationships—should we continue to procrastinate, others will eventually make the decision for us.

We also live on the cusp when we are preoccupied by matters over which we have no power. Obsessing about something we have done in the past or something that might happen in the future leaves little room for present possibility. If you suffer from this form of anxiety, a therapist may be able to help, but the best medicine might simply be to surprise an old friend with a call or go to a stupid movie. Anything to get you out of your own head.

In a third instance, our lives rest even more precariously on the cusp of existential paralysis. We know we need to do something to jump-start or redirect our lives but lack clarity as to what that might be or how we might begin to work a change. Then life lives us, not we it.

Finally, we may know precisely what we must do to change our lives for the better yet somehow cannot act on this knowledge. At such times the cusp becomes a blade. Unable to free ourselves from the pain we feel, we can escape it only by numbing our consciousness. And then the present disappears.

Cusp is an old astrological term. Having been born "on the cusp" between Virgo and Libra, I know it well. Had I been born but hours earlier, I would have been certified a Virgo: pure, rigid, disciplined, left-brained, an impeccable life player. Arriving on life's doorstep a few hours later than I did, I would have been an obvious Libra: artistic, open, creative, right-brained, the holy fool, seeking all that is harmonious. Born the hour I was, if astrology were the state religion, I wouldn't just be on the cusp; I'd be on the rack. Next time you read a horoscope in the paper, try putting the Virgo and Libra forecasts together. If Virgo reads, "This is the day you've been waiting for, so go for it—love, money, everything—don't miss a single opportunity to make a new connection," Libra is sure to say, "Take the day off, better yet don't even get out of bed; you might break your leg on the way to the bathroom."

For this reason among others I have never been tempted to take astrology seriously. Yet the cusp metaphor remains a good one. Balancing radically different options can prove bracing. It reminds us of how important our choices are. Yet, no matter what we choose, nothing good comes without the risk of failure or disappointment. And almost nothing good comes without pain.

Pain is the body's way of telling us that it is doing everything possible to help make us well again. The same thing holds true for the soul. For instance, the pain of a bad conscience reminds us that we have done something wrong. Having a bad conscience doesn't mean that you are a bad person. It means that you are a good person who has done something wrong and doesn't know what to do about it. By contrast, postponing pain by muting its symptoms has no redeeming qualities whatsoever. It signifies a life lived according to the principle of avoidance. For this, the best metaphor I know is Limbo.

It may strike you as strange that one would escape *to* prison and not *from* it, but that is the way Limbo works. It's understandable, really. By walling ourselves in, we wall the world out and with it all danger of risk, embarrassment, and honest pain. On the most meager of spiritual rations—our daily allotment of work and rest, with unlimited TV rights—we can set up house in Limbo quite nicely. Besides, there is no better place in which to nurse injuries. Wallowing in victimhood is by far the sweetest pastime of a sorry life. Safe in prison, we are free to tick off our precious list of grievances to our heart's content. We can lament the mess our parents left us, curse the cruelty of lovers and fickleness of so-called friends, not to mention all the other cards that life unfairly dealt us, leaving us a hand that we might as well fold as play. Victimhood is perversely sweet. From its pains one can wring more pleasure than might be imagined.

The problem is, when we lock up our lives and throw away the key, God can't gain entry. This may be fine for a while, but when death knocks or love beckons—when the walls close in around us or we remember to dream again—our safe house becomes a tomb. Having freed ourselves from the dangers of disappointment, we are bound in the captivity of regret.

In Catholic theology, Limbo is a special precinct reserved for innocents. Translated into our daily lives, it is where good people take themselves not to freeze or burn, just to exist until its spell is broken or they die.

- *Limbo is not going out because you aren't sure that you'll have a good time.*

- *Limbo is not speaking out when injustice is done because you're afraid that no one will listen.*

- *Limbo is holding out for the wheel of fate to spin in your direction.*

- *Limbo is dropping out the moment life gets difficult, when the going gets too "interesting" for you.*
- *Limbo is for people who postpone decisions, who want to ensure that they'll never be wrong.*
- *Limbo is where we remain every day we determine that we will change our lives beginning tomorrow.*

Limbo has its advantages. Until the recognition of where we are and who we have become finally catches up with us, there is little sharp pain in Limbo, only the dull throb of regret, uncertainty, and fear. We can elevate these things to the status of pain, but none compares with the honest pain of those who embrace experience more openly. For instance, when someone we love dies, the grief we feel is equal to our love. And whenever we entrust our heart to another, we risk having it broken. In either case, as a measure of our love, the pain of loss can be almost unbearable. Nothing, however—no act of betrayal or crushing blow of loss—can break an armored heart. This is one advantage of Limbo. Spiritually, the advantage is worthless: it destroys what it protects.

We imprison ourselves in Limbo, yet here the lock that holds us captive opens from within. God or those who love us can bang on our door as loudly as they wish, but they can gain entry only if we let them. One of my favorite spiritual guides is Frederick Buechner, who writes, "We are captives in the house we have built for ourselves, which is in many ways a haunted house—a house haunted, a world haunted, by the dark spirits we ourselves have raised—and to see it for what it is, even as little as we do, is to feel as estranged as slaves must feel in the place of their captivity. It is to feel, inside our own lives, as helpless to escape as slaves are helpless, because of course the one thing we can't escape is ourselves."

When Buechner was a boy of ten, his father put an end to depression by committing suicide. Haunted by this act, yet all the more determined to wrest from life a meaning that might sustain him through its inevitable trials, Buechner sought first for meaning within himself. But as long as he continued drawing only from his own resources, he remained a wanderer. Having won great success with his first novel and living comfortably as a teacher, Buechner confesses, "I felt I needed somehow to be cleansed of the too-muchness and too-littleness of my life, to be cleansed as much as anything, I suppose, of myself." On the flyleaf of his copy of *Gone with the Wind,* Buechner's father had written, "I am no good." From this the son caught a glimpse of the horrors of existential isolation. Finding his own refuge from self not in death but in God (on a journey that led him to the ministry), Buechner discovered that nothing, "not even ourselves, can separate us forever from that last and deepest love that glimmers in our dusk like a pearl."

~ ~ ~

Having learned this same lesson, no one teaches it more memorably than St. Augustine in his *Confessions.* The first modern book (if modernity can be said to commence with the emergence of introspection), Augustine's memoir of his pilgrimage from the secular city to the city of God has played a role in countless spiritual awakenings. Not only did luminaries such as Petrarch and John Bunyan take up and read Augustine's story but untold others equally well educated in skepticism trace their liberation to the self-recognition they experienced when reading his words. I am one of many to have seen my reflection in Augustine's dark yet illuminating mirror. His penchant for procrastination strikes a particularly familiar chord. Before finally entrusting his heart to God, Augustine was wont to pray, "Oh, Lord, grant me chastity and continency, but not yet." I can't count the number of times I have uttered a version of this same prayer.

From bargaining to temporizing, the games we play to keep ourselves trapped in Limbo are legion. I always have a ready excuse not to act. "My life is hard right now; I should wait until it gets easier." Or "My life is sailing along quite smoothly; why mess with a good thing?" One friend of mine calls this "better living through rationalization." "It might rain." "My plate is full enough already." "She won't really mind if I don't join her." And, besides, "Smoking helps guard against Alzheimer's."

Even as I write these words, I have no burning desire to pay the bills, make a dentist appointment, call my mother, or stop smoking. In fact, since my afternoon is more or less free (which invites procrastination), the closest I may get to setting a fire under myself this morning is by lighting a cigarette. I light a cigarette. Having thus struck "Stop smoking"—the most easily postponable of resolutions—from today's agenda helps me focus full attention on the unattractiveness of everything remaining on my plate. Nonetheless, I determine to take action. Do I pay my bills? Not exactly. I make a list instead, placing "Pay bills" right at the top of it.

To the seasoned procrastinator, list making is an art form. To begin with, one must not rush things. For instance, on this particular occasion I supplement my list with as many little items as possible. This strategy serves two purposes. First, prolonging the list-making process delays immediate action. Second, an overwhelming list can prove sufficient disincentive to taking any action whatsoever. A case in point: by adding lots of little tasks after "Pay bills," I confect a splendid buffer against "Dentist appointment," which is now so far down my list that I risk no danger of actually getting to it today. Moreover, since I cannot possibly tackle everything on my new, expanded list of tasks, why should I bother with any of it? I do pay that one bill (annotated in threatening bold print by what feels to be a very judgmental computer) announcing that "your telephone will be disconnected if we have not received payment for outstanding charges one week from the date listed below." All my other (less outstanding) bills can easily wait until tomorrow. As for the dentist, I might as well wait until he calls me. I spoke to my mother last weekend. And all the additional items on my list were afterthoughts. My process of rationalization thereby complete, in block caps on the top of my list I write the sweet words TO DO TOMORROW and reward myself with a cigarette and a day free for writing.

The strange thing is, I enjoy talking to my mother. I feel great about myself when my desk is clean, and I don't mind visiting the dentist nearly as much as I mind fretting about visiting the dentist. In fact, most of the things that I ought to do I take pleasure in having accomplished, not to mention the joy I get from ticking them off my list. Some unwelcome tasks I even relish completing, yet knowing this may still fail to provide sufficient incentive. The promise of postponed gratification is sometimes not enough. Something deep within me wants to skirt life's flame. If I can't raise it to the burning point of action or put it out, at least I can put it out of my mind. It's simple. All I have to do is quench my conscience.

For years my preferred solution to almost any discomfiture I might feel was a drink or two, that and a couple of newspapers (one was never enough)—anything to take me outside of myself and put my niggling conscience to sleep for a while. Since the absence of pain feels like pleasure, I could even view this as doing myself a favor. Besides, sins of omission are far easier to cover up, even from ourselves, than are sins of commission. Other people are rarely aware of things that we meant to do but didn't. Apart from my conscience—which is eminently mutable—I am less likely to get punished for skipping a hospital visit than I am for declaring false business expenses to the IRS. Should we need permission for our sins, it too is ready at hand. When on the lookout for convenient counsel, we can always find some co-conspirator or innocent who will happily or unwittingly oblige us by letting us off the hook.

I do my best these days not to seek out major mischief. We have trouble enough resisting the devilry that finds us on its own; why compound it by becoming collaborators? Yet, from long repetition, Augustine's prayer remains etched in memory. Anyone who has inhabited that grim circle in the Hell of good intentions reserved for those who resolve to reform on a regular basis knows its mantra all too well. Over the years during which I sporadically attempted to cut down on my drinking, my own version went as follows: "Both to save myself and also to free my loved ones from the whirlwind of my self-absorption, this time at long last I shall do what I know I must do. I shall mend my ways. I swear this on the Bible of everything I honor and hold sacred. Nothing will stop me. I shall no longer permit deceitful pleasures or the seductions of oblivion to undermine my will. Unlike all those other times when I made the same vow, this time I promise to change. And I will make good on this pledge. I shall turn my life around, finally and completely. Beginning tomorrow."

I didn't have to wait for New Year's Day to make this

resolution. Any morning after would suffice. Once it was made, I even found ineffectual ways to act on it. When my life would jump out of the shadows and mug me, I would dust myself off, stare in the mirror, recognize the harsh truth reflected there, and swear a solemn oath to change. Where a thousand casual glances had revealed a Dr. Jekyll, I could now see only a Mr. Hyde. Nothing cosmetic could redeem the specter of my life, this I knew. So I would take the pledge right there and then. Not only would I do this but, signing myself up for a full makeover, I would vow to work the impossible. "Henceforth I shall give up Scotch, cheeseburgers, and tobacco. I shall meditate upon waking, pray before sleeping, go to the gym every day, attend to every one of my parishioners' needs, and never again forget my mother's birthday." That I could make good on this final intention only the following February rendered it moot. Nonetheless—if but for short periods of time—in most other respects I did manage to honor these vows to myself. I could white-knuckle it through a week or two of perfection before arranging a transfer back from this new maximum-security prison to my accustomed captivity in the "country club" reserved for criminals who pose no real threat to society. Though it is also a prison house, at least there I could sign myself in and out whenever I wished. "God, grant me release from my self-imposed bondage," I continued to pray. "Soon, but not yet."

One can languish in Limbo without being guilty of a serious crime. Certainly this was true of St. Augustine, whose trademark offense was a mere peccadillo. As a boy of sixteen, he stole a few pears from a neighbor's tree. If I could trace my own problems to the theft of two pumpkins from a patch of thousands when I was nineteen, redemption would be a snap. Augustine's childhood infraction is a metaphor, of course. And the real crime was committed against himself. Necessity (poverty or hunger) didn't force him to steal. He had more and better fruit in his own backyard and didn't even enjoy the pears. The motivation for his thievery was idleness and mischievousness, both common to adolescence and therefore matters of little concern. Yet for Augustine this act symbolized both the heartlessness that stems from misplaced love and the willfulness of self-involvement and pride. Augustine recognized that he had been playing God. "In truth I was a prisoner," he confesses, "trying to simulate a crippled sort of freedom, attempting a shady parody of omnipotence by getting away with something forbidden."

For the first thirty years of his life, Augustine chased knowledge and pleasure with equal avidity. Brilliant and libidinous (though raised in a Christian home by a pious mother), he won acclaim for his intellectual precocity and personal magnetism. Augustine had everything, including the promise of worldly success, but everything was never quite enough for him. Haunted by the existence of evil in the world and in his own heart, he set out on a pilgrimage for wisdom. This took him on a tour of the popular fourth-century philosophies, his mind particularly captured by Manichaeanism (which posited dueling forces of good and evil) and Neoplatonism (which held evil to be an illusion caused by material appearances that veil the pure spirit of the Good). He even spent a brief time toying with astrology. Certainly he was on the cusp. Though he quickly became a noted rhetorician of every school of philosophy in which he temporarily enrolled, Augustine remained homeless.

After years of effort, Augustine's mother succeeded in persuading him to look to the church for guidance. Augustine's experience of life resonated with the Christian teaching that a good God created the world and that evil springs from human willfulness and sin. In Christianity, he knew he had found his true home. But his soul was wedded to pleasures that weakened his will to convert and make his dwelling there. "I was displeased that I led a secular life," Augustine confesses. "Now that my desires no longer inflamed me, as of old, with hope of honor and profit, a very grievous burden it was to undergo so heavy a bondage. For, in comparison of Thy sweetness, and the beauty of Thy house which I loved, those things delighted me no longer. But still I was enthralled."

It was love for his mistress that captivated Augustine most completely. Our own fleshly preoccupations may differ but, in describing his bondage to lust, Augustine well depicts the general nature of Limbo.

> With the baggage of this present world I was held down pleasantly, as in sleep: and the thoughts with which I attempted to meditate upon Thee were like the efforts of people who are trying to wake up, but are overpowered and immersed once more in slumberous deeps. No one wants to be asleep all the time, and sensible people agree that being awake is a better state, yet it often happens that a person puts off the moment when he must shake himself out of sleep because his limbs are heavy with a lassitude that pulls him toward the more attractive alternative, even though he is already trying to resist it and the hour for rising has come. . . . I was convinced by the truth and had no answer whatever except the sluggish, drowsy words, "Just a minute," "One more minute," "Let me have a little longer."

Even as Petrarch found what his heart had been seeking by randomly opening St. Augustine's *Confessions,* Augustine at last was converted by the same device. At his darkest moment, convinced that he would never escape the prison that held his soul captive, Augustine prayed, "How long, O Lord, how long? . . . Why must I go on saying, 'Tomorrow, tomorrow'? Why not now?" At this very instant, weeping in contrition and helplessness, Augustine heard the voice of a child from a neighboring house, as if chanting the words "Take up and read. Take up and read." He picked up a volume of the Apostle Paul's Epistles, which he happened to have with him. "I seized, opened, and in silence read that section on which my eyes first fell: 'Not in dissipation and drunkenness, nor in debauchery and lewdness, nor in arguing and jealousy; but put on the Lord Jesus Christ, and make no provision for the flesh or the gratification of your desires.' I had no wish to read further, nor was there need. No sooner had I reached the end of the verse than the light of serenity flooded my heart and all dark shades of doubt fled away."

In *Look Homeward, Angel,* the self-destructive yet self-knowing American novelist Thomas Wolfe writes: "The world was filled with silent marching men: no word was spoken, but in the heart of each there was a common knowledge, the word that all men knew and had forgotten, the lost key opening the prison gates, the lane-end into heaven, and as the music soared and filled him, he cried: 'I will remember. When I come to the place I will know.' " After a lifetime of bondage, Augustine came to that place and knew. As he repeats throughout his *Confessions,* "Our hearts are restless, until they rest in Thee."

❧ ❧ ❧

The one-time Richard Nixon aide Chuck Colson knew freedom behind bars. Charged with conspiracy for his Watergate crimes, in 1974 he pleaded guilty to obstruction of justice and served seven months in Maryland's Fort Holabird Prison. One year earlier, Colson became a born-again Christian. At the time many people dismissed his as a conversion of convenience, but since his release Colson has built an impressive prison ministry, devoting much of his attention to criminals suffering from addiction. To prisoners he preaches the gospel of Jesus, himself a prisoner: "That prisoner, Jesus, will be in your cell with His hand on you. He will make you God's own son or daughter. At that moment, a new life begins for you." Colson speaks from personal experience. It was not while he was serving his sentence that Colson's heart was imprisoned but during his years as special counsel in the White House.

On the other extreme of the political spectrum, the Black Panther and author Eldridge Cleaver tells a similar story in recounting his own conversion. For seven years Cleaver exiled himself from the United States to avoid serving time for the part he played in the 1968 Oakland police battle in which his fellow Black Panther Bobby Hutton met his death. Traveling throughout the world as a lecturer and organizer, Cleaver was hosted by the governments of North Korea, North Vietnam, China, Russia, and Cuba. He settled in France, continued his writing, and slowly lapsed into depression. One night he turned to the Bible and searched for the Twenty-third Psalm and the Lord's Prayer. He found them with difficulty. It had been years since Cleaver had rifled through his Bible. Yet that night, for the first time in ages, his heart found rest. "I slept the most peaceful sleep I have ever known in my life," Cleaver writes in *Soul on Fire,* his sequel to *Soul on Ice*. "I woke up the next morning with a start, as though someone had touched me, and I could see in my mind the way, all the way back home, just as clear as I've ever seen anything. I saw a path of light that ran through a prison cell." Shortly thereafter, Cleaver returned to America. He was greeted by a team of prosecutors and delivered to prison, where he served out his time. That is to say, Cleaver surrendered; *surrender* is another word for turning one's life over to God.

There is nothing unusual about Chuck Colson's and Eldridge Cleaver's stories. Untold numbers of people surrender to escape from prison every day, no matter the nature of their bondage. The annals of redemption contain millions of such tales.

Let me close by sharing another one. I discovered it in a letter posted from prison to Gilda's Club International, an organization that devotes its money and lobbying efforts to aid those suffering from cancer. Joanna Bull, executive director of Gilda's Club (founded in memory of the comedian Gilda Radner) sent a copy to her sister-in-law, my All Souls ministerial colleague Jan Carlsson-Bull, who passed it along to me. The childish hand in which this letter is written cannot disguise the brilliance of a remarkably acute mind. I share this letter unaltered and in full.

To Whom It May Concern:

I hope this missive finds you in high spirits. Your ad in *U.S.A. Today* put me in very high spirits. If a little guy like that [the child pictured in the ad] can stand up and fight cancer, then a 215-pound, 6 ft. man can go a round or two. But the significant feature of cancer reveals itself when you meet other people directly or vicariously and you experience real kindness. Someone to strain with, to strain to see you as you strain to see yourself. Someone to understand; someone to accept the regard, the love, that cancer sometimes forces into hiding. It's strange. The day I saw your ad in the newspaper a relentless rainstorm struck. It rained all through the night. I think you understand the emptiness a person can feel inside when they have cancer. That morning the storm abated to a drizzle, and suddenly it stopped. We were out in the yard—there is only one way to describe a prison yard with seven or eight hundred inmates interacting at one time—it's like the New York Stock Exchange. Suddenly an inmate pointed at the sky and shouted, "Look!" I looked where he was pointing. There, filling the whole sky, was the first complete and perfect end-to-end rainbow I've ever seen. Above it, like a technicolor shadow, was a second ghost rainbow about half as bright as the first. Above that, a third echoed, half as bright as the second, shimmering in and out of existence, leaking tears of color into the dome of the sky. At first only a few other inmates looked up and then those few began to shout. And then others took up the cry, tugging at their friends, gesturing at the sky. Everything ceased and the ambient background noises of the prison yard diminished into a silent symphony of spiritual wonder. For perhaps five eternal minutes nobody could speak. As I stood there looking at this rainbow hanging like a warm cloud in the arctic sky, a vivid picture of the little boy in the Gilda's Club ad appeared in my mind. A peace flowed through me so profound that the tears began to flow from my eyes. This was God's way of letting me know I wasn't alone. You have my sincerest regards.

May God shower you with peace and happiness,

Robert

The body that contains it may be cancer-ridden and behind bars, but any heart that can receive such abundant joy and express such perfect love is nothing if not free.

5 *Home After Dark*

Whither shall I go from thy Spirit?
Or whither shall I flee from thy presence?
If I ascend up into heaven, thou art there:
If I make my bed in Sheol, behold thou art there.
If I take the wings of the morning,
And dwell in the uttermost parts of the sea;
Even there shall thy hand lead me,
And thy right hand shall hold me.
If I say, Surely the darkness shall overwhelm me,
And the light about me shall be night;
Even the darkness hideth not from thee,
But the night shineth as the day.

Psalm 139:7–12

A quarter of a century ago, in the middle of his thirty-third year, lying one cold winter morning in the darkness, James Fowler awakened fully and suddenly to the fact that he was going to die. In the introduction to his book *Stages of Faith,* Fowler writes that for the first time he saw clearly that "this body, this mind, this lived and living myth, this husband, father, teacher, son, friend will cease to be. The tide of life that propels me with such force will cease and I—this *I* taken so much for granted by *me*—will no longer walk this earth." At first he was frozen by a feeling of remoteness, from the room itself and from his wife sleeping in the bed beside him. As his many little triumphs and accomplishments raced through his mind, each felt vaporous and fictive. His faith as a Christian minister too seemed to have no real substance, appearing to him to be as shapeless as an overcoat hanging on the door of his room. Fowler got out of bed. "I seemed to stand completely naked—a soul without body, raiment, relationships, or roles. A soul alone with—with what? With whom?"

Reflecting that faith is like an overcoat covering our nakedness, Fowler sought first to recover himself and then better to understand the many differing ways faith connects us to God. Sparked by a night of existential anguish, Fowler's search not only led to a rekindling of hope but also—as is evident from his book—invested his work with new-felt purpose. Fowler's contemporary, the Roman Catholic theologian Henri Nouwen, coined the phrase "wounded healer." "Hope means to keep humming in the dark," he wrote. Such humming is by no means futile. As Fowler's experience suggests, the music of hope can harmonize the darkness. Life can lift its song from death's score.

Nothing tests our spiritual mettle like a proverbial dark night of the soul. Whatever casts us into the abyss—the specter of our own death, some self-inflicted agony, or a twist of fate—the journey through midnight toward morning can be excruciating. Yet it carries a gift. Much as the consciousness of being alive is enhanced by a heightened sense of death, our awareness of needing to be saved springs most surely from the experience of being lost.

My own dark nights descend sometimes without warning, often with unwelcome news their harbinger. I endure them in the usual way. After an initial bout of denial, arguing, and bargaining, I reconcile myself to whatever fate reality has deposited at my door. Less tractable is the trouble I bring down upon myself. The cost to our sense of well-being is particularly steep when its bill of particulars is a lengthy self-indictment for all the things we might have done to avoid harming our own or others' lives. When we can answer the question "What have I done to deserve this?" by saying "Nothing," at least we don't augment the pain we are experiencing. But when we ourselves are to blame, time stops at midnight. Our minds haunt us with things that we can't change, words we can never take back, deeds that are fixed in the record of our days. As one girl in our church school puts it, life doesn't come equipped with erasers.

A saving paradox is at work here, however. Spiritual opportunity visits more readily when we in fact *are* responsible for getting into the thicket through which we find ourselves wandering. About another's actions we can do little. But if we own our culpability—admittedly a big *if*—we may discover that we hold it in our power, if not to rechart our steps, at least to proceed in a new direction. Life may not come equipped with erasers, but we can always resharpen its point.

Though we alone may be responsible for our predicament, to escape the grip of self-imposed agony we often need outside assistance. Don't think of this need as weakness or a crutch. When we fall, it takes more courage to ask for another's hand than it does to attempt to lift ourselves up by broken bootstraps. I was reminded of this again last winter when—unexpectedly, almost miraculously—the books closed on an unfinished chapter of my life.

As it turns out, my memory was mistaken. I thought I had found the letter tucked under my study door; a decade later she tells me that she sent it through the mail. I am quite certain of the season (Lent and therefore winter), for I quoted her note in my Easter sermon. I should ask her if my memory is playing tricks on me here as well. In any event, it came to me out of the darkness.

Dear Mr. Church,

What is the meaning of adversity? I don't think I can handle it anymore. Nothing it seems has gone right in my life. I am very tired of this stupid life. If you can tell me the reason for suffering or pain or adversity, please tell me. I know people do not have an answer, and I know many people overcome adversity but I am tired of it. I feel absolutely hopeless. Is there a god or is there not a god? If I feel there is not a god what is the sense of going on? And for whom?

I know this letter sounds crazy, but I am tired of it. I feel absolutely hopeless.

A Parishioner

P.S. Yes, I've had therapy and medication—now you must really think I'm crazy—but I remain hopeless. Please help me.

How could I be of help? I knew nothing about this person's identity. Asking my staff for assistance, together we tossed around a few possible names. A sometime parishioner had just lost his wife and children to a tragic accident. Perhaps he was the one. Another was facing bankruptcy after more than a year without work. Both were deeply depressed, and with good reason. We thought of the man who had gone off his medication and was acting strangely, and of the woman who had checked herself out of rehab and clearly was drinking again. But we were in touch with these people. Whoever had written this cry for help was nowhere on our screen.

I soon realized the enormity of our task. Even should the author have chanced into our midst, we wouldn't have known it. Any of our parishioners could have written that letter. Shortly before my arrival as minister, a successful investment banker and leader of the congregation closed a lucrative deal one day and took his life the next. I myself remembered the boy with a perfect report card and perfect family who no longer could bear the weight of perfection. Attempting suicide, he too sought to end his secret pain. I should have known this lesson by heart.

For almost a decade I remained in the dark about the author of this letter. Clearly he or she was depressed, perhaps even suicidal, but I could do nothing. I thought that the sermon—or my inclusion of the letter in my book *Life Lines*—might prompt a visit. Still not a word. And then the miracle happened. Two weeks before I started working on this chapter, I was leading the usual check-in before Wednesday evening prayers in our chapel. During the service everyone participates in Quaker fashion, praying in silence or out loud—as the spirit moves us. A sensitivity to what people are struggling with in their lives helps me open the service on the right note and also assists them in preparing their hearts for worship.

"I have been wondering whether or not to tell you this," she said.

"What's that?" I asked.

"I'm Anonymous," she replied.

"That's just fine," I said, not at all sure what she was getting at. "Anonymity is an honored tradition in twelve-step programs. On the other hand . . ."

"No, Forrest, that's not what I'm talking about. I'm Anonymous, the one who wrote you that letter, the letter you put in your book."

This revelation left me almost speechless. I scarcely knew this woman, not even by name until a month before, when she joined our prayer circle. Had you asked me, all I could have told you about her was that her prayers were always prayers of thanksgiving. She spoke often of the joy she received from life and from our church. In eloquent, simple words, she mentioned little acts of kindness, given and received. "This is real wealth," she said once. "Kindness is life's true miracle. Love, life's greatest joy."

One day I shall ask her how she managed to get from Hell to Heaven. She did say that my sermon and book both helped. Reaching out for help, she found it on her own. Experience teaches that, even as Hell comes cloaked in many guises, there are at least as many means to uncover Heaven beneath them. Clearly this woman found a way that worked. I'm sure it was hard. None of these ways is simple or painless. On earth, to get from Hell to Heaven, one must always pass through Purgatory.

When our lives are dark, with everything we see but a reminder of our soul's estrangement and alienation, the clearer our predicament, the more hopeless it may seem. Depression is like that. Leaving us impervious to beauty, joy, or laughter, like Fowler's solitary bout with death and darkness, depression severs our felt connections to anything that might rescue us from ourselves. It can hold us prisoner for months, even years.

Unmitigated darkness may even alternate with unnatural light. The work of the eighteenth-century poet William Cowper—who wrote, "God moves in a mysterious way/His wonders to perform"—reveals a wild swing between manic ecstasy and abject despair. "Laugh at all ye trembled at before," Cowper wrote at a moment of exultation. Soon thereafter he attempted to take his life with an overdose of laudanum, another time by hanging. Mysterious indeed. Cowper's poem "Lines Written During a Period of Insanity" describes his mood during one such midnight hour:

Hatred and vengeance, my eternal portion,
Scarce can endure delay of execution,
Wait, with impatient readiness, to seize my
Soul in a moment.

Clinical depression freezes life at midnight. The joy that others seem to take in life is irrelevant, if not insulting. Depressed individuals feel alone in company, estranged from the very people who most wish to offer aid. When I am counseling those who are suffering from depression, sometimes the most helpful thing I can do is shake my head and say, "Isn't it awful." Not tell them to go to the gym, or to set out and accomplish at least one thing every day, or to think about what a gift life is. Simply to love them and say so, this and how sorry I am for the misery they are enduring.

This is not much, I know. Nor is it enough. I also make sure that they are seeing a real doctor. If almost unbearably slow to kick in, psychotropic drugs can work wonders for people whose depression is triggered by a chemical imbalance. I have them promise me one more thing as well: that they won't kill themselves until they make a phone call. Together we write down at least six numbers (including my home and office numbers) for them to keep in their wallets. No deeply depressed individual can honestly pledge not to commit suicide, but keeping a promise to pick up the phone first falls well within the realm of possibility. One or two numbers is not enough, by the way; nor is the assurance "I will call you before I do anything." If the phone is busy or an answering machine chirps its sensible greeting on the other end of the line, anyone contemplating suicide will take this as one more sign (when almost none is needed). However—excluding vengeful final calls to punish others and thereby make one's suicide sweeter—merely to connect with the sound of another's live voice can be enough to break the spell of death.

The only way in which the most severe forms of clinical depression illuminate God's nature is by defining the limits of divine intervention. Neither Jesus nor anyone can save someone who is helpless to receive salvation. Psychiatrists and friends can provide a safety net and a measure of understanding, but beyond this we can do almost nothing. That such depression may lift on its own or by virtue of the right medicinal agent may teach patience and gratitude, but little more.

In the great majority of cases, though, the power of love and understanding works magic in helping to free one from the grip of depression. And when a depression does lift, the light, however flickering, is strangely more radiant. Witnesses to the dawning of hope are among the most clear-sighted observers of life's beauty. Through their keen eyes, we can see things we tend to overlook when preoccupied by the demands of daily living. Able once again to unwrap the present, those who return from Hell on earth have much to teach concerning how we might find Heaven here.

The primary symbol of Purgatory in Roman Catholic theology is fire. Not only does the fire of judgment accompany many of God's acts in the Jewish scriptures but the New Testament too suggests that fire that will separate human gold from dross in the final reckoning. Fire offers a wide range of symbolic nuance. It illumines, warms, incinerates, and purifies. As symbols of judgment, the latter two images are especially apt. Fire discriminates between substances, turning some to ash while tempering and perfecting others.

The third-century Christian philosopher Origen (who believed in Purgatory but not in Hell) was graphic in his description of the fires of judgment burning in Purgatory. "This fire consumes not the creature, but what the creature has himself built. . . . It is manifest that the fire destroys the wood of our transgressions, and then returns to us the reward of our good works." By this reading, the fire illuminating Purgatory's darkness is not the fire of Hell, it is the fire of Heaven. The word's etymology suggests a like interpretation. *Purify* (related to the word *pyre*) stems from the Greek root for fire. It means literally "to manufacture by fire, to make more perfect by testing in flames." Thus interpreted, the fires of Purgatory are fires of purification, not fires of punishment.

The problem with Purgatory as popularly understood is that Heaven is missing. This is especially true in common parlance. When Shakespeare's contemporaries Francis Beaumont and John Fletcher wrote, "There is no other purgatory but a woman," they were not bearing witness to women's power to cleanse men of their sins or free them from their pain any more than is the old adage "Marriage with strife is this world's purgatory" intended to suggest that we might perfect our marriages by adding a little unpleasantness to them. Such witticisms color Purgatory with a prejudicial pen.

Another obstacle to our employment of Purgatory as a metaphor is sectarian scruples, particularly among Protestants. The sixteenth-century reformers didn't drop Purgatory because it lacked a scriptural basis. They were upset by corruptions of the indulgence system—itself a corruption of the original doctrine of Purgatory—whereby people were enticed to give money to the church in order to purchase masses for the liberation of "poor" dead souls. In 1517, when Archbishop Albert of Mainz appointed a Dominican monk, Johann Tetzel, to sell indulgences, it was the latter's unprecedented success in the soul-brokering business that prompted Martin Luther to nail his Ninety-five Theses to the church door at Wittenberg. Luther's passion may also have been fired by the perverse little rhyme that Hans Sachs ascribed to Tetzel: "When in the box the money rings, the soul from Purgatory springs."

If common usage inverts the true meaning of Purgatory by replacing purification with punishment, the indulgence system subverts it further by preempting the process by which a soul is cleansed. There is no cheap grace in Purgatory, no matter how much someone is willing to pay. According to Dante, the soul's cleansing is complete when we feel ourselves to be purged and sound. This is a matter of self-recognition, not bestowed from without but confirmed from within. Here the doctrine of Purgatory can prove telling, even for life on earth. Purgatory is Hell tempered by Heaven. We receive salvation not despite our pain but because of it.

My favorite story of Purgatory is told about St. Patrick. Legend has it that when Patrick visited County Donegal, Ireland, brandishing a muscular gospel well-suited to vanquish the tired remnants of a once-thriving Druidical cultus, Christ appeared to him in a vision. Among those places holy to the Druids was a dark cave on the tiny island of Lough Derg. Because it was rumored to be the mouth of Hell and altarplace for dark priestcraft worked by Druid elders in the ancient days, no one dared approach this cave.

"Go there," Christ said to Patrick. "Enter the cave. Then return to the people with word of what you've seen. Great wonders will be revealed to you."

Valiantly his followers tried to dissuade Patrick from accepting Christ's dare. Druidical lore held that anyone who entered the mouth of Hell would not return. Even newly baptized Christians, protected by the seal of Christ, lacked the temerity to test their faith against the spell of Druid magic. But Patrick would not be moved. Correctly he perceived that this single act of valor, itself a reenactment of the victories of Yahweh over the priests of Baal, would do more to remove the veil of superstition than a thousand sermons. So he set sail at nightfall to enter the mouth of Hell.

All night long Patrick crouched in a damp, cold chamber deep within the cave. Just before daybreak his eyes opened upon a miraculous sight: the torments of Hell and the ecstasy of Heaven juxtaposed in a single image. *Loca purgatoria ostendit Deus*—"God showed him the places of Purgatory."

If, as scholars vow, St. Patrick's Purgatory in Lough Derg—once feared as the mouth of Hell but henceforth a place of penitential pilgrimage for Christians—has no connection with the saint, it hardly matters. Legends need not be based on fact to be grounded in truth. The truth revealed here is that Purgatory isn't someplace halfway between Hell and Heaven. It is Heaven and Hell at once. In Purgatory, people suffer well in order to be saved.

So understood, in literature Purgatory has many heroes. Some know that their lives are hell, others discover this fact along the way. But all heroes of Purgatory share one thing: out of the darkness they discover a light they had lost sight of, or never before knew existed. Through this discovery—born of an intimate acquaintance with despair—they experience redemption.

One such hero is Ebenezer Scrooge, from Charles Dickens's *Christmas Carol.* Unconscious of the hell his life has become, Scrooge seeks only to preserve himself from the soilage of the world. Early in life he had put together a formula to ensure his freedom from earthly care: attend to your own business, never meddle in other people's, work hard, secure a financial buffer against exigency, avoid sentimental attachments. As he himself explains, "It's enough for a man to understand his own business and not interfere with others."

"You fear the world too much," Scrooge's fiancée tells him during their parting conversation. "All your other hopes have merged into the hope of being beyond its sordid reproach."

Aptly enough, Scrooge's dark night of the soul takes place on Christmas Eve, one of the longest yet among the most cherished nights of the year. The story is familiar. His old partner, Jacob Marley, returns from beyond the grave, a ghost "doomed to wander through the world and witness what it cannot share, but might have shared on earth, and turned to happiness." Marley informs Scrooge that three spirits (the ghosts of Christmas past, present, and future) will visit him. As a gift from his old partner, Scrooge receives the opportunity before he dies to harrow Hell and enter Purgatory.

Not since he was a young man has Scrooge experienced pain. From early on he had perfected a technique for insulating his life. It was easy. Simply avoid the risks that accompany attachment to others. Having been hurt as a child, he would never be hurt again. At least not until that fateful night.

The first spirit tells him, "The memory of what is past makes me hope you will have pain in this." Scrooge begs release. "Spirit," he pleads, "why do you delight to torture me?" Yet after a night of torment, visited by visions from the past, present, and future (children mocking him at play, relatives suffering by virtue of his selfishness, the jocularity of his business associates upon hearing word of his death, his untended grave), Scrooge awakens transformed. For the first time in his life, he celebrates Christmas properly, with lavish gifts, imprudent tips, hearty greetings to strangers, charitable be-quests, family celebrations, and generous bonuses. He abandons the security of his private Heaven, which happened to be Hell. Home after dark, Scrooge's life is illuminated with a ray of hope. "I am not the man I was; I will not be the man I must have been except for this."

In the first chapter of the Book of Genesis, God doesn't just "let there be light, and there was light." It takes four days (in God's time) before the proper balance is struck between light and darkness. And still the darkness remains—in the firmament, between the waters, in our own lives. It is as if God keeps toying with the balance. Our lives are a little like that. We keep toying with the balance too. The hope contained in these first few verses of the Bible is that, at the end of each, God says, "It is good."

The question remains, How can we distinguish the light of God, whether shining through the darkness or in the bright of day? As always, theology offers many answers. To illustrate the varied ways in which God's presence might become apparent, consider three images drawn from optical technology: the magnifying glass, the prism, and the holograph.

With a magnifying glass, on a sunny day we can go outdoors, focus the otherwise imperceptible rays of the sun on some dry leaves, and they will catch fire. The rays of the sun beat down everywhere, of course, but—lacking the focus offered by the glass—they are not transformed into a tangible power that can turn tinder into ash. According to this model, two things are required for God's power to evidence itself. First, the human soul must be prepared. Even as wet leaves won't ignite in response to the sun's rays, an unreceptive soul is immune to the outpouring of God's grace. Second, God's presence must be focused. In traditional Christian parlance, the magnifying glass that focuses God's presence upon a receptive soul is the gospel. This metaphor offers a "hot" model of the way God might become manifest. It also explains why God's presence is not universally felt. God is with us always but, lacking focus and our own receptivity, we lack evidence. Only those who experience God through the glass of the gospel are set afire by the Holy Spirit and transformed, even as dry leaves are ignited and transformed by the focusing of the sun's rays through a magnifying glass.

The prism offers a different, cooler model, by which God—still transcendent—might be experienced objectively. A prism catches the light and breaks it into its component parts. God's light too is evident only with the aid of an instrument, in this case not the gospel but the human mind, through which life's manifold appearances are filtered in search of some pattern to explain not only their complexity but also their symmetry and orderliness. The cool model has long been a favorite among rationalists. During the Enlightenment it led to the argument from design. Focused through the prism of thought, the spectrum of reality was perceived to be so intricate and orderly as to demand the original efforts of a creative mind. If the hot view of God tends, in the West at least, toward a personal God who invokes a pietistic response in the hearts of his children, the cool view elicits a distant and respectful reverence for a much more impersonal divine master of ceremonies. By worshiping this God, many of my own Unitarian forebears earned the epithet (now shared with Episcopalians) "God's frozen people."

The third optical image, one more promising to twenty-first-century theology, is the holograph. Both hot and cool, the holograph differs from the magnifying glass and prism even as they resemble each other, offering a reflexive (both transcendent and immanent) image for God. The holograph works in conjunction with a laser, which records images on a photo plate made up of thousands of tiny lenses. The result is a three-dimensional hologram, like those you have seen in the Haunted Mansion at Disneyland or on your charge card. Mysteriously, if the photo plate is broken to bits and only a single shard of the original is employed for projection, the entire image, however faint, will be replicated.

Our bodies too are holographic. Each of our cells contains the full genetic coding or DNA for our whole being, an even more telling metaphor for the reflexive nature of divinity. As each organism is a colony of cells and organs, all marked with the same DNA, might not everything that lives be said to create a larger living system marked with the DNA of God? Far from unknown to past theologies, the same idea echoes throughout ancient scriptures. "The Kingdom of God is in a mustard seed." "The Father and I are one." "Atman [individual consciousness] and Brahman [universal consciousness] are one." "The Kingdom of God is within you." As with Paul's image of the cosmic Christ (one body, many members, each with the same signature of divinity), the holograph suggests God's reflexive nature in a way that transforms our relationship not only with the divine but with one another as well. Spun out of star stuff, illumined by God, we participate in the miracle we ponder.

You may have noted that I exclude mirrors from this array of optical images. If you wish to refract God's light into meaning, don't look to mirrors. They almost never work. As Scrooge did, we can learn lessons by looking back on our behavior with clear eyes, but almost never can we balance the light and darkness in our lives in the mirror of the past. Reflecting lost or stolen happiness, mirrored images are reminders of dreams that we have let slip away or that others have dashed. Whether recollecting another's actions, our own misdeeds, or things otherwise fated—by our given parents, the color of our skin, our gender, sexual orientation, or the economic stratum into which we were born—such reflections may help us apportion blame, but they do little to lift life's burden.

To abandon our hopes to the future—consumed by worry about things that may never happen—serves us no better. God's light shines on the present alone. Only an ability to discern the light within each passing moment can redeem our days from the pain that abides within them.

One witness to unexpected hints of light, illuminating the shadows of life and marking the path home, is the poet Kathleen Raine. In her poem "Exile" she writes:

Sometimes from far away
They sign to me;
A violet smiles from the dim verge of darkness,
A raindrop lands beckoning on the eaves,
And once, in long wet grass,
A young bird looked at me.
Their being is lovely, is love;
And if my love could cross the desert self
That lies between all that I am and all that is,
They would forgive and bless.

My once-anonymous parishioner's love crossed the desert self, leading her home through the light-riddled darkness from a personal Hell to the doorstep of Heaven. And for Scrooge, light pierced a darkness he didn't know existed. I have witnessed both miracles many times, in my own life and in the lives of others. Like Easter after Good Friday, we rise from the ashes. Life shines forth with meaning once again.

In the Russian Orthodox Church, out of the cool darkness of an early spring evening, the celebration of Easter begins with the blessing of new fire. Struck from flint, this new fire passes from one candle to another until the church is filled with light. Thomas Merton describes how, long ago on Easter night, peasants would carry the new fire back home to their cottages. "The light would scatter and travel in all directions through the darkness, and the desolation of the night would be pierced and dispelled as lamps came on in the windows of the farmhouses one by one." Emerging from the darkness out of deathly shadows, new fire is kindled from candle to candle, lighting home after home. "Even darkness, even evil, even death, seen by the light of the sacramental fire . . . can contribute accidentally, but existentially, to the life, growth, and liberty of our souls," Merton observes. "And [in] the night, then: the night of inertia, anguish, and ignorance . . . is the passage through non-being into being, the recovery of existence from non-existence, the resurrection of life out of death."

To practice spreading light in the darkness does not mean to extinguish the darkness. This we cannot do. But we can—if free from the grip of depression—see that shadows are only the actions of light being cast. By catching but a glimmer of the powering light, we can perceive strange beauty, emerging from our waking dream of death to appreciate life more fully. As our eyes grow accustomed, we discover that we can see in the dark.

Perhaps this is all we can hope for here on earth: Heaven and Hell at once, stark in juxtaposition, inviting us to enter the flames, to undergo the pains of suffering with those who suffer and share the joys of those whose lives are visited by joy. If so, all we can hope for is enough.

6 *Where the Heart Is*

Pilgrims on the way! Where are you?
Here is the beloved, here!
Your beloved lives next door
wall to wall
why do you wander
round and round the desert?
If you look into the face of Love
and not just at its superficial form
you yourselves become the house of God
and are its lords

Rumi, "Pilgrims on the Way"

My children and I were almost killed once, crossing the street right in front of our apartment building. It happened years ago but remains vivid in memory. The circumstances could not have been less ominous. I was walking them to their last day of school when—three-quarters of the way across, with the light in our favor and all of us dutifully holding hands—a car burst out of nowhere, hurtling around the corner at breakneck speed, ricocheting off the curb, and swerving into our path. I saw the driver clearly. She was a striking woman with wild eyes. Missing us by inches, her car skidded, fishtailed back into control, and disappeared. I could barely breathe; my knees buckled, my heart beat like a pile driver.

I try to teach my children about life's dangers. All parents do. Look both ways. Wear white after dark. Don't take candy from strangers. We answer their questions and dearly wish they'd ask us more. But put a crazed or drunken driver behind the wheel and our lessons mean nothing. On this particular occasion, I was horrified. In stark contrast, my kids just laughed, romping blithely down the sidewalk, jumping from tree to tree as they always did, trying to touch the leaves. Deeply shaken, not knowing what to think or say, I did the obvious thing. I got angry. Not at the driver. She was gone. I vented my anger at the children. I decided to teach them a lesson they had obviously failed to learn from experience.

"Never, ever let your guard down when you're crossing the street. Did you see that car? It almost hit us. It really did. We could have been killed."

"Come off it, Dad," my son Frank replied nonchalantly, jumping a second time at a branch that had eluded him. By this time my daughter, Nina, was skipping around the next corner almost out of sight. That did it. I exploded. If they remember anything about our somber walk to school that morning, it is that their father sometimes goes completely out of his mind. And they were right. Neither of them had done anything wrong. They were holding my hands, walking with the signal. I had no lesson to teach them. But life had a lesson to teach me: how fragile it is, and how precious.

How could I forget? Every Sunday, when I am closing worship, my benediction contains a reminder:

And now in our going
May God bless and keep us.
May the Light of God shine upon us
And out from within us,
And be gracious unto us,
And bring us peace.

For this is the day we are given,
Let us rejoice and be glad in it.

How often do we instead postpone our lives to some tomorrow, until one day when tomorrow doesn't come?

Think of all the things you plan to do tomorrow, or as soon as you can clear the space or find the time. "I'm going to do that when I get my life back," people say. The problem is, every opportunity we squander waiting for some life-transforming experience—every moment we fail to seize because our hands are too full—is lost to us. We will never get it back.

If our children can't awaken us to what really matters, nobody can. Sometimes they come right out and tell us. Children are by nature unafraid to speak their minds (at least until we teach them otherwise). Not that they are perfect, only to be ruined by their elders. After all, children are human too. But they do have much to teach us, simply by the way they view the world.

One of my favorite "out of the mouths of babes" love stories comes from a parishioner. I question it a bit, perhaps because I cannot quite imagine having this particular conversation with my own children. However, we tell moving stories not because they are completely factual but because they testify to a deeper truth.

This parishioner took his nine-year-old son camping one summer. Until recently—when my family and I went down the Middle Fork of the Salmon River and I learned better—my memory of camping was trout for breakfast: you catch it, you clean it. With a far more reverent outlook, this fellow pulled out all the stops when introducing his son to the grandeur of the creation.

As he regaled me with details of their adventure together in the High Sierras of California, I felt a twinge of jealousy, but only a twinge. After all, if die-hard high-rise dwellers had backyards, I too might spring for a tent and take my wife and children camping right here in New York City. Imagine the six of us in sleeping bags on a concrete balcony gazing out at the stars (all three of them), with me pointing out that the unflickering one is not a star at all but the planet Venus. But I know better. In places like New York, even planets flicker like stars through the shimmering haze of an artificially lit sky.

This other child's father is an architect. Judging by his buildings, I would conclude that the mountains and stars inspire him, though the towers he designs also supplant nature, domineering the heavens with their brilliant luminosity. When camping together, he and his son gazed out upon a different sky, its heavens gently darkening until, one by one, the stars came out.

"This is the eighth wonder of the world," the man said to his son.

"What are the other seven?" asked the boy.

Can you name the Seven Wonders of the World, a group of remarkable creations of ancient times? When my parishioner shared this story with me, off the top of my head, I conjured up three: the Egyptian pyramids, the Hanging Gardens of Babylon, and the Colossus of Rhodes. Not bad. But just in case one of my own children should ask the same question on some future virtual camping expedition, I took out a little insurance, looking up the other four in my encyclopedia. Here they are: the tomb of Mausolus at Halicarnassus; the temple of Artemis at Ephesus; the statue of Zeus by Phidias at Olympia; and the Pharos (or lighthouse) of Alexandria. Of course.

When it comes to the Seven Wonders of the World, my

friend the architect has a built-in advantage: architects designed five of them. But he didn't tell the story to boast of his craft. Quite the opposite.

He answered his son's question, describing each of these marvels in considerable detail. Then the two of them stood silently together, until the sky wound itself into a riot of stars. Minutes passed. The man lost himself in the heavens. The boy pondered his father's words.

"Daddy?"

"Yes, son?"

"Those things you told me about. They aren't the real Seven Wonders of the World."

"What do you mean, son?"

"The first wonder of the world is a baby being born. Don't you think so, Dad? The second is being able to see. Then comes being able to talk and walk. That's four. Hearing makes five. Then either touch or smell, maybe both?"

Looking upon the creation with new eyes, his father said, "How about love?"

"Love," his son repeated. "You got it, Dad. That's the eighth wonder of the world."

In both power and gentleness, no wonder compares with love. Not to see love is to miss almost everything, yet we can see love only through loving eyes.

Samuel Beckett wrote his play *Krapp's Last Tape* about a self-absorbed man who celebrated the end of every year by dictating his successes and accomplishments on tape while they were fresh in mind. At the end of his sixty-ninth year, Krapp decides to try something different. He plays all the old tapes over again. Listening, he discovers something about his life he hadn't noticed before. The memories that stand out—that give him greatest pleasure and, in retrospect, invest an otherwise meaningless life with a hint of significance—are not his victories, promotions, or private coups against some long-forgotten adversary. Instead, they are offhand moments of connection, when momentarily he became part of what little he had loved.

In contrast, when sorting through the files of his past for evidence of meaning, Danish scholar Johannes Jørgensen dismissed the value of everything (clippings, letters, and keepsakes) he had saved. A materialist and skeptic who had lost his faith in secular philosophies, Jørgensen despaired at the vanity of his existence. "Old newspapers, old Press notices, old joys and feuds—layer upon layer of the past. . . . The most varied handwritings, conventional, dashing, honest, affected, vague, firm. Old addresses, post-marks and dates. All my old life—arrangements about work; prescriptions and bills, engagement cards of friends, and continually my own name, which seems to me like the name of one dead—over and over again on all the hundreds of envelopes—the estate of one deceased. . . . I felt as one who is at home nowhere, belonging neither to the day nor the night."

Surveying his life, however vain, Krapp catches at least a glint of meaning in refelt moments of affection. Jørgensen saw no evidence whatsoever of redemption when contemplating the tokens of his own past. Reflecting on the Copenhagen of his formative years—and including himself in the circle of emptiness—Jørgensen observed that "such a state of spiritual ignorance had been reached that no one knew what love was."

Jørgensen's possessions made him poor. His house was full; his heart, empty. On the eve of his conversion, in catching his first glimpse of God's love, Jørgensen gazed through this emptiness to see a new life waiting, one "prepared for me who wandered lost." He prayed, he writes, "in exile, to an image strange to me," and received an answer within his heart. In an act of love another child of privilege, St. Francis of Assisi, sold all his possessions to aid the poor. After his conversion to Catholicism, among the books Jørgensen wrote was a biography of St. Francis. Though in his lifetime Jørgensen was never quite able to find the perfect peace that Francis promised, he knew his heart was finally in the right place.

The Book of Proverbs teaches us that "home is where the heart is." But our hearts can dwell in the wrong residence. It may house every manner of longing, only to be filled with an aching awareness of all that is missing within it. By their very nature, most of our desires can never be fulfilled. For instance, there is no such thing as enough money for those who fix their hearts on the accumulation of wealth. In fact, many of our dreams—for power, peace of mind, freedom, or happiness—recast themselves upon attainment.

- *As with money, a lust for power is insatiable.*
- *Apart from the larger peace of God, peace of mind can masquerade as an absence of pain.*
- *Freedom is worthless unless we expend it on some freedom-limiting responsibility.*
- *And happiness is particularly fickle as an object of our affections.*

Having pursued happiness with mixed success my entire life, I am especially well acquainted with the last of these idols. Our nation's founders understood the pursuit of happiness as a vocation not a chase, viewing happiness itself (by the light of Utilitarian philosophy) as the greatest good for the greatest number. As a personal quest not a social virtue, happiness often will elude those who pursue it. Since its meaning derives from the word *hap,* or chance, at root happiness is a chancy business. Depending on a thousand things, many outside of our control, we may happen to be happy one day, only to see our happiness evaporate the next.

Other idols of the heart disappoint as surely. For instance, if we devote our full attentions to the maintenance of health, we pledge them to something we can guard but cannot keep. Nor does the cultivation of knowledge or a devotion to work offer a secure home for our affections. With knowledge, our awareness of ignorance grows apace, and the work will go on without us. Money, power, peace of mind, freedom, happiness, health, and work all hold their own attraction and utility. They furnish our lives with more than a little joy. But to be fully at home in ourselves, to uplift and redeem all lesser affections, we must clear a place within our hearts for love.

The ancient Greeks distinguished among three forms of love: *eros* (romantic love), *filia* (brotherly love), and *agape* (divine love). Each is good, but romantic and brotherly love are only so to the extent that divine love—both God's love and the love of God—completes them. If *agape* is absent from the altar we erect to love, we risk worshiping an idol. For instance, brotherly love may foster hatred toward the siblings in another family. And, if we have eyes only for our beloved, romantic love can blind us to both *filia* and *agape.* Though celebrated as the greatest of the seven Christian virtues, love possesses a power to destroy equal to its power to save.

Witness the story of David and Bathsheba, as recounted in the eleventh and twelfth chapters of the Second Book of Samuel. While lolling about on his veranda late one afternoon, King David catches sight of his beautiful neighbor, Bathsheba, naked in her bath. On a king's prerogative, he calls her to his bed. Before the evening is over, Bathsheba is carrying David's child. As it unfolds, this story offers a perfect case study of love's idolatry and its consequences.

On learning that Bathsheba is pregnant, David recalls her husband, the soldier Uriah, from the field of battle. Were Uriah to lie with his wife quickly, the question of paternity might be blurred. But when Uriah returns, he refuses to comply with his sovereign's request, choosing instead to sleep fully armed on David's doorstep. Anxious to avoid the consequences of his actions, David asks Uriah—who surely must be weary after such a long journey—why he is so stubborn as to resist a bit of refreshment in his own home. "The ark and Israel and Judah dwell in booths," Uriah replies, "and my lord Joab and the servants of my lord are camping in the open field; shall I then go to my house, to eat and to drink, and to lie with my wife? As you live, and as your soul lives, I will not do this thing."

Faced with this testimony of honor, David concocts a second plan to subvert Uriah's will and attain his own end. The next night he gets Uriah drunk. But once again, upon suggesting man to man that Uriah might enjoy a nightcap with his wife, David is disappointed. The good soldier plants his feet firmly on high ground. With this David sends Uriah back to the field of battle, carrying a message to Joab: "Set Uriah in the forefront of the hardest fighting, and then draw back from him, that he may be struck down, and die." And so it comes to pass. Bathsheba performs a suitable period of mourning. The two lovers then marry and await the birth of their child.

An angry God sends the prophet Nathan, who confronts David with a parable. There were two men, one very poor, the other enormously rich. The poor man owned a single ewe lamb, which he loved as his very daughter, even inviting her to join him and his family at their table. The rich man had more sheep than he could number. One day, having invited a guest to dine with him, the rich man decided to spare his own flock, instead ordering his servants to seize the poor man's lamb, slaughter it, and prepare it for his supper.

As with most parables, Nathan's has two messages, the first obvious, the other veiled. Latching on to the obvious meaning, David expresses his outrage, vowing that the man who committed this unspeakable act deserves to die. To which Nathan responds, "You are the man."

In recognizing the self-deception of others, we may sometimes be Nathans, but when it comes to our own self-deception we are almost always Davids. Until Nathan brought the word of God to him, no one confronted David with his sin, because he was king. For us a veil of self-absorption—even absorption in a loved one—serves the same dysfunction as did David's protective mantle of royalty. This is no ordinary veil. It has the peculiar property that, though others may be able to see through it, we are blocked from seeing out.

The German Christian theologian and martyr Dietrich Bonhoeffer wrote of *eros* that it "makes itself an end in itself, . . . an idol which it worships." Such "human love has little regard for truth. It makes the truth relative, since nothing, not even the truth, must come between it and the beloved person." That was certainly true of King David.

Romantic love can also ransack the habitations of the heart. One reason hatred and love slip so easily in and out of one another's clothing is that, when *eros* is not reciprocated on its own terms, it turns against its object. In Bonhoeffer's view, *eros* "desires the other person, his company, his answering love, but it does not serve him. . . . So long as it can satisfy its desire in some way, it will not give it up, even for the sake of truth, even for the sake of genuine love for others. But where it can no longer expect its desire to be fulfilled, . . . it turns into hatred, contempt, and calumny." Conceived in future longing, such hatred is born of disappointed expectation. Tomorrow becomes yesterday, and the dream of love, a nightmare.

Hatred is rooted in the past; desire, in the future. God's love dwells only in the present. Hope can inspire us to reach for things that will invest our lives with meaning, even as memories of past illumination may prompt us to look for divine tracings where we are, not somewhere far away. But apart from these exceptions, nothing bound to past or future is of much utility in advancing our spiritual quest. This is as true of nostalgia as it is of expectation. Since both nostalgia and expectation are fickle, in our every present need they betray our heart's desire.

Nostalgia is a form of sentimentality that looks backward. We conjure up images of life as it once was, or as we wish to remember it, and pine away for the good old days. This is a highly selective process. We distill and embellish our memory. The result is a kind of fantasy, purified of imperfections, even of reality. We long for what never really was, regret its passing, and rue the present for its absence. Expectation is no less misleading. Expectation is premeditated resentment. Measuring some future reality against our lofty expectations, when tomorrow finally delivers the present we find only disappointment in it.

Recognizing that I shall never sate it entirely, I have developed and occasionally remember to practice a couple of tricks to satisfy my appetite for nostalgia and expectation, without permitting them to rob from the present the one gift that is surely mine to receive. The first I call nostalgia for the present. Today is that "good old day." I look wistfully at that which is mine this very instant to have and to love. As the Roman emperor Marcus Aurelius writes in his *Meditations,* "Do not indulge in dreams of having what you have not, but reckon up the chief of the blessings you do possess and then thankfully remember how you would crave for them if they were not yours." We can practice the same trick on our expectations by "looking forward to the present." Take something you already have and then wish that it was yours. Too often we think to desire only what we lack. Yet nothing is sweeter than to want what we already have.

Both nostalgia for the present and looking forward to the present enhance our well-being. At the very least they remind us to seize and thereby to redeem the day. Beyond this, they may open the gates of Heaven.

According to its root, the word *salvation* implies health. When Roman citizens greeted one another they would say, "*salve,*" or "good health to you." The Teutonic words *health, hale, whole,* and *holy* share a like etymological kinship. If salvation is health, it is also a state of wholeness or holiness. Following the same logic, sin is sickness or brokenness: we are conflicted within ourselves, divided against others, and separated from God. (The word *diabolic* means "divided.") So long as we remain divided within our hearts, alienated from others, and estranged from God, we are uprooted from the ground of our being—whether being alone, being together, or being alive.

Healing the division within us, salvation issues in integrity (or oneness). Through self-acceptance and right living, we come to love ourselves. With respect to neighborly love, the agency of salvation is reconciliation (union with others). Should another person not accept our offer of forgiveness, by extending such an offer we still may free ourselves from unhealthy preoccupation. Besides, we all need forgiveness. Nothing is more human than to squander or misplace our love.

We can budget our love also in the very name of love: the love of self. But this strategy doesn't work. As with freedom, we possess love's blessing only by investing it. Healthy self-love works along similar lines. To love our neighbor as ourselves is a cruel injunction if we despise ourselves. Given how hard it is to love ourselves sometimes, we are fortunate that love (like grace) is something we receive not because we deserve it but by opening our hearts to make room for it. When I could not pretend to love myself, my wife, Carolyn, rescued me from self-hatred through her love. By returning the gift of my wife's devotion—also by accepting her forgiveness and thereby finding self-acceptance—I made room for love within my heart.

In the largest sense of the word, salvation is oneness with God, our receipt of *agape,* the promise of grace. "Love is the reconciliation of man with God," Bonhoeffer wrote. "The disunion of men with God, with other men, with the world, and with themselves, is at an end. Man's origin is given back to him." Receiving back our "origin," we bring God home.

Dietrich Bonhoeffer spent the final years of his short life

in prison, awaiting execution for having knowledge of the assassination plot against Adolf Hitler. Pondering there both the love of enemies and the pain of separation from his loved ones, by drawing on his faith Bonhoeffer did something quite remarkable. He found room within his prison cell for his heart to flourish. Bonhoeffer's receptivity to grace receives eloquent expression in one of the last letters he wrote before he died. He sent it to his fiancée, Maria von Wedemeyer-Weller, just before Christmas 1944.

> These will be quiet days in our homes. But I have had the experience over and over again that the quieter it is around me, the clearer do I feel the connection to you. It is as though in solitude the soul develops senses that we hardly know in everyday life. Therefore I have not felt lonely or abandoned for one moment. You, the parents, all of you, the friends and students of mine at the front, all are constantly present to me. Your prayers and good thoughts, words from the Bible, discussion long past, pieces of music, and books—[all these] gain life and reality as never before. It is a great invisible sphere in which one lives and in whose reality there is no doubt. If it says in the old children's song about the angels: "Two, to cover me, two, to wake me," so is this guardianship, by good invisible powers in the morning and at night, something which grown-ups need today no less than children do. Therefore you must not think that I am unhappy. What is happiness and unhappiness? It depends so little on the circumstances; it depends really only on that which happens inside a person. I am grateful every day that I have you, and that makes me happy.

We can go for weeks without experiencing this same peace of mind. Instead, we slink through our days in the hope of getting through each without conspicuous incident. When night falls we sometimes think only to tick off our little list of grievances, not to give thanks for the honor of having one. Dietrich Bonhoeffer counted past gifts as present blessings. Even though he was about to die, his list was not an enemies list but a friends and lovers list. How could Bonhoeffer experience such peace on the eve of death, whereas we find so little in the midst of life?

Bonhoeffer drew inspiration from St. Paul. Writing from his prison cell to the Greek church in Philippi, Paul assures his brothers and sisters in Christ that they need not fret about his circumstances. Thanking them for their concern, he tells his friends not to worry, he is fine. "I have learned, in whatsoever state I am, therewith to be content. I know both how to be abased, and I know how to abound: everywhere and in all things I am instructed both to be full and to be hungry, both to abound and to suffer need."

If your own freedom is less liberating than Bonhoeffer's or Paul's bondage—which for most of us almost certainly is the case—you might try practicing those tricks of mind that often work for me. Imagine that today is tomorrow and also yesterday. Instead of pining over a past that is no more or longing for a future that may never be, greet the present with a wistful and anticipatory welcome. This perspective has nothing to do with living *for* today, disregarding consequences that might follow on self-indulgent or thoughtless behavior. It requires living *in* today, being fully present, awake and alive. It consists of reminding oneself that this is the day we are given, and then rejoicing and being glad in it.

In a piece he wrote for *Harper's* magazine, the essayist Peter Marin epitomizes nostalgia for the present in these wonderful words: "It is a passion beyond all possessiveness, a fierce love of the world and a fierce joy in the transience of things made beautiful by their impermanence. I would not trade this day for heaven, no matter what name we call it by. Or rather, I think that if there is a heaven, it is something like this, a pleasure taken in life, this gift of one's comrades at rest momentarily under the trees, and the taste of satisfaction, and the promise of grace, alive in one's hands and mouth."

Come to think of it, my kids had the right idea all along. We had just escaped from a brush with death. Why didn't I think to jump and touch the leaves?

7 *The Home Fires*

Keep the Home-fires burning,
While your hearts are yearning
Though your lads are far away,
They dream of Home.
There's a silver lining
Through the dark cloud shining;
Turn the dark cloud inside out,
Till the boys come Home.

Lena Ford, "Keep the Home-Fires Burning"

These boys from the old World War I song are soldiers, but they could be any of our children. When our children—be they dutiful or prodigal, settled or wandering—are far from home, we keep the home fires burning for them. In our spiritual search also, it never hurts to ask, Who keeps the home fires burning for us? Who tends our hearth, awaiting our return, when we are far away?

In his poem "The Death of the Hired Man," Robert Frost offers a solemn, if reassuring, definition of home: "Home is the place where, when you have to go there,/They have to take you in." Taken out of context, this definition is often couched in discussions of blood duty. Should our moral delinquencies shut every other door to us, we can always knock on our parents' door and it will open. This promise, most memorably recounted in the story of the prodigal son from the Bible, repeats itself from family to family throughout the generations. If but one person weeps for a mass murderer, it will be his mother. No wonder then—for most parents anyway—that lesser crimes lock neither parental heart nor home to the pleas of a wayward child.

The definition of home in Frost's poem is broader than this, however. It arises during the course of a conversation between a farmer and his wife. Mary proposes to her husband, Warren, that they offer a room to their farmhand Silas, an undependable sometime field worker who once again has returned from his wanderings. The man is no good, Warren argues; he will not have Silas back. "Who else will harbor him?" Mary asks. Warren mentions Silas's brother, a well-healed bank director who lives but sixteen miles down the road. "I think his brother ought to help," his wife replies. "But have some pity on Silas," she begs. Silas is like family. If he wishes to stay with them, their home should be open. Tweaking Warren's conscience further, Mary shares an additional piece of information. Silas is dying.

To help make up his mind, Warren looks to the heavens. He picks out a "small sailing cloud" from the sky and watches to see whether it will hit or miss the moon. It hits the moon. Taking this as a sign, Warren goes to talk to Silas and offer him a room in their home. When Warren returns too quickly, Mary senses that something is amiss. "Warren?" she questions. "Dead," he replies.

During the course of their conversation, it is Warren who acknowledges that home is the place, when we go there, that they have to take us in. In her rarely cited response to Warren's observation, Mary speaks in the language of grace: "I should have called it something you somehow haven't to deserve." Fixed in the constellation of life and death—and coupled with the heavenly sign that opens Warren's heart to Silas—through Mary's humble, all-forgiving observation, home is here consecrated into a sacrament.

In the original parable of the prodigal's return (as told by Jesus and recorded in the fifteenth chapter of the Gospel of Luke), a wealthy man has two sons, the younger of whom asks his father to divide the family estate and give him his inheritance. His father agrees, upon which his son promptly turns his portion into cash, leaves home, and squanders his inheritance in a life of riot. After years of self-indulgence, the young man is left with nothing (and with the country suffering a famine, his prospects for recovery are further crimped). The only work he can find is slopping pigs at the estate of another landowner. With the pigs better fed than he, he asks himself, "How many of my father's paid servants have more food than they can eat, and here am I, starving to death. I will set off and go to my father, and say to him, 'Father, I have sinned, against God and against you; I am no longer fit to be called your son; treat me as one of your paid servants.' " The reconciliation that follows is an archetype for unconditional love. Catching sight of his prodigal child approaching home, the father runs to kiss and embrace him. The boy protests that he is not worthy. His father will have none of this. He calls for his best robe to be given to his son and a fatted calf killed for a celebratory feast.

Upon hearing this extraordinary news, the elder son steps forth to defend the claims of justice. As always, they are remarkably persuasive. Refusing his father's plea to enter the family home and join in the festivities, through tears of righteousness and rage the good son complains, "You know how I have slaved for you all these years. I never once disobeyed your orders; and you never gave me so much as a kid, for a feast with my friends. But now that this son of yours turns up, after running through your money with his women, you kill the fatted calf for him." His father answers him as God might answer: "You are always with me, and everything I have is yours. How could we help celebrating this happy day? Your brother here was dead and has come back to life, was lost and is found."

It is no wonder that Augustine read Jesus' parable of the prodigal son as a script for his own flight from and return to God, for it has all the markings of a classic conversion narrative. Both Augustine and the prodigal son leave home, where they enjoy yet find no satisfaction in an abundance of everything, including love. Both wander lost through distant lands, indulge their every appetite only to end up famished, and then return as penitents to their fathers' houses, to new gifts and unprecedented welcome.

Augustine interprets this progression as a journey of the soul. To God he confesses, "We do not go away from you or return to you on foot or by spatial measurement. Nor did that younger son in the Gospel get horses for himself or chariots or ships; he did not fly away on any visible wings or travel by any motion of the limbs that in a far country he might waste in riotous living what you gave him at his departure." The distance we travel from God is spiritual not physical. As in every conversion narrative, the journey is one of self-loss (or self-alienation) and self-recovery. Yet the pilgrim remains lost until he finds his way home. Home is our reference point for self. The base of identity remains, no matter how far we may range away from it. Augustine confesses to God, "Your light was within, and I was outside."

Augustine's and the prodigal son's adventures are but records of return: they lead inexorably from home to home. The journey between is necessary only to the extent that neither can appreciate what is his to begin with until he loses it. Augustine naturally interprets Jesus' parable in ways that illuminate his own conversion. Replying to questions about its meaning, he casts the story in terms of loss and recovery. First the prodigal has, then he loses, and finally he regains wealth, security, and love.

This paradoxical pattern of losing oneself to be found echoes the promise of redemption that Moses makes to God's people in the midst of their forty years of wandering in the wilderness:

> If you turn back to him and obey him heart and soul in all that I command you this day, then the Lord your God will show you compassion and restore your fortunes. He will gather you again from all the countries to which he has scattered you. Even though he were to banish you to the four corners of the world, the Lord your God will gather you from there, from there he will fetch you home. . . . When you turn back to the Lord your God with all your heart and soul, he will again rejoice over you and be good to you. . . . It is not in heaven, that you should say, "Who will go up to heaven for us to fetch it and tell it to us, so that we can keep it?" Nor is it beyond the sea, that you should say, "Who will cross the sea for us to fetch it and tell it to us, so that we can keep it?" It is a thing very near to you, upon your lips and in your heart ready to be kept.

Here (as recorded in the thirteenth chapter of the Book of Deuteronomy) Moses couples God with home and home with life. "I offer you the choice of life or death, blessing or curse," Moses says to God's people. "Choose life." All conversion stories narrate life and death choices that lead to a homecoming: the self who was lost is found; the prodigal returns. In every such story, to find our way home we must first find ourselves. Yet there are two parties to conversion, sinner and forgiver. The good news—at least according to the Torah, Jesus, and St. Augustine—is that, no matter how far we stray, God keeps the home fires burning.

There is nothing easy about opening our hearts and homes to those who have done nothing to deserve our hospitality. To forgive may be divine, but we humans find it more natural to err than to forgive. Not only miscreant field hands and sons who run riot but also the most ordinary children have been known to do their human worst to undermine the prospects for unconditional love. There is logic at work here. It is hard to open our arms to embrace another's problems when they contribute to our own. Keeping our houses in order is difficult enough without adding someone else's mess to them. And a returning prodigal, especially one who has lost everything, carries a load of emotional baggage. When we are the victims of our supplicant, it is far easier to turn our back than to turn the other cheek. The reason love can turn to hate so quickly is that the sins of our loved ones tend to unsettle our lives far more than do the sins of other people who may happen to wrong us.

As in enlightened society, in our families we do our best to strike a balance between love and justice. The problem is that love and justice operate according to very different sets of rules. We mete out justice on a crime-and-punishment or virtue-and-reward basis, whereas love, especially unconditional love, is based on a sin-and-forgiveness model. Rather than a reward for good behavior, love, like home, is something we somehow haven't to deserve. Therefore, love entails forgiveness. Love is not "never having to say you're sorry." Love is having to say we're sorry over and over again. Love is also having to say, "I forgive you," to a child, spouse, parent, or friend who has done nothing to deserve our forgiveness.

In almost every household, love and justice models collide in classic fashion during the period of adolescence, when children test their parents' authority in a fierce attempt to establish their own identities. In the most basic sense, a power struggle occurs between children (who wish to have the privileges of grown-ups without the attendant responsibilities) and their parents (who feel responsible to establish the same level of control over their nearly grown-up children that their own parents failed to establish over them).

For instance, my seventeen-year-old son Jacob breaks what he considers an unreasonable curfew. In response, his parents ground him. He refuses to accept their authority. The ensuing argument—in which both parties demonstrate just how childish we all can be regardless of how grown-up we appear or how much we wish to be treated like adults—is hateful and hurtful to everyone. Yet, from one blowup to another, most parents and adolescents manage to ride this roller coaster of passion without being thrown off its track. Given the heat intrinsic to internecine battles and the anger such arguments inspire, without the renewal of love by forgiveness (received and reciprocated) to maintain such equilibrium would simply not be possible.

When the car does go off the track, the result can be tragic, and ironic as well. I know of parents who refuse to let their teenage child return home in punishment for having run away from home. More generally, repeated attempts to impose or escape authority can lead to an estrangement so deep that years must intervene before true reconciliation is possible. In my experience, those who have the hardest time forgiving themselves for being human tend to be most judgmental of other's imperfections. In parent-child relationships I call this throwing stones at mirrors. Even as we cannot piece shattered mirrors back together, when the home fires grow cold it is hard to rekindle them by blowing on the ashes.

A loving parent or spouse recognizes that to overlook repeated instances of destructive behavior only encourages its continuance. Nonetheless, saying, "I love you, but you cannot ever do this in our home again," is very different from saying, "I hate you because you did this in our home" or "Because you did this in our home, you can never return." By closing our hearts to another, not only do we lock them, precluding the penitent prodigal's return; we also imprison ourselves within them. When we impose a life sentence on a loved one in punishment for a crime against love, justice may be done but love dies.

However idealistic it may seem, religion offers a contrasting model, enjoining love as an absolute in all of our relationships. Following in the spirit of Jesus, we love not only God but also our neighbor as ourselves—the two commandments Jesus singles out in his Sermon on the Mount to sum up "all the law and the prophets." The paradox is, when Jesus tells us to love our enemies, it is not for their sake that he asks this of us but for our own. In Frost's telling, as well as in the scriptures, the story of the prodigal son illustrates this point perfectly. Unconditional love sanctifies the lover's own heart.

I could illustrate both the difficulty and the importance of keeping the home fires burning with many examples from my own youth. In fact, on my continuing quest to bring God home, I have spent a considerable amount of time reflecting on my childhood, especially on my relationship with my parents. I had attempted to unpack this relationship before, especially in therapy, which I always found helpful. But by this time I was looking for something different. No longer had I any interest in revisiting the past to augment my list of grievances, because—though dog-eared from use—that list was no longer serviceable. Regret may be perversely sweet, but its seductions lure us into arms that offer neither comfort nor release. Nor did I wish further to indulge in self-justification; the self I had so long attempted to justify was precisely my problem. However mixed my inheritance, having squandered so much of it, I alone stood squarely between God and myself. And yet, in a strange way, the road home to God still passed through my parents' house. To make room in my heart for God I needed to empty it of preoccupations over things I could not change, only let go. To free my spirit from ineffectual obsession over my own sins and sins committed against me, I needed to confess and forgive. And to cleanse my soul in preparation for receiving God's blessing, I needed unconditionally to bless my parents and the life they gave me.

As a boy, when I demonstrated need for moral instruction, the all-purpose adage in our household was "The chickens will come home to roost." Though not given to cliché, my father was enamored of this particular bit of wisdom. Whenever I was tempted to rationalize "ends justify the means" misbehavior, the roosting chicken metaphor hit uncomfortably close to the mark. Its moral was both obvious and, as with most truisms, demonstrably true. Our misdeeds come home to haunt us.

My father, Frank Church, served in the United States Senate from Idaho for twenty-four years, incidentally spanning most of my youth and my entire adolescence (at least that part of my adolescence that was age-appropriate). In retrospect, I recognize that the lessons he tried to impart to me had broader application. For example, during his investigation into bribery of foreign governments by American-based multinational corporations, as well as in the Church Committee exposé of CIA assassination plots (against foreign leaders not international terrorists), my father iterated the danger to our nation's soul whenever we fight "crime with crime, evil with evil, or delinquency by becoming delinquents." He reminded straight-faced executives—who said that they had to break the law in order to do business overseas—that their excuse "is written plainly in the adage, 'When in Rome . . . ' but the excuse is hollow. The bad habits of Rome are brought home to America." He argued that "ours is not a wicked country and we cannot abide a wicked government." And (later adopting a phrase from my Harvard professor George Huntston Williams) he employed similar logic to defend his early opposition to the Vietnam War: "We must choose our enemies carefully," he said, "because we will become like them." Chickens come home to roost for misbehaving nations as well as for children who cut corners in order to get what they want.

You might have thought that having a liberal father would have curbed the prodigal tendencies of even the most clichéd late-sixties adolescent. For me this turned out not to be the case. The gulf between my father and me was enormous. That we both were affected by it is evident from the events leading up to my wedding in the spring of 1970. I had spent my last quarter of college as a bit player in the revolution, manning the barricades at Stanford University. That my father at this very juncture in our history was writing the legislation that would finally put a stop to the bombing of Cambodia—that he and a handful of others in the U.S. Senate had struggled for years within the system to bring the Vietnam War to a close—made little difference to me. The system he was fighting to preserve from its own folly was finished, or so I passionately believed.

That May, my first wife and I got married. Of course we wrote our own ceremony. As a minister who has now performed hundreds of weddings, I still inwardly (and unfairly) cringe when a couple tells me that they are planning to do the same. Our vows were not really vows. They were more on the order of a manifesto. Among other things, I proclaimed that I would never serve in the military.

My father almost missed the ceremony. The Cooper-Church Amendment (designed to put a cap on our growing involvement in Southeast Asia) was under debate on the floor of the Senate, and he barely broke free in time to make the last plane west. When my parents arrived, I proudly showed them our vows. My mother was audibly appalled. My father just got a little quieter than usual. Not until years later did I realize how often my parents had bent over backward to avoid getting in my way. They must have been especially conscious of how my father's position complicated my life. I, by contrast, was all but oblivious to how my positions or actions might complicate his. As I recall, my father simply said, "Forrest, I am not going to tell you what you can or cannot say in your wedding vows. Your pronouncement of pacifism, however, could not be more poorly timed. All I ask is that you not release it to the press." Honoring his wishes, we did not distribute the handsomely printed commemorative copy of our vows to the guests. But this compromise did not keep the gist of what we had pledged to each other from being reported. Among other places, it turned up in the Idaho papers and also in the armed forces magazine *Stars and Stripes*.

This was far from the worst moment in my relationship with my father. Two years earlier, during his 1968 reelection campaign, I was known among the Frank Church staff as George Hansen's (his opponent's) secret weapon, a ticking time bomb that could go off any second and dash my father's hopes. Their concern was well-founded; I was a political father's nightmare. Taking advantage of my mere existence, someone from the Hansen campaign mischievously hired a band of disreputable-looking longhairs to canvass door to door in northern Idaho, saying that they were members of my San Francisco "Hippie Club" and importuning terrified housewives to be sure to vote for my father. (I remember how offended I was that anyone could possibly couple my existence with anything as bourgeois as a club. Cell perhaps, but not club.) Sporting a Cossack beard, I kept a stash of marijuana in the boiler room beneath our house. I had turned this dank cellar into a romantic grotto, painting the pipes black, silver, and gold, and furnishing my makeshift bookshelves with hard-rock records and unread communist tracts. Between my music (from Frank Zappa to Cream) and my books (from Trotsky to *The Communist Manifesto*), I had everything needed to supply the least ambitious investigative reporter with a front-page story crippling to my father.

The story was never written, and my father won reelection. Today, with four adolescents of my own, I wince when I read that my father wondered whether I loved him and questioned whether he had been a good father to me. Perhaps more troubling, I have forgotten what one biography of my father describes as a partial reconciliation between us that appears to have taken place midsummer that year in the Idaho mountains. Evidently we embraced one evening by the Salmon River. I cried. Tears welled in my father's eyes. We apologized to each other, begging forgiveness and confessing mutual love. Recollecting our conversation that evening, my closest friend, Peter Fenn, told my father's biographer that "it was the kind of thing that a lot of people wish they had done with their fathers at some time." So there I was, experiencing what every son prays for; yet I have no recollection whatsoever of the encounter during which this prayer was answered. That I have forgotten my reconciliation with my father in the summer of 1968—while remembering so vividly the tension between us leading up to it—illustrates how difficult it is to compose a fair representation of our past from remembered images. It also underscores the decided advantage unconditional love holds over retributive justice in interpersonal relationships. If our hearts were ledgers, we could never balance them.

I could fill these pages with the sins of my parents as easily as with my own. There is no question parents complicate the lives they bequeath, and we can all apportion some blame on our parents for who we have become. To balance disappointment in ourselves with an appropriate measure of disappointment in our parents invests our lives with a healthy equilibrium. This is the goal of therapy. But for me, dredging up old grievances has lost its appeal. We must assume responsibility for who we are; certainly we have much greater power to shape our future than to change our past. Accordingly, we serve ourselves better by taking our own moral inventory than by taking someone else's. We may be innocent of the pain others inflict on our lives, but—as my father taught me—when our misdeeds come back to haunt us, it is we who need forgiveness.

❧ ❧ ❧

To place all this in a larger context, consider our child-parent relationship with God. According to Christian teaching, as children of God we are always welcome in God's house, whatever our sins may be. The seventeenth-century poet and preacher John Donne writes, "We are all prodigal sons, and not disinherited; we have received our portion, and misspent it, not been denied it. We are God's tenants here, and yet here He our Landlord pays us rent; not yearly, nor quarterly, but hourly." Remembering that we too are prodigal children, to make room for God we must find room in our hearts for others. To see this dynamic more clearly, reverse the characters. When God knocks, does the prodigal child refuse his holy parent entry? You wouldn't think so, but that's the way the story often goes.

Madeleine L'Engle is both a novelist and a confessing Christian. "The Lord's table is the prototype of the family table," she writes. "If I think in terms of the family table, I know that I cannot sit down to bread and wine until I've said I'm sorry, until reparations have been made, relations restored." The same holds true for her children. "When one of our children had done something particularly unworthy, if it had come out into the open before dinner, if there had been an 'I'm sorry,' and there had been acceptance, and love, then would follow the happiest dinner possible, full of laughter and fun."

Beyond our doors, the world is rife with injustice and undeserved tragedy. Perhaps the old adage should be reversed:

"To err is divine, to forgive, human." Without judging the Creator, the best we can come up with is that to forgive is both human and divine. Through forgiveness, in L'Engle's words, "reparation is made, relations restored, love returned."

As manifest in churches, mosques, and temples, the House of God itself is (or should be) always open to welcome home God's children. Madeleine L'Engle and her husband, the actor Hugh Franklin, began building a relationship with God when they moved to the country and, for the sake of their children, joined a local congregation. Inspired by the ideal of Christian community, they expanded their family by becoming foster parents to orphans. On returning to New York City, L'Engle became active at the Cathedral of St. John the Divine and began testifying (both there and nationally) to the saving gift of grace.

Two other novelists, both prodigals who experienced God's grace by returning to church, are Dan Wakefield, whom I've already mentioned, and Anne Lamott. Both subsequently won freedom from addiction and have gone on to serve as guides for countless others in spiritual writings of unforced power. Wakefield—a cultured despiser of religion who looked first to Freudian analysis to find escape from what he later recognized as self-imposed bondage—saw his own story in the parable of the prodigal son when he began attending King's Chapel, a Unitarian church in Boston. "I was particularly moved especially by the moment the prodigal son knew it was time to go home and so—in that simple and profound summation—'he came to himself.' "

It was Thanksgiving. The Reverend Charles Forman spoke of exile in his sermon. "I was struck by how each of us lives those stories, and repeats variations of them, in our inner as well as our outer journeys," Wakefield remembers, as he does the preacher's words: "If this year your story is one of loss, and you are as an exile in a strange land, remember that even in such a place the Lord's song will yet be sung. In God's good time, even exiles at last come home."

Wakefield's exile continued awhile longer before he found release from his addiction to alcohol and drugs. Even then he realized that he still had "much more 'housecleaning' " to do. In the chronicle of his spiritual journey, *Returning,* Wakefield reminds us that the story of the prodigal son too continues after his homecoming. "How nice it would be if exiles could end their troubles and live happily ever after simply by coming home. But those are the endings of fairy tales. We aren't told what happened to the prodigal son after his father welcomed him back, but the anger of his jealous older brother does not portend a future of sweetness and light." Yet by returning to God's house "not only for inspiration but for solace, a respite from the all too common afflictions of the human condition," Wakefield did find some of the comforts that had been missing from his life.

Anne Lamott's story is akin to Wakefield's. She too languished in the self-destructive throes of addiction, finally crossing over the threshold of St. Andrew Presbyterian church in Marin City, California, one step before consigning her life to the abyss. "When I was at the end of my rope, the people at St. Andrew tied a knot in it for me and helped me hold on," Lamott writes in her book *Traveling Mercies*. "The church became my home in the old meaning of *home*—that it's where, when you show up, they have to let you in. They let me in. They even said, 'You come back now.' "

The child of a writer and herself an accomplished novelist, Lamott drew inspiration from her own resources until the well of self ran dry. It is evident from her writings that she is still searching for her earthly father—for some kind of closure that will open her to the possibility of a more abundant life. But when she showed up drunk at church one day, even through an alcoholic fog Lamott sensed the possibility of a homecoming. She describes this encounter in her graceful text on writing, *Bird by Bird*. "A black man at my church who is nearing one hundred thundered last Sunday, '*God* is your home,' and I pass this on mostly because all of the interesting characters I've ever worked with—including myself—have had at their center a feeling of otherness, of homesickness. And it's wonderful to watch someone finally open that forbidden door that has kept him or her away."

Lamott shares a parable her pastor told from her own childhood about a friend who got lost one day. "The little girl ran up and down the streets of the big town where they lived, but she couldn't find a single landmark. She was very frightened. Finally a policeman stopped to help her. He put her in the passenger seat of his car, and they drove around until she finally saw her church. She pointed it out to the policeman, and then she told him firmly, 'You could let me out now. This is my church, and I can always find my way home from here.' " For the same reason, Lamott stays close to her church—"because," she says, "no matter how bad I am feeling, how lost or lonely or frightened, when I see the faces of the people at my church, and hear their tawny voices, I can always find my way home."

For both Lamott and Wakefield, homecoming was impossible until they stopped drinking. Yet the embrace of forgiveness and acceptance they received in God's house gave each of them a promissory note for subsequent redemption. Because they lived the story of the prodigal, their appreciation for home is all the greater, something that one who has lived the life of the elder son might post on his or her mirror.

~ ~ ~

I am grateful to have reconciled with my father long before he died. Fortunately, I can remember other occasions when we shared tears and expressed our love for each other. I took time off from my doctoral work when he ran for president in 1976. We even won a few primaries together. I say together because the campaign was a family operation. Cheap help is a necessity when you are running for president on next to no money. I also had the privilege of sharing my father's death. He almost died of cancer when I was a baby. The miracle that saved him (a then-experimental radiation treatment) was so intensive that even at the time the doctors told him it would take years off the other end of his life. In his fifty-ninth year cancer revisited, and within three months my father was dead.

Years before he told me that his chosen way to die would be a massive heart attack. "One moment I would be walking down the street playing with a thought, the next moment I would be dead." What he feared most, and secretly expected, was a recurrence of cancer. How fortunate it is that we are not in charge of our own destinies. Though he was basically at peace with himself, during the final months of his life my father was able to make a closure that in tangible ways was redemptive. For one thing, he was surprised by the outpouring of personal affection and gratitude for the work he had accomplished. As one whose only belief in immortality was cached in the bank of personal and historical memory, he was sustained by this gratitude. As for those of us who gathered first around his hearth and then at his bedside, this gift of time offered one more chance to say how much we loved him.

We had long since forgiven each other, he and I. And I still had miles to go before I awakened, before I realized how far I had drifted away from God. But that I was welcome in my parents' home—fully welcome—foreshadowed how it might feel to be at home in myself. Even today I get warmth from my father's fire. My heart shares his laughter and receives his blessing.

When Walt Whitman was a nurse in the Civil War, he sat by a campfire one night, "the darkness lit by spots of kindled fire," and dreamt of home:

> *O tender and wondrous*
> *thoughts,*
> *Of life and death, of home and the past and loved, and of*
> *those that are far away;*
> *A solemn and slow procession there as I sit on the ground,*
> *By the bivouac's fitful flame.*

However prodigal our footsteps—however great the distance we have traveled in our wanderings away—if we know that somewhere the home fires are burning, we are never far from home.

8 *Be It Ever So Humble*

Not because of victories
I sing,
having none,
but for the common sunshine,
the breeze,
the largesse of the spring.

Not for victory
but for the day's work done
as well as I was able;
not for a seat upon the dais
but at the common table.

Charles Reznikoff, "Te Deum"

Three weeks before he died, my father chose the words for his tombstone. Knowing that a slab of Idaho granite would long outlast living memory, he weighed what message to post for strangers who might visit his neighborhood some century hence. I wasn't privy to his thoughts, but the words he chose give an inkling of what he had in mind. When we wander through graveyards, we weigh our own mortality. Mindful of this, rather than filling the space on his little pyramid with vainglorious information, my father thought to strike a more universal chord. As "final instructions," the words Frank Church left for future generations to ponder are humble words yet more than worthy of the splendid stone into which we carved them:

I never knew a man who felt self-important in the morning
after spending the night in the open on an Idaho mountainside
under a star-studded summer sky.
Don't forget to spend some time in nature,
where you can bear witness to the wonder of God.

I never thought of my father as religious. He quit the Catholic Church when he was fourteen. I sensed that for him the Catholic Church was the one true church; it just happened to be false. What I should have known—having preached it so often—is that organized religion and personal spirituality can exist completely independent from each other. At the root of all direct human experience of the Holy are two things that organized religion may even discourage: awe and humility.

The word *human* has a telling etymology, my very favorite. All the words that relate to it—*humane, humanitarian, humor, humility, humble,* and *humus*—are illuminating. From dust to dust, the mortar of mortality binds us fast to one another. Jews, Christians, and Muslims alike trace their ancestry to the third chapter of the Book of Genesis, where God proclaims to Eve and Adam (whose name means "out of red clay"), "In the sweat of thy face shalt thou eat bread, till thou return unto the ground, for out of it wast thou taken: for dust thou art, and unto dust shalt thou return."

For this reason alone, life requires not only a measure of humility but also a leavening sense of humor. I love G. K. Chesterton's quip that "angels can fly because they take themselves lightly." Just a little lower than the angels, we too can lift up our sights by lowering our pretensions. And just a little higher than the most humble creature, we are wise to remember our mortal kinship and destiny. We may be "valiant dust" (in Shakespeare's words) but, whether we perceive ourselves as spun out of stardust or fashioned from earthly loam, when we die we inherit the same earth.

Next to "Home Sweet Home," which in cross-stitch and needlepoint adorns so many homespun icons, no domestic adage is more familiar than "There's no place like home." Its source is the libretto of John Howard Payne's all-but-forgotten operetta *Clari, or, the Maid of Milan,* from a song titled—appropriately enough—"Home, Sweet Home." The complete couplet reads as follows:

'Mid pleasures and palaces though we may roam
Be it ever so humble, there's no place like home.

I can certainly subscribe to this sentiment. From my tiniest studio apartment to our present parsonage—a spacious Manhattan high-rise perched across from the steeple of All Souls Church, my spiritual home for a quarter century—I have loved something about every one of my many residences. I counted them up recently. Typical of today's peripatetic Americans, over my fifty-odd years I have resided for six months or more in twenty dwelling places: three in Idaho; one in Washington, D.C.; one in Bethesda, Maryland; four in Stanford, Woodside, and Los Altos, California; three in Cambridge and Concord, Massachusetts; one in Hanover, New Hampshire; and six in New York City. For the past decade my family has been blessed with a second home as well, on Shelter Island, New York, with a lighthouse in the distance and beyond it the open sea.

When I visit my children at school, I am reminded of how intimate and revealing the most humble residence can be. The room of our eldest son, Frank, is like a rabbit warren, cozy, dark, and carpeted with mattresses. Nina's room is a bright, chaotic shrine to friendship, chockablock with photographs and mementos. The room of our youngest son, Nathan, is papered with edgy posters celebrating the heroes of contemporary adolescent culture. Jacob's room at home is a temple of irony, its walls mocked up with all manner of expressionistic kitsch (his most recent addition, a refrigerator door). At a recent college reunion, my freshman roommate presented me with a collage of pictures taken in our dorm room more than three decades ago. I had forgotten the life-size headless plaster statue that we used as a clothes rack but not the red overhead light with its unintentionally ironic stenciled reminder, "Sex alone is not love."

One reason there is no place like home is that no place is more completely ours. Some say that we are what we eat. More aptly, we are what we keep. The amalgam of belongings we collect and display at home both illustrates our past and presents it as a composite work in progress, as unique as individual identity itself is, each of our lives a living canvas layered with patinas of memory. Yet there is another part to the saying: "*Be it ever so humble,* there's no place like home." What happens when we create living spaces for ourselves that boast of our material accomplishments, advertising good and expensive taste? When we return every nightfall to roam through "pleasures and palaces," is this cause for celebration or concern?

I think of George Herbert's quest for more capacious lodgings in which to house his soul. "Not thriving," he determined to cancel his present lease and seek a finer residence. First he looked to Heaven. As in the parable of the mountain, when he got there he discovered that God had gone down to earth "about some land, which he had dearly bought . . . to take possession.

> *I straight return'd, and knowing his great birth,*
> *Sought him accordingly in great resorts;*
> *In cities, theatres, gardens, parks, and courts:*
> *At length I heard a ragged noise and mirth*
> *Of thieves and murderers: there I him espied.*

Not only is God where we last might think to look, but even the company God keeps is (to say the least) surprising. Such evidence fosters humility. Because of humility's saving power, medieval Christian theologians rightly numbered pride the greatest of all sins. "An exile from home," Payne writes, "splendor dazzles in vain."

The seven deadly sins fall into two categories, sins of the flesh and sins of the spirit. Because their wounds are often self-inflicted rather than inflicted on others, the fleshly sins (laziness, gluttony, and lust) are generally considered less deadly than are the sins of the spirit (avarice, envy, anger, and pride). For instance, when we act on our laziness, we literally do nothing. As for gluttony and lust, when we eat too much or waste fifteen minutes of our life hoping that some neighbor in the apartment building across from ours will undress before she closes the bedroom curtains, nine times out of ten the world will look the other way. Conversely, when we explode in anger or indulge in the kind of backstabbing that envy fosters, our sins are flushed into the open, exposing the condition of our souls. In one sense, the relative privacy of their dominion makes sins of the flesh more insidious than sins of the spirit. Neither the world nor we are as likely to detect the subtle tyranny they exercise over our souls.

Pride operates in a category of its own. When our mirrors reflect pride, not only do we miss seeing it for what it is but we also tend—fittingly enough—to boast in it. By way of demonstration, try this brief idolatry test. Given how tough pride is to recognize, I have made it as difficult to cheat on as possible.

1. DO YOU PRIDE YOURSELF ON YOUR SOCIAL CONSCIENCE, CONCERN FOR OTHERS, LOVE FOR HUMANITY?

Have you called your mother lately?

2. DO YOU PRIDE YOURSELF ON YOUR KNOWLEDGE OF CURRENT EVENTS, READ ALL THE RIGHT MAGAZINES, WATCH THE NEWS TWICE A DAY?

Did you vote in the last municipal election? Did you write to your congressperson about his or her stand on gun control? Perhaps you ought to boycott the paper for a day or two and read a trashy novel, one you couldn't mention in proper company.

3. DO YOU PRIDE YOURSELF ON YOUR HONESTY, HIGH SENSE OF PURPOSE, AND DEPENDABILITY? DO YOU COME TO WORK EARLY AND STAY LATE?

Call in sick at once. Go directly to a ball game or a B movie. The work will go on without you. The question is, Can you go on without the work?

4. DO YOU PRIDE YOURSELF ON YOUR HEALTH, TAKE GOOD CARE OF YOUR BODY, EAT WELL, EXERCISE, DRINK IN MODERATION, AND NEVER SMOKE?

Fine. There may be any number of good reasons to do all this, but living forever doesn't qualify.

5. DO YOU TAKE PARTICULAR PRIDE IN YOUR PIETY? DO YOU ATTEND CHURCH OR SYNAGOGUE EVERY WEEKEND?

If so, skip a week or two. If you are proud of your spiritual life, there must be something wrong with it.

Idolatry tests can be useful, because pride is blinder than love.

Given that humility is easier to boast of than to practice, it is also useful for those presumptuous enough to preach on pride to illustrate their pronouncements with examples from their own lives. For instance, in one of its many disguises, pride wears the robes of judgment. Yet we are attractive to no one but ourselves when, by damning others, we play God. One of my congregants gave up gossip for Lent last year; I can think of almost nothing more difficult. Though I tell people I read them for the sports pages, I feed my appetite for gossip almost daily by devouring two New York City tabloids. My wife has pointed out to me how often I chuckle when I happen upon some particularly salacious tidbit. Though this pinches my own heart, much worse is when I indulge in backbiting—delighting with others in sharing our condescending disappointment in the behavior of colleagues, friends, or presidents. Yet I couldn't tell you how often I have quoted from the pulpit Jesus' injunction to "judge not, lest ye be judged," or cautioned against throwing the first stone while having it at hand in my own pocket.

In another of its manifestations, pride paradoxically serves as a cloak for low self-esteem. Some folks given to self-aggrandizement are not covering for their sense of insecurity, but precious few fall into this category. Name-dropping illustrates this fact perfectly. Clever insecure people can even name-drop and feign humility in the same breath.

During the first year of my ministry, I officiated at the funeral of Thomas Finletter, past secretary of the air force. Arthur Schlesinger, Jr., and Norman Mailer offered the eulogies. In our church parlor before the service—mustering every bit of my twenty-nine years' worth of authority—I instructed the participants as follows: "Norman Schlesinger will speak first, and you, Arthur, will follow." To which Mailer replied, "You're not nervous are you, kid?" This little story is a perfect example of pride parading in humble drag.

My preferred sins are sloth and gluttony, but pride abets both. Take the sin of sloth. It may not seem that way—few people boast of their laziness—but indolence and pride are roommates. Selfishness powers indolence, and whenever we act on selfish motives, we act out of pride. I know from experience how deftly pride conspires with sloth to excuse me from my responsibilities, enticing me to cut corners in my work, even encouraging me not to call my children to see how they are doing (fearful perhaps of bad news). Severing connections that support and sustain our being, pride always begs special treatment for the grubby little ego. Pride also promotes sloth as an escape from being tested. After all, if we refuse to try our hand at something, we cannot fail at it. By taking cover in indolence, we shelter our egos. The fear of failure and the fear of success both are expressions of demonstrably false pride.

Whenever I choose not to do something simply because I don't feel like it, by choosing to play at life according to my own private rules I exclude myself from duty in a gesture of superiority. My rationalizations may seem self-serving, but they are certainly self-driven and have a cumulative diminishing effect on my soul. I have noticed of people as they grow older that, as they become practiced in avoiding things that may not please them, over time—with fewer and fewer activities falling outside the compass of ensured satisfaction—the circle of their lives begins to close. They may be safe in their gardens, but as the walls grow higher the sun shines in more fleetingly with each passing season of their life. My own indolence tells me to ignore this observation. After all, if I can somehow shirk engagements that don't guarantee some pleasure, I can liberate my life from pain. I can avoid the dangers of disappointment and embarrassment, and especially the risk of discovery. The risk of discovery cuts both ways, of course. I may avoid being discovered for who I am, but also, less happily, I preclude myself from the discovery of meaning beyond my mere subsistence.

Gluttony and pride collaborate in a slightly different fashion. At least with respect to alcohol—the object of my own sometime desires—pride encourages its servant to drink on gluttony's demand. Yet gargantuan appetites arise from a famished ego. In consequence of this intrinsically unstable coupling, pride and low self-esteem alternate in possession of the psyche, provoking mood swings from complete self-aggrandizement to absolute self-abasement. A temperate drinker has no direct experience of this dynamic, but anyone unfortunate enough to live with an alcoholic knows just how fragile and imperious his or her ego can be. Highs are precipitously high, lows pathetically low. Yet in each instance King Baby's ego is completely engaged, to the exclusion of all others. Certainly there is no room for God in the melodrama of such a life.

I have pondered why I drank so much and for so many years. To any but the most attentive observer, it would not appear to have been from a lack of healthy self-esteem, but looking back I wonder. I certainly used alcohol to subdue unwelcome feelings. I was afraid of looking too deeply within myself, for fear of what I might find there.

More prideful expressions of my egoism were more obvious in my drinking. I dictated my own set of rules and then slavishly followed them. Nonetheless, having counseled many addicts and alcoholics over the years, I didn't recognize myself in their glass. My work won me the respect of others, and my spirit—whether elevated artificially or not—contributed to the general bonhomie of most of the company I kept. For the most part, I lived life in the manner I wished and did what I chose to do.

To ease my conscience, I also prided myself on not being a moral perfectionist. I wrote books with titles such as *The Devil & Dr. Church* and *The Seven Deadly Virtues*. I even edited a twelve-step book while drinking. I have discovered it to be useful to me now that I have stopped. At the time, however, I accepted drinking as a lubricant to creativity. If Faulkner, Hemingway, and Fitzgerald could write drunk, who was I to question such a muse? It even appeared to work for me. I found that Scotch muted self-criticism and thus facilitated my productivity. I would never be guilty of committing a best-seller, but that was fine also. Until my awakening began to complicate matters (when the emptiness of my life became unendurable), I was enjoying a good time and hardly raising a sweat as I did so. My appetites for both indolence and gluttony were well served and, far from being a bad person, I was merely a self-indulgent one. I believed that the world, on balance, was a better place during those years of my residence within it, and in retrospect I think it probably was.

As things turned out, for me pride didn't lead to a fall; it simply took slow possession of my soul. Fortunately, when I awoke one day to discover that God was nowhere in my life, I knew enough to recognize that alcohol (though symptomatic of more general self-absorption) was part of the reason. I wasn't humiliated into humility as so many others have been, merely lost in the desert of self. I felt an emptiness I could no longer medicate against and to which I had to either respond or succumb.

Love gradually turned me from the bottle, which had become a kind of mistress. I discovered that I could fulfill my own hopes only by answering the needs of those I love. Old habits are hard to break, but over time love's responsibilities tempered and deepened this awakening. At first I simply cut my drinking back, and my pilgrimage progressed, albeit slowly. Were it not for my wife, Carolyn, I doubt that I would have attempted to continue it sober, for to do so entailed the loss of fond and familiar comforts. Notwithstanding her concerns, comfort triumphed over love for years. I walked toward God with a half-full bottle in my suitcase. I tried to cut a bargain between my appetites and my responsibilities. As most drunks will tell you, this didn't work. So I swallowed my last bit of pride and, at long last, found my way out of the thickets of addiction.

In retrospect, I am grateful today not only for my wife but, in a strange way, for my addiction also. It established the parameters of a God-shaped hole that I could fill only with God. Each of us has his or her personal version of this hole, and we attempt to fill it in our own private ways. Yet no God substitute can fill the God-shaped hole. For this reason alone—since little contentments disguise our spiritual emptiness by taking the edge off our hunger for spiritual renewal—we should welcome discontent when it visits.

At the outset of my search, one prayer in particular touched my heart. Written by a hero of my youth, whose tempestuous life and insistence on his freedom had inspired my emulation, it is a tragic prayer. I read it to remind myself how lost I was, and how profoundly I needed God's help to find peace.

And what do I owe You, God, for my gifts:
I owe You perspiration and suffering and
all the dark night of my life:
God I owe You godliness and diligence,
God I owe You this blackest loneliness,
and terrified dreams—
But humbleness, God, I have none and
I owe it You: for I would have You
reach down a hand to me, to help me
up to You—Oh I am not humble.

Jack Kerouac wrote this poem, one of many found after his death in a satchel of prayers, hymns, and personal essays. Kerouac's book *On the Road* served as the anthem for a generation of lost, if liberated, souls. His incandescent brilliance was equaled only by his magnificent pride and self-destructive addiction to alcohol and drugs. For all his devotion to freedom, like Chris Antley, Kerouac could not escape from self-imposed bondage. He could not receive the help for which he so desperately prayed. And he hated himself for this. In words that suggest they were written in an intoxified state of depression, Kerouac pleads:

> *Spit in my soul, God, for asking and*
> *always asking, and for not giving and*
> *owing what I have given, and give,*
> *and shall give: God make me* give.
> *Old Job there of the three thousand five*
> *hundred years a-moldering in his grave,*
> *old Job there is your servant, God:*
> *forgive me for my youth, then forgive*
> *me for it, God, oh make me a giver.*

Nothing is emptier than a life in which God is palpably absent. Kerouac died an angry, prideful, repentant, and broken man. God could not make him a giver, because another god held possession of his soul.

Humility may not be as central for you in your journey as it has been for me. A dose of humility enhanced my self-worth. For someone else, a double shot of pride might be necessary to work the same change. People who have had the pride beaten out of them may discover self-esteem to be far more important than humility to the advancement of their spiritual quest. Without a healthy sense of self-esteem, we may not feel worthy to invite God into our homes. I know women who accept humiliation as if it were their birthright, and others who argue angrily that indeed it is just that. For Jesus or anyone to tell a person who is already empty of self that she should empty herself and be filled is nothing less than cruel. Perhaps one can go to a store and redeem a coupon that isn't worth anything, but the same does not hold true for a human life.

We may journey from dust to dust, but our life need not be ashes in between.

Far from being sins, Black Pride, Gay Pride, and Feminist Pride are in fact virtues when they unite people. In contrast, the sin of pride divides us, leading to mutual alienation and estrangement from the ground of our being. Both selfish pride and self-abasement leave little room in our hearts, for giving or for gratitude. As long as we don't confuse humility with humiliation, its presence will open our lives to one another and make room in them for God. In his notebook, *Markings*, the Swedish statesman and UN Secretary-General Dag Hammarskjöld wrote, "Humility is just as much the opposite of self-abasement as it is of self-exaltation. To be humble is *not to make comparisons*. Secure in its reality, the self is neither better nor worse, bigger nor smaller, than anything else in the universe. It *is*—is nothing, yet at the same time one with everything."

Fifteen years after my father's death, our family (both Carolyn's and mine) took a weeklong raft trip down the Middle Fork of the Salmon River, the same river on whose banks I had reconciled with my father decades before. With our three living parents, my brother, and three of our four children, we traveled one hundred miles down a wild and scenic river protected by legislation Frank Church had written during his tenure in the Senate. Our entire journey took place within the compass of the Frank Church River of No Return Wilderness Area, 2.2 million acres named in his honor shortly before he died. At night, around the campfire, amazed by the heavens, I could not help but follow my father's instructions and bear witness to the wonder of God. He was right that it is impossible to feel self-important in such a setting, and (for a time at least) I got out of God's way and felt the presence of the Holy infuse my being.

We don't need to go into the mountains to experience this. Evidence of the divine is manifest throughout our everyday experience. Whether in New York City or on the shores of Shelter Island, when I remember to look at my life with eyes that see, I too (with Whitman once again) witness "nothing else but miracles,

> *Whether I walk the streets of Manhattan,*
> *Or dart my sight over the roofs of houses toward the sky,*
> *Or wade with naked feet along the beach just in the edge of*
> *the water,*
> *Or stand under trees in the woods,*
> *Or talk by day with any one I love, or sleep in the bed at night*
> *With any one I love,*
> *Or sit at table at dinner with the rest.*

A miracle is anything, be it ever so humble, that helps us greet our given days with gratitude. In speaking of home, Robert Payne was right: "A charm from the sky seems to hallow us there/Which, seek through the world, is ne'er met with elsewhere." With home being graced by miracles such as these, there is simply no place like it.

9 *Open House*

You take a risk when you invite the Lord
Whether to dine or talk the afternoon
Away, for always the unexpected soon
Turns up:

. . . The table set for four
Must often be enlarged and decorum
Thrown to the wind. It's His voice that calls
them
And it's no use to bolt and bar the door:
His kingdom knows no bounds of roof, or wall,
or floor.

Marcella Marie Holloway, "The Risk"

Hell is oneself," T. S. Eliot said. No, Jean-Paul Sartre proclaimed, "Hell is other people." Both are 100 percent half right. Hell is oneself *apart* from other people. The quest for salvation may have all the markings of an individual pilgrimage—and certainly at times can be a lonely one—but rarely do we meet success traveling alone. Not only does the path to God pass through the human village but we find our destination there as well.

I have been lucky. My homes have always been oases, not alone for my rest and refreshment but also as hubs of neighborly commerce and hives of activity. In part for selfish reasons, my mother opened our home to all my friends. The one place we knew we could always gather, it served us as a clubhouse. Every afternoon after school, rarely were fewer than three of us in my basement listening to the Beatles and playing pool. Because my mother didn't really care whether I did my homework or not, my best friend, Peter Fenn, often stayed for dinner and long into the evening. I say for selfish reasons only because my own expansive hospitality as a parent is predicated partly on the knowledge that if our children are at home—no matter how great a crowd may tag along—Carolyn and I will always know right where they are.

Growing up, I especially loved dinner parties. My parents were generous in including me, and I welcomed the opportunity to enjoy my father's company, never ceasing to be amazed by his bounteous gift for hospitality. Being a minister ensures that my home too is regularly open for business and pleasure both. My wife and I recently counted up the guests we have hosted over the past three years; they number more than a thousand. At times I find myself pondering the novelist Norman Douglas's observation that "many a man who thinks to found a home discovers that he has merely opened a tavern for his friends." No matter. We love our parsonage and take delight in sharing it.

The American writer Polly Adler is credited with the coinage "A house is not a home," from her book of the same name published in the 1950s. This was the decade—when I and so many other baby boomers were growing up—that family suddenly was all the rage. Yet the distinction remains a good one. What makes a house a home is love given and received. This doesn't require crowding one's apartment with strangers, only welcoming our neighbors, wherever we may encounter them, with open hearts.

W. H. Auden had his most memorable mystical experience when enjoying the company of three colleagues one evening after dinner. As they casually discussed everyday matters, Auden felt his being invaded by a higher power. "For the first time in my life I knew exactly—because, thanks to the power, I was doing it—what it means to love one's neighbor as oneself." This sensation lasted a full two hours. Later, one of Auden's colleagues—they were not close friends—confirmed having experienced the same feeling. It was so powerful that it prompted Auden to return to church and publicly proclaim his refound Christianity. In retrospect he writes, "The memory of the experience has not prevented me from making use of others, grossly and often, but it has made it much more difficult for me to deceive myself about what I am up to when I do."

Neighborly love's intimate connection with the love of God is explicit throughout Christian literature. In the Legend of the Holy Grail, the pilgrim who finally secures the Grail is not among the many knights who attempted to wrest it from its guardian by force but rather the one who alone acted lovingly toward him. To employ force was tempting I am sure, given that the Holy Grail's guardian was nearly a quadriplegic. Years of defending this treasure from knights on pilgrimage had left him with the use of only one limb. Yet in his ravaged state the guardian still could fend off the mightiest foe, as many in their final moments learned. Far from being the finest swordsman, the knight who finally won possession of the Holy Grail (thereby securing his own salvation) was instead the one whose heart went out to his adversary, the one who thought to ask, "What are you going through?"

Jesus teaches that the realm of God is within us. The Greek preposition *entos*, translated in English Bibles as "within," also means two other things: "between" and "among." Not until we perceive the myriad connections within us, between us, and among us—thereby becoming part of all we encounter—

do we enter God's realm. And what did Jesus say to the man who wanted to know what example he must follow to enter the Kingdom?

> *I was hungry, and you gave me to eat;*
> *I was naked, and you covered me;*
> *I was thirsty, and you gave me to drink;*
> *I was sick, and you visited me;*
> *I was a stranger, and you took me in;*
> *I was in prison and you came to me....*
> *Inasmuch as you do the same unto one*
> *of the least of these my brethren,*
> *you have done it unto me.*

Following the spirit of the Torah rather than its letter, Jesus was anything but a biblical literalist. Throughout the entire body of his teachings, Jesus quoted the Hebrew scriptures only once. And he got in trouble with the fundamentalists of his own day by placing humane action over religious law. In like manner, I do not follow the letter of Jesus' theology; I embrace its spirit as summed up in the great commandments of love. Trumping all lesser injunctions, Jesus' commandments to love God and our neighbor as ourselves are themselves not divisible. Unless we love our neighbor, we cannot love God.

Paradoxically, loneliness can be compounded in company and assuaged by solitude. Nonetheless, according to Jesus we cannot hoard God's treasure for ourselves without losing it. The Japanese spiritual writer Akutagawa Ryunosuke illustrates this point in his story "The Spider Thread." During his short life (he died in 1927 at the age of thirty-five), Ryunosuke wedded Christian and Buddhist imagery in ageless parables. In this brief morality play, Ryunosuke illuminates the tragedy of an individual who chooses to estrange himself from community for personal gain by telling the tale of Kandata, a bandit and murderer who has died and gone to Hell.

The Compassionate Buddha chances one day to walk by a lotus pond in Paradise and, while delighting in the pearl white blossoms, glimpses between the lotus leaves the netherworld below. Languishing in Hell, Kandata catches the Buddha's eye and wins his pity. Though he had lived a life of crime, Kandata did perform one good deed, sparing a spider that happened to be creeping on the roadside where he was walking one day. Lifting his foot to stamp on the spider, Kandata held back when compassion got the better of him. "No, no," he sighed. "Small though it is, it must be endowed with a life. It is a pity to take that life."

To reward him for this singular (if sole) act of kindness, the Compassionate Buddha picks up a spider spinning its silvery web on a lotus leaf and holds it so that the silken thread may go down to Hell, offering Kandata a means of escape. When he sees the thread, Kandata claps his hands in joy. "If I take hold of it and climb up, I might be able to get out of Hell. And if I am lucky, I may even get to Paradise." So he grasps the spider thread as firmly as he can and begins his ascent. Carefully yet surely he climbs from the pit of darkness toward the light. Higher and higher he ascends, until Paradise is almost within reach. "I have done it. I have done it," he cries. But then, casting his eyes downward for one last look upon the realm of his damnation, Kandata sees behind him countless other sinners climbing up the spider thread like a parade of ants. How, he asks himself, can the thread possibly hold himself and so many others? "Should it break, I would tumble down back to Hell, despite all the pains it took me to get up this far." As Kandata panics, the sinners below continue their progress up the thread, itself weakly shining in the dark. At the top of his voice, Kandata shouts, "Hey, you sinners! This spider thread is mine. Whose permission did you have to get up here? Get down! Get down!"

With this the spider thread—which until that very instant had proved so resilient—breaks but a hand's breadth away from Paradise, right at the place where Kandata is dangling, sending his body plummeting through the darkness back to the bottom of the abyss. "Shakyamuni Buddha was watching everything from the edge of the lotus pond in Paradise," Ryunosuke concludes. "Seeing Kandata sink into the pond of blood, he was very sad and resumed his walk."

Charity may begin at home—we cannot take care of others unless we remember to care for ourselves—but if charity ends at home, everyone (including us) will be impoverished. Love is not a zero-sum game, in which the love we give to others comes at our expense. It is more like a compliment, kind words that enhance both giver and recipient. When others have no access to what is ours, it becomes worthless. By acting selfishly we close both heart and hearth to God. To paraphrase Wordsworth's poem "Guilt and Sorrow," we are left standing "homeless near a thousand homes," and "near a thousand tables" we pine for food.

~ ~ ~

Love to neighbor presents most people with a greater ethical challenge than does love to family and friends. Yet the virtue of hospitality can be practiced in enlightened self-interest as well as out of duty. Remember the three strangers who appeared to Abraham on the plain of Mamre. He invited them to supper, fetched water to wash their feet, and suggested that they rest before moving on. His wife, Sarah, prepared them a fine meal of fresh bread and butter, milk, and veal. Abraham set it before their guests and stood by as they feasted under a tree. After receiving Abraham and Sarah's free offer of hospitality, they announced that Sarah, already an old woman, would give birth to a son. Sarah and Abraham had been entertaining angels.

Not only in ancient Israel but in the heroic age of Greece as well, virtue was understood in direct reference to both household and community. Though the Greek word for virtue (*arete*) had the primary connotation of courage or fortitude, fortitude itself was not initially an individual virtue, such as might be demonstrated by a mountain climber or a marathon runner. Instead, it was the hinge upon which the survival of the community turned. In his book *After Virtue,* the ethicist Alasdair MacIntyre writes, "What is alien to our conception of virtue is the intimate connection in heroic society between the concept of courage and its allied virtues on the one hand and the concepts of friendship, fate, and death on the other. Courage is important not simply as a quality of individuals, but as the quality necessary to sustain a household and a community."

Virtue's hospitable connotation expanded, first to include the city-state, as in the Golden Age of Greece, and then, during the Hellenistic and Roman periods, to embrace the entire cosmos. According to one philosophical school, the Stoics, virtue is "conformity to cosmic law both in internal disposition and in external act." The Stoics honored natural law—the key to spiritual understanding—as a mandate for hospitality.

This conviction echoes in a metaphor favored by St. Paul. Adapting Stoic teaching concerning one body with many members, Paul understood cosmic law and its obligations in terms of the body of Christ. To Paul, every resident of the House of God is a member of Christ's body. Accordingly, individual virtues are subject to corporate judgment. Paul invokes this same image to reconcile adversaries within the Christian community who differ over the observance of Jewish dietary laws. As he sees it, since the earth is the Lord's and the fullness thereof, when it comes to eating, all things are lawful. That which enters our bodies cannot corrupt us, only things that issue from us, such as cruel words or thoughtless deeds. Paul divides his Christian brothers and sisters into the strong and the weak, with strength not a virtue but a gift carrying an obligation. Should the strong happen to eat the meat of an animal that has been sacrificed on a pagan altar, they know it can do them no harm. The other Christians are weak, fearing that they might be polluted by such food. Both groups assign themselves a quotient of virtue, the latter protecting their faith by abstinence, the former by disregarding such scruples. But Paul doesn't see it that way. Since all virtue is corporate, good Christians must honor their neighbors' scruples (however foolish) by adapting their own behavior.

To Paul, all that matters is that the body of Christ (the church) not be torn asunder by disputation and rancor. Rather than exhort his compatriots to demonstrate their fearlessness of "tainted" food (in the hope of converting those whose scruples have led them into superstitious error), he urges the strong not to offend the weak by eating in their presence meat known to have been sacrificed to idols. "Pursue what makes for peace and for mutual upbuilding," Paul writes in his Letter to the Romans. "Do not for the sake of food destroy the work of God. Everything is indeed clean, but it is wrong for anyone to make others fall by what he eats. . . . Let each of us please his neighbor for his good, to edify him."

The consequences of neighborliness extend far beyond our households, whether of family or of faith. Yet much in society militates against its cultivation. The Jewish theologian Martin Buber framed recent history by reminding his listeners that modern government was originally founded on three principles: liberty, equality, and fraternity. Over the years liberty traveled west to be enshrined in capitalism; equality gravitated east and became the linchpin of communism. In each instance, fraternity got lost. Buber called fraternity (the kinship of all people) the spiritual principle.

In the United States the spirit of fraternity is most painfully compromised by the legacy of slavery, which lingers in the ongoing scourge of racism. A house divided is closed to God because it offers no quarter to an entire family of God's children. At my own church we continue to struggle with the de facto racism that a predominantly white congregation unintentionally represents. A recent weekend antiracism workshop that we sponsored to raise consciousness and prompt action in this regard reminded me once again of how trenchantly prejudice is rooted in the most liberal of institutions. The currents of fear in our society run so very deep.

Thank God for my daughter, Nina, and P.S. 158—an old battleship of a school overrun with children of every color. Years ago I attended a memorable talent show there in which my then six-year-old daughter was featured. She and a friend had worked up a number called "The Doughnut Shop" (something about doughnuts and nickels both having holes in them). They don't vote on winners at P.S. 158. Given the competition, this is probably a good thing.

Among my favorite noncontestants were the Latino third-grader singing "La Bamba," with his little Jewish buddy on the sax; a stirring rendition of "Blue Suede Shoes" sung as a trio by two first-graders and a kindergartner (two energetic boys, Italian and Irish, trying to keep up with a black girl twice their size); "Edelweiss" from *The Sound of Music*, performed by the daughter of the assistant U.S. attorney; the pop song "Donna"—"I had a girl/Donna was her name"—hilariously sung by a Greek girl; and the only pure-bred WASP in the bunch belting out "Somewhere Out There," a song from a Disney film about an immigrant mouse. But the real tearjerker was "Carry Me Back to Old Virginny" played on the piano by a second-grader from Japan. "Carry Me Back to Old Virginny" was the first record in history to sell a million copies. Anticipating her little Asian American follower, the singer was none other than that good old girl, the opera diva Alma Gluck.

If the talent show at my daughter's school suggests the true American dream, for Nina that dream certainly seems to have caught hold; at Georgetown her favorite extracurricular activity is a gospel choir, and she is majoring in Chinese. Buber was right about fraternity getting lost, but our nation's founders—imperfect as they were—inscribed it in the proclamation that launched our experiment in government. As set forth in the Declaration of Independence, the American creed is a union of faith and freedom, in which liberty is tempered by justice and elevated by faith. When we forget this—whether in the House of God or our own homes—we bar God entry.

~ ~ ~

We also lock God out when—though devoting full attention to "loving" service—we neglect those we love. Here charity begins at home in a different sense: through thoughtful attention to the needs of one's immediate family, needs too many of us take for granted.

Leo Tolstoy's life offers eloquent testimony to the peril of sacrificing a spouse's needs to one's personal program for self-improvement and social justice. In fact, his wife got so angry at him that Tolstoy might aptly have employed Jesus' most plaintive observation to lament his own family predicament: "Prophets are not without honor, except in their hometown, and among their own kin, and in their own house." Better, he might have acknowledged that some prophets bring this curse down on their own heads, for Tolstoy was one such prophet. He so loved God that he sacrificed his only wife. Devoutly following the commandment to love our neighbor, Tolstoy forgot that his wife too was his neighbor, in fact his closest neighbor. For example, to redeem himself from the burden of worldly success, Tolstoy donated all his future earnings (including all rights to and royalties from his books) to the poor. Madeleine L'Engle shares her impressions of the Tolstoy family home (now a museum) as follows: "I was fascinated, when in Russia, to see the family line-up in Tolstoy's house, bedrooms plain and monastic for those of the children who agreed with Papa and bedrooms with French furniture and fancy bed- and window-dressings for those who agreed with Mama, giving the impression that it was a divided household and not a happy one." When his wife proved less than understanding of the distance Tolstoy had imposed between them, he wrote an eloquent novella, *The Kreutzer Sonata*, championing celibacy. Shortly after its publication, Sonya Tolstoy gave birth to their thirteenth child.

She tried to understand. "Obviously nothing can be said against the assertion that it is good to be perfect," she acknowledged in a letter to her husband. "[I suppose] that it is necessary to remind people constantly that they should be perfect, and to point out to them the ways in which they can reach perfection. But I must confess I find it difficult." Actually, far better than to be perfect is to be kind.

I learned this lesson from experience. Throughout the decade of my thirties, having devoted the better part of each year to my parish, I spent much of the summer at home with my wife and children. But I was so completely absorbed in my writing that I never fully acknowledged their existence, even when we were together, at table or in bed. It shouldn't have come as a surprise, therefore, when my wife suggested divorce. When she told me that she wanted to go out for a drink with me, I thought the occasion was to celebrate my completion of that summer's manuscript. No doubt she must have been as pleased as I was over my triumph in meeting yet another deadline. Instead, she told me that our marriage was dead. The conversation made no sense to me. Our life together was uneventful. We never argued. We had just spent two months as a family at her parents' home. I hadn't a clue that anything was amiss between us. But she knew better. She could find no room in my life for herself, because I had filled it entirely with me.

Self-absorption comes in many guises, only a few so conspicuously unattractive that the world will force it on our attention. By publishing books I even received extra credit for my self-absorption. Following this rude but just awakening, I added a postscript to that summer's book, reminding myself and others to watch out for the people in white, for they might be Klansmen, and not to forget that the Church of the Beatitudes in Nazareth was funded by Mussolini. I still had no true sense of how profoundly my self-absorption diminished my wife's existence. I failed to recognize that when fully preoccupied we put out a No Vacancy sign; there is no room in our lives for others. My wife and I lived alone together for almost three more years. Our house was not a home.

Years before, in 1971—in one of the rare real vacations we took together—my wife and I sailed around the world on an oil tanker. I learned two lessons that summer, one of which hit me at the time, the other only long after my divorce. They were the same lesson actually; I simply failed to connect the dots of my life into a picture.

Our ship, the *Pathfinder,* was a supertanker built specifically to fit the Panama Canal. Her only passengers, we were like pilot fish, tiny, colorful human hangers-on, just along for the ride and for the pleasurable company of all those books, carefully packed in four of our five bags, texts I had been assigned but had not read during my undergraduate years at Stanford. I had heard of people who spent their summers working for the Forest Service as fire watchers living all alone above the treetops in Robinson Crusoe–type houses. This trip was a little like that. Every night we watched the sea catch fire as the sun went down. Sailing from Portland, Maine, across the Atlantic, around the horn of Africa, through the Singapore Strait, and then back over the Pacific to El Segundo, California, we spent sixty-three days on water and ten long hours on land. Our friends thought we were crazy.

Among the fascinating things about this ship was its social and political structure. It reminded me a bit of the American regency in Japan following the Second World War. In charge was the captain, an amiable American with whom, other than a passion for baseball, I shared little in common. Second in rank was the chief engineer, Austrian and a fairly good chess player. The four of us had large forward cabins. We ate dinner together every night in the captain's dining room. Everyone else on the crew, from the officers to the lowly purser who waited table for us, was Japanese. They slept in tiny quarters aft. Morito, who must have been in his mid-forties then, was the purser. He cleaned our cabin, brought us lunch, kept me well supplied with Scotch, and did the cooking—hearty American fare to suit the captain's taste. By demeanor as much as by instruction, the captain discouraged us from fraternizing with Morito, the one Japanese crew member who spoke excellent English. Not only would familiarity have been inappropriate but also Morito himself would have found it painful. This, anyhow, is what we were led to believe.

Two days before we reached home port, Morito came into our cabin and asked if we would mind terribly if he took a few moments of our time. Having noticed that I was reading Thomas Mann, he told us about how he had walked the streets of Tokyo all night long with tears welling in his eyes upon finishing *The Magic Mountain* for the first time. The reason he came to sea was to have uninterrupted time for reading and study. And also for his poetry. I asked Morito about his poetry. He ran back to his room and produced a handsome volume of ancient Japanese haiku. He sat with us and shared in simple, elegant words the principles of haiku. And then he wrote us a poem.

The Bible speaks of how, as Abraham and Sarah did, we sometimes entertain angels unawares. This visit reminded me of that passage. I remember being at least half aware of angels outside my window dancing on the waters, but to a soul mate my heart was closed. I managed to read every book I brought with me that summer, but didn't think to open and share the book of this man's life. In one simple yet eloquent human gesture, Morito touched me in a way that nothing else had on that voyage.

I preached about this epiphany and wrote about it as well. It became a kind of touchstone for me. Yet I failed to appreciate something far more important. All summer long I had been almost as oblivious to my wife's existence as I was to Morito's.

When a marriage breaks up, the blame is almost always shared. But—as with my relationship to my parents—in looking back over my first marriage, I choose today to weigh only those sins for which I bear responsibility. I can do nothing about the past. But by acknowledging my sins, I may at least be more mindful of not compounding them by repetition. As Senator Bob Kerrey wrote in a recent letter (reflecting on his Vietnam War experiences), "We are not our memories. We are what we make of them."

What I have learned—to my own regret and others' sorrow—is this. When wholly self-contained, the most dedicated life is inhospitable to God and barely habitable for the rest of us. With respect to our larger ethical obligations and to our more personal moral responsibilities as well, how much more hospitable to our hopes is this humble advice from the old nursery rhyme:

Crosspatch, draw the latch,
Set by the fire and spin:
Take a cup and drink it up,
Then call your neighbors in.

10 *Our Heavenly Home*

I thought I saw an angel flying low,
I thought I saw the flicker of a wing
Above the mulberry trees; but not again
. . . why
Do our black faces search the empty sky?
Is there something we have forgotten? Some
precious thing
We have lost, wandering in strange lands?

Arna Bontemps, "Nocturne at Bethesda"

She settled uneasily into a chair in my ministerial study. Before posing the question that was preying on her mind, the young woman apologized. It was a silly question, impossible to answer; how embarrassed she was to be wasting my precious time. All this came in little staccato bursts as she wrestled free from her coat.

Why are some of us so quick to apologize when things are grating at us? Are we supposed to solve life's questions all by ourselves? I can think of no better way to invest another's time, especially a busy person's time, with value than to interject a bit of unanticipated perplexity into his or her day. In my experience with such meetings, one of two things happens. Either one person receives useful counsel from the other and both feel better about themselves, or both are left bewildered, which leads each to feel less alone in his or her bewilderment.

On this occasion the question my parishioner posed was a brilliant one. It came from her three-year-old daughter. Children don't know enough to refrain from asking magnificent, impossible questions. As it turned out, this particular question numbers among the best I've ever had the privilege of pondering. Curious by nature, the child wanted to know where she was before she started growing in her mommy's tummy? In response her mother did the sensible thing. She sat her daughter down and said, "Honey, that is a very good and very hard question. I will think about it carefully and come back to you with an answer a little later." She could then have taken the easy way out. The attention span of a three-year-old is limited. Once tabled, the girl's question would surely have removed itself from this woman's already full plate. But she took her daughter's concerns too seriously for that. So she went off in quest of an answer.

Our children have great, if unwarranted, confidence in us. This story underscores just how great and how unwarranted. The first place this young woman turned for an answer was the library. Acting on a hunch, she took out a popular book called *The Magic Years* and started searching for clues.

"What are you doing, Mommy?"

"I am looking for the answer to your very good, very hard question," her mother replied.

If you do not have this particular volume in your library and are interested in the answer for your own purposes, I can promise that you will not find it in *The Magic Years*. For the little girl, however, the book lived up to its title by taking on magical significance. Later that evening her father found her reading it upside down in the bathroom.

"What are you doing, sweetheart?"

"Mommy told me that I can find out where I was before I was in Mommy's tummy by looking in this book. But, Daddy," she said, "there aren't any pictures." At this point this little girl's mother resolved to come to me in search of an acceptable answer to her daughter's question.

Two days later I visited the hospital to say farewell to a longtime parishioner, a gentle but tough-minded woman who had been a member of All Souls for almost fifty years. We had a wonderful conversation, one from which I received much of the shared benefit. She was in good spirits, something I find true more often than one might expect of people who are dying. Nonetheless, given the trouble she had been having lately, her hale, almost chipper manner surprised me. In any event, our conversation tripped along lightly. The church was fine, I thanked her. The snow should stop by tonight or tomorrow morning. She certainly hoped so. And then, sudden as a shift in springtime weather, she grew serious. "Forrest," she asked, "what do you think happens to us after we die?" In that instant something struck me with the force of divine illumination. Not the answer exactly. I don't know the answer to this question either. What hit me was that these two questions, hers and that of the little girl, were very much the same. Where were we before we were conceived? What happens to us after we die? The former is of existential moment to the very young; the latter—posing itself death by death through the course of our lifetime—assumes greatest significance when we know we are reaching life's close.

We are the religious animal. Knowing that we will one day die, we question what life means. Our answers to questions of meaning need not include a God, but being life-and-death questions they demand some kind of religious response, if only an "antireligious" one. Sigmund Freud, for example, dismissed religion as a repressive construct thwarting autonomy while at the same time adapting a classic religious frame for his teachings. To Freud, the basic human drives were *eros* (the fearful desire for what we do not possess) and *thanatos* (the fearful desire for death). To embrace his "reality principle," we must disentangle our minds from dysfunctional dependencies rooted in childhood, particularly the love-hate relationship with our parents, who are as gods until we free ourselves from their stewardship over our psyches. Following this model, by exchanging comforting illusions for freedom, we put aside our fears and attain a kind of stark autonomy.

If death, as Freud suggests, is life's ultimate goal, we nonetheless return to our original—if uninhabitable—home when we die. By this reading, our journey is from dust to dust with ashes (or embers) in between. As the sixteenth-century Roman Catholic poet Chidiock Tichborne wrote on the eve of his beheading for participation in the plot to kill Queen Elizabeth, "I sought my death, and found it in my womb." Though bereft of hope, this view of life is faithful to death as we observe it. Bodies decay and turn to dust, and we must liberate ourselves from attachment to the womb to achieve a measure of liberty before we die. Despite its godless faith in the reality principle, Freud's approach follows the same arc as do many explicitly religious narratives. The literary critic Allan Bloom goes so far as to say that "Freud is another of the authors of the Jewish myths of exile, and psychoanalysis becomes another parable of a people always homeless or at least uneasy in space, who must seek a perpetually deferred fulfillment in time."

The original Jewish myth of exile is the story of the fall. As recorded in the Book of Genesis, when God created our original ancestors, Adam and Eve, he blessed them with the gift of immortality. As long as they continue to honor but one restriction on their freedom—not to taste of the fruit of the tree of knowledge—Adam and Eve are free to bask for an eternity in the Garden of Eden. Lolling in the shade, babbling mindlessly by the brook, naming the occasional animal, theirs is a life free from stress and burden. But then the serpent sidles up to Eve and puts a bug in her ear: "Don't be a simp, dear. God put that tree off limits only because it bears the sweetest fruit of any tree in the garden. Take but a single bite and its mind-expanding elixir will bestow the one divine possession that you lack, the knowledge of good and evil." The serpent wasn't lying. Coupled with immortality, this fruit of knowledge would indeed endow Adam and Eve with godlike powers, for knowledge and immortality together constitute the divine portfolio. If in retrospect satanic, the serpent's logic strikes Eve as unimpeachable. Adam buys in quickly, and they eat the forbidden fruit. But then God trumps the Devil's ace. In punishment for stealing the knowledge of good and evil, God strips Adam and Eve of their most prized possession, eternal life.

For Christians, the third and final chapter of this saga opens with the birth of Jesus, whom God sends to die for the sins of those who believe in him that they may return to a life of eternal rest. The journey is from Eden to Heaven, with earth as a way station or proving ground between two worlds of paradise for those who would gain reentry. During the course of our pilgrimage together, we have witnessed the same story many times. Banished (or distanced) from home, we wander for a spell in the wilderness, seeking a path that will lead us home again.

❧ ❧ ❧

No one knows whether Heaven actually exists. But when we conjure up images of what it might be like, we tend to imagine ourselves in a familiar if idealized setting, leading a life liberated from stress, responsibility, and disappointment. All I can say about the afterlife is that it cannot be any stranger or more unexpected than life *before* death. The least prepared pilgrim could not be more startled by Heaven the moment following death than a preternaturally prescient embryo would be astounded by life on earth the moment following birth. Nonetheless, we can learn something about the appropriateness of our earthly desires from the images we create of Heaven. Many of them really are quite silly, something Mark Twain illustrates in his inimitable fashion in the unfinished tale "Captain Stormfield's Visit to Heaven."

When Captain Stormfield marched into Heaven, he was in for a mighty surprise. St. Peter met him—things were in order as far as that was concerned. The problem was, as Stormfield perceived it and Twain reported it, Peter appeared to be out to lunch. "I beg pardon, and you mustn't mind my reminding you and seeming to meddle," Stormfield says to Peter, "but hadn't you forgot something?" Peter shakes his head. "Think," Stormfield says. So Peter thinks, but he has to admit, "No, I can't seem to have forgot anything."

Put yourself in Captain Stormfield's shoes. After thousands of church services, many devoted to the advantages of Heaven over earth, a truly good man arrives at the Pearly Gates and the gatekeeper doesn't seem to know what Heaven is all about. After all, if you were doing a crossword puzzle and the clue was "heavenly item"—four letters, first letter *h*—there would be only three obvious possibilities, *hymn, halo,* and *harp*. "Look at me," Captain Stormfield complains, "look at me all over." Peter looks. "Well?" he asks. "Well!" Stormfield cries. "You don't notice anything? If I branched out amongst the elect looking like this, wouldn't I attract considerable attention? Wouldn't I be a little conspicuous?"

Peter remains nonplussed. "I don't see anything the matter. What do you lack?"

"Lack! Why, I lack my harp, and my wreath, and my halo, and my hymn-book, and my palm branch—I lack everything that a body naturally requires up here, my friend." As amazing as it may seem, the gatekeeper of Heaven is truly puzzled. After pondering for a while, Peter finally says, "Well, you seem to be a curiosity every way a body takes you. I never heard of these things before."

Captain Stormfield looks at St. Peter in astonishment. Then he puts it on the line. "Now, I hope you don't take it as an offense, for I don't mean any, but really, for a man that has been in the Kingdom as long as I reckon you have, you do seem to know powerful little about its customs."

To please Captain Stormfield and free the Pearly Gates for other arrivals, Peter gives in to Stormfield's request, providing him a harp, wreath, halo, hymnbook, and palm branch. Fully equipped and in a state of perfect bliss, the good captain settles down on a cloud with about a million other angels, gives his palm branch a wave or two for luck, tunes up his harp strings, and starts to sing. About seventeen hours later, the angel next to him asks, "Don't you know any tune but the one you've been pegging at all day?"

"Not another blessed one," Stormfield confesses.

"Don't you reckon you could learn another one?"

"Never, I've tried to, but I couldn't manage it."

At this his companion shakes his unhaloed head. "It's a long time to hang to the one," he says. "Eternity, you know." To which Stormfield replies, "Don't break my heart. I'm getting low-spirited enough already."

They sit in silence next to each other. Finally the veteran angel asks, "Are you glad to be here?" To which Captain Stormfield replies, "Old man, I'll be frank with you. This *ain't* just as near my idea of bliss as I thought it was going to be when I used to go to church."

Whatever happens after we die, I hope it isn't this. So defined, Heaven might best be described as punishment for good behavior. An eternity of anything would be intolerable. A vacation forever; Sunday seven days a week; everyone in uniform, harps, hymnals, and halos commissioned upon arrival from the PX. Just think of your favorite pastime, one you love more than anything else in the whole wide world—a millennium of lying on the beach reading a good book, or an eternal game of bridge, or having your back scratched forever.

Heavenly respite is certainly called for in our lives. When longing for something wonderful to happen, we think to ourselves, Wouldn't it be Heaven! We fantasize possessing the one thing most wanting in our life, and dream about how everything would be different if only it were ours. Depending on our circumstances, this could be love, the right job, a two-week vacation, or simply a full night's sleep. Wherever we were before we were born or may go after we die, at times like these we may wonder whether anything like "Heaven" is possible here on earth.

We will always have troubles. Life is unimaginable without them. Even when things are going well, disappointment interrupts our lives. Distraction and frustration fill our days with uncertainty. And when things are going badly, the level of difficulty heightens. If Heaven on earth is anything more than a pipe dream, we will find it only in a neighborhood that itself is anything but heavenly.

All of us, even the most pious of pilgrims, must reconcile ourselves to this reality. Henry Vaughan, who wrote volumes of devout verse, is no exception. Among his finest metaphysical poems are confessions of self-doubt and bewilderment. In his poem "Man" Vaughan laments:

Man hath still either toys, or Care,
He hath no root, nor to one place is ty'd,

But ever restless and Irregular
About this Earth doth run and ride,
He knows he hath a home, but scarce knows where,
He says it is so far
That he hath quite forgot how to go there.

If the way home is something we have forgotten, how can we recover this knowledge? After all, in the biblical story of the fall, it is in punishment for stealing forbidden knowledge that God strips us of our immortality. In the Christian salvation story, not knowledge but belief holds the key to our redemption. By contrast, many ancient Greeks, Plato among them, turn this archetypal myth from Genesis inside out. By their reckoning, we begin our lives in possession of both divine knowledge and immortality. When we are born, our immortal souls are trapped in mortal bodies and forget their heavenly origin and destiny. For the Greeks, knowledge is not our curse but our goal. To achieve enlightenment we must recapture the knowledge of who we truly are.

In the best-known telling of this story, Plato's dialogue *Phaedrus,* Socrates leads his student to conclude that the human soul is immortal because it reflects the divine nature. "By reason of her nature," Socrates avows, "every human soul has had contemplation of true being; else would she never have entered into this human creature." By this reading, in its original freedom (with wings to soar to the highest reaches of the heavens), the soul remained fully conscious of God's presence. At birth, trapped in an earthly body, she shed her wings and with them her celestial range. To describe this mortal state, Plato employs the term *forgetfulness.* Upon being born, we forget who we are; life's object is to remember what we have forgotten.

Freud postulated that the first thing we forget in a dream

(and must therefore work hardest to remember) is by far its most important element. To Plato, our very ability to try to remember our distant, divine dwelling place is proof of our original residence there. However lost we may be in human forgetfulness or misled by the soul's mortal casing, we instinctively, if unconsciously, know where to uncover the secret to our immortal origin and destiny.

The attempt to regain this knowledge has moral consequence as well. "Knowledge is virtue," Plato said. That we have experienced knowledge of God in the "beforelife" explains why on earth "the human babe shall grow into a seeker after wisdom or beauty, a follower of the Muses and a lover." By this interpretation, once we begin to remember that our true nature is coded and its journey plotted on our soul map, by turning there for directions as we come to know ourselves we grow in virtue.

In the meantime (to cite another Platonic metaphor), the soul is like a chariot attached to two steeds, one responsive to the urgings of the Good, the other unruly and led by destructive passions. By evoking this image, Plato explains the familiar human experience of dueling instincts, one driving our conscience, the other firing our lusts. These two steeds pull us in different directions, thus contributing to our uncertain progress down life's way. Insofar as we continue in ignorance of our true nature, we remain prey to the seductions of flesh and perversions of spirit that conspire to divert us from the path that leads to knowledge.

Walker Percy recasts this myth of the soul's journey in his essay "The Message in the Bottle." In a Platonic vein Percy writes, "Suppose that a man is a castaway on an island. He is, moreover, a special sort of castaway. He has lost his memory in the shipwreck and has no recollection of where he came from or who he is. All he knows is that one day he finds himself cast up on the beach." The man makes friends, keeps up with "island news," finds useful work, passes his days one after the next. "Yet all is not well with him," Percy continues. "Something is wrong. For with all the knowledge he achieves, all his art and philosophy, all the island news he pays attention to, something is missing. What is it? He does not know. He might say that he was homesick except that the island is his home and he has spent his life making himself at home there. He knows only that his sickness cannot be cured by island knowledge or by island news." This impasse continues until one day the unself-knowing castaway finds a bottle cast up on the shore. In it a message bringing news from his true home awakens him from amnesia.

Percy's parable of the castaway mirrors another tale from the ancient wisdom literature. Contained in the Acts of Thomas, an extracanonical early Christian romance, the Hymn of the Pearl is arguably the most colorful quest narrative in all of literature. Few narratives more closely approximate my own spiritual journey. As you read my paraphrase, remember not only the little girl's question ("Where do we come from?") and that of my elderly parishioner ("Where are we going?") but also the question at the heart of the castaway's quest ("Who am I?").

Here is the story the pilgrim prince tells of his own religious journey from his heavenly home through earth and back to Paradise once more.

> When I was a child I dwelt in my father's palace. Every luxury was mine for the asking. I delighted in the wealth and splendor of my surroundings, and in the love of those who raised me. One day my parents sent me forth on a

journey out from their Kingdom in the East unto Egypt. Having stripped me of my robe of glory, they fitted to my form a new garment, so light its burden that I scarcely knew I carried it woven upon my breast. They swore me to a sacred covenant, which was this: "When thou goest down into Egypt and bringest the One Pearl which lies in the middle of the sea which is encircled by the snorting serpent, thou shalt put on again thy robe of glory and thy mantle over it and with thy brother our next in rank be heir in our Kingdom."

I left my home in the East, traveling down the hard and treacherous path into Egypt. I found the serpent and awaited for him to slumber that I might seize the One Pearl and return unto my home. So as not to arouse suspicion while waiting, I clothed myself in the Egyptian fashion. So like unto them did I appear that my hosts gave me of their meat and drink. Intoxicated by the wine, I fell into a deep slumber and lost all sense of my true self. I forgot that I was a King's son, and also the errand on which my parents sent me, to bring back the One Pearl. For years I languished in forgetfulness.

Upon hearing of my plight—that I was lost with no memory of home—my parents wrote me this letter:

"From thy father the King of Kings, and from thy mother, mistress of the East, and from thy brother, our next in rank, unto thee, our son in Egypt, Greeting. Awake and rise up out of thy sleep, and perceive the words of our letter. Remember that thou art a King's son: behold whom thou hast served in bondage. Be mindful of the Pearl, for whose sake thou hast departed into Egypt. Remember thy robe of glory, recall thy splendid mantle, that thou mayest put them on and deck thyself with them and thy name be read in the

> book of the heroes and thou become with thy brother, our deputy, heir in our Kingdom."
>
> This letter took on the form of a great eagle, which, alighting beside me, became wholly speech. At its voice and words I awoke and remembered my nature, that I was a son of kings. I remembered the One Pearl. Enchanting the serpent by chanting my father's name, I seized the Pearl, put off the impure garment I had borrowed, and repaired unto my home in the East. Guided by their letter (become again a great eagle), I found my parents' house and donned the robe of glory that I had last seen or worn in my childhood. It seemed to me to become a mirror image of myself: myself entire I saw in it, and it entire I saw in myself, that we were two in separateness, and yet again one in the sameness of our forms. And the image of the King my father was depicted all over it. Clothed therein I ascended to the gate of salutation and adoration and entered with my gift, the One Pearl, to place before my father's throne.

The symbolism of this story is not hard to decipher. The Kingdom of the East is Heaven; Egypt, the earth. The pilgrim prince's father is God and his older brother, Jesus. The serpent is the god of the fallen, material world; the impure garment, fleshly existence; the robe of glory is the divine image, the transcendental self. As for the One Pearl, in Gnostic literature the pearl is a metaphor for the soul. Here, adapted more generally, it may represent the immortal treasure hidden within the creation, a treasure that can be recognized and recovered by spiritual seekers only once they have remembered where they have come from, who they are, and where they are going. In Greek the word *gnosis* means knowledge. As illustrated in the Acts of Thomas, Gnostic Christians adapted Greek teaching, substituting knowledge for belief as the catalyst for salvation.

Plato speaks of "jewels of the soul" that we perceive "through a glass dimly" as the most valuable prizes on our human treasure hunt. Given that he was schooled in Greek philosophy, St. Paul may have had Plato's words in mind when he wrote, "Now we see through a glass darkly, then face to face." Jesus suggests something akin to this in his parables of the treasure in the field and the pearl of great price. Elsewhere, in the Gnostic-influenced Gospel of Thomas, Jesus tells his disciples that "the Kingdom is inside of you, and it is outside of you. When you come to know yourselves, then you will become known, and you will realize that it is you who are the sons of the living Father. But if you will not know yourselves, you dwell in poverty and it is you who are that poverty." He goes on to add this promise: "Recognize what is in your sight, and that which is hidden from you will become plain to you. For there is nothing hidden which will not become manifest."

Even if this is true, divining the sacred through the veil of mortal existence remains dauntingly difficult. As for the premium that the Gnostics (including many of their New Age cousins) place on secret knowledge to decode life's mysteries, this too presents a problem for most of us. Despite the charm of Plato's myth of the soul or the Gnostic Hymn of the Pearl, knowledge is hardly a dependable guide. Even Socrates said that he was the most ignorant man in Athens; knowing so much more than others, he was more conscious than anyone of how little he actually knew. The Russian mystic P. D. Ouspensky offered a like paradox. "The nearest we come to self-remembering," he often would say, "is when we know that we do not remember ourselves." This realization may not change our human predicament, but I find it comforting nonetheless. It lightens my burden to acknowledge that, regardless of how well my search for meaning may go over the course of a lifetime, upon my death I will have caught but a glimmer of what life was all about.

In a universe of more than 100 billion galaxies, human knowledge is limited and humility therefore a requisite for human wisdom. For all the things that divide us, whether intellectual, cultural, or religious, we mortals are far more alike in our ignorance than we differ in our knowledge. Remembering this may help us to be less inclined to judge, and certainly less driven to destroy one another. Both are worth the effort. Religion sponsors more unholy violence than any other force on earth. Anything that promotes humility cannot help but foster peace. Nonetheless, when coupled with a sense of God's absence, our lack of knowledge (especially self-knowledge) can leave us feeling homeless, the cloud of unknowing an impenetrable fog. "Oh how I long to travel back," Vaughan laments, "but (ah!) my soul with too much stay is drunk, and staggers in the way."

Divine disorientation being common to human nature, drunkenness is an apt and oft-chosen metaphor for those in search of heavenly directions. The Sufi mystic and poet Rumi writes of his own soul's journey,

My soul is from elsewhere, I'm sure of that,
and I intend to end up there.
This drunkenness began in some other tavern.
When I get back around to that place,
I'll be completely sober.
. . . What is the soul?
I cannot stop asking.
If I could taste one sip of an answer,
I could break out of this prison for drunks.

A dedicated drunk blacks out entirely, unable to remember in the morning where he was the night before, or what he did or said while he was drunk. We may even drink too much—or lose ourselves in work or some other escape from consciousness—precisely in order to forget that we have forgotten who we are. When indulged to excess, almost anything can temporarily fill the God-shaped hole within our lives. Rumi, Plato, Percy, and the Gnostic Hymn of the Pearl go one step further, suggesting that this state of complete forgetfulness describes the human condition itself, with the earth a kind of drunk tank or, at best, a rehab facility for those who are fortunate enough to break free from bondage. In either case, the distance we need to travel to return to God seems daunting. "God is at home," the Christian mystic Meister Eckhart says. "We are in the far country."

Fortunately, as the Qu'ran (touchstone of Rumi's faith) promises, "We are all returning." On this point almost every religious tradition stands in agreement. Despite our apparent ignorance, to seek the way of return is our birthright. We may be lost, drunk, and forgetful of our true nature, but we appear to be born with a homing instinct, a capacity for self-transcendence that can lead to salvation or enlightenment.

The question remains, Is God our home here on earth or only in Heaven? Are we castaways on an island, marooned far from our souls' true residence? Is human life merely a scavenger hunt for treasure hidden in earth's field, which we gather only to store for eternity? Or is our treasure where our heart is, as Jesus teaches? And, if our hearts are in the right place, can we therefore find our way home here and now?

This is the conundrum posed in Paul Gauguin's masterpiece, the Tahitian triptych he painted in answer to three questions: "Where do we come from? Who are we? Where are we going?" Gauguin sets his human tableau against the backdrop of a garden, a naturalistic sylvan glade at once earthly and Edenic. On his canvas the countenances of those he depicts in this garden shift dramatically, not according to their proximity to birth represented on the right side of the canvas or death on the left, but from one person to the next. One native is suffering, the next worshiping, another lost in self-absorption. Three chat together, one stands darkly alone, another stands alone also yet is bathed in light. It is as if—from before our birth through the journey of life to our arrival at death's door—we dwell forever in God's creation, yet only some of us are at home in God's garden. Others suffer as if trapped in a prison house, strangers in paradise, lost in self-absorption or damned to languish there.

Two figures stand out in Gauguin's painting. Near its center, an androgynous Eve picks fruit from a tree in the garden. To the left of center, nearer to death than birth, is a Buddhist figure, in Gauguin's own words "a statue symbolizing the Divinity that is inherent in humanity." With the former image, Gauguin reconsecrates the earth as Eden; with the latter, he symbolizes God's fixed presence in the creation. Though we "come from" birth and "are going" toward death, Gauguin's answer to the question "Who are we?" is that, whether we perceive it or not, we are children of God.

More at home on earth than Gauguin (who, riddled with syphilis, attempted suicide the moment he completed his masterwork) was the naturalist Henry David Thoreau. When a minister asked him on his deathbed if he believed in an afterlife, Thoreau answered, "One life at a time." Another questioner wondered if he had made his peace with God. "I wasn't aware that we had quarreled," he said.

As did Gauguin, Thoreau found evidence of God in the details of the creation. More promising for our own journey, he also delighted in that evidence and tended to find housekeeping here a pleasure. In fact, when he built his little hut on the bank of Walden Pond, he could not have better practiced his dear friend Waldo's Transcendental preachment:

> Every spirit builds itself a house (Emerson wrote); and beyond its house, a world; and beyond its world, a heaven. Know then, that the world exists for you. . . . All that Adam had and all that Caesar could, you have and can do. Adam called his house, heaven and earth; Caesar called his house, Rome; you perhaps call yours a cobbler's trade; a hundred acres of ploughed land; or a scholar's garret. Yet line for line and point for point, your dominion is as great as theirs, though without fine names. Build therefore your own world, . . . a Kingdom you shall enter without more wonder than the blind man feels who is gradually restored to perfect sight.

After my conversation at the hospital, I called the young mother and told her I had a tentative answer to her child's question. It is an answer as ancient as recorded thought, yet as fresh as its most recent discovery. Before we are conceived ("in our mommy's tummy") we dwell in God; after we die we return to God. In the meantime, during the span of days represented by that little dash between dates on our tombstone, we hold the key to Heaven in our pocket.

How easily we forget.

11 *Carry Me Home*

Our birth is but a sleep and a forgetting:
The Soul that rises with us, our life's Star,
Hath had elsewhere its setting,
And cometh from afar:
Not in entire forgetfulness,
And not in utter nakedness,
But trailing clouds of glory do we come
From God, who is our home.

William Wordsworth, "Ode: Intimations of Immortality"

If eternity surrounds us and immortality looms ahead—with life on earth our mortal lot between—death is a gate through which we pass into the House of God forever. The literature of the spirit sounds this common refrain: when we die, we return to God. "Surely unto God all things come home," affirms the Qu'ran. "Our rendezvous is fitly appointed," Walt Whitman writes. "God will be there and wait till we come." Or, as that fine old spiritual beckons, sounding from the fields of oppression, facing death we sing the song of liberation: "Swing low, sweet chariot, coming for to carry me home."

I haven't the faintest idea whether we live on after death. For me, to bring God home right here and now is—as they say—to die and go to Heaven. It may be all of Heaven we will ever know. I certainly don't believe in Hell. However bad I may have been at times, the God I believe in is too good to sentence me (or any of God's creatures) to eternal damnation. I am confident that when we die we will all experience peace. To be sure, the peace of extinction is different from the peace of fulfillment. Yet, whether to fulfillment or extinction, when God carries us home it will be to a place of eternal rest. No promise is more comforting and none, for me, more certain. Having passed through the valley of the shadow of death, we will dwell in the House of the Lord forever. Wherever we are, you and I will be with Jesus.

When I was ten years old, my father presented me with a copy of the Jefferson Bible. He had received it as a gift two years earlier, upon his election to the U.S. Senate. Over three nights in 1803, when Thomas Jefferson was in the White House, he cut up the Gospels, excising the miracles and arranging Jesus' life and teachings (in English, French, Latin, and Greek columns) into a single narrative. He entitled his personal Bible "The Life and Morals of Jesus of Nazareth." Jefferson's Bible (my first) led me, if unknowingly, to take tentative steps down the path toward divinity school and into the parish ministry. Years later I wrote the introduction for the most recent edition of the Jefferson Bible. My father would have been surprised had he suspected the role he played in my religious vocation, but no more surprised than I was hearing him invoke God in the words he selected for his tombstone.

Jefferson performed this pruning operation for his own spiritual purposes—he had no intention of sharing his Bible with a world that surely would have scorned his act as arrogant and impious. Yet, according to the few surviving letters that allude to it, Jefferson understood himself in fact to be rescuing Jesus from the captivity of his biographers (whom he considered unlettered and superstitious) and from what he called the "sophistications" of Christian theology. Though his confidence in choosing Jesus' authentic words was overweening, by separating what he believed to be the teachings *of* Jesus from the teachings *about* Jesus, Jefferson sought reverently to construct for his evening devotions the ultimate in Christian commonplace books. As edited by Jefferson, the passages that remain of Jesus' teaching show a master spiritual guide, one (according to Jefferson himself) whose "system of morality was the most benevolent . . . ever taught, and consequently more perfect than those of any of the ancient philosophers." Describing Jesus to his friend and onetime secretary William Short, Jefferson spoke of "the innocence of His character, [and] the purity and sublimity of His moral precepts." What Jefferson omits, save through capitalization, is any hint of Jesus' higher status among mortals. Jefferson opens his Bible not with the annunciation but with Jesus' birth. Its final words are these: "There laid they Jesus, and rolled a great stone to the door of the sepulchre, and departed."

What an extraordinary revelation for a ten-year-old boy, a boy who knew how the story was *supposed* to turn out. The resurrection was missing. The tale of God's son—preaching salvation and proclaiming the advent of the Realm of God—ended in the ordinary, all-too-human way. Having for a brief time lived, even having loved and served so memorably and well, the hero died. This realization is the first of many that have shaped my understanding of religion. If religion is our response to the dual reality of being alive and having to die, *the purpose of life is to live in such a way that our lives will prove worth dying for.*

Whether he was resurrected on Easter Sunday or not, Jesus' Good Friday tribulations bear witness to an all-too-human death. Suffering, uncertainty, reconciliation, and resignation are all manifest in his final words, as recorded in the Gospels. Jesus questions God ("Why hast Thou forsaken me?"). He suffers

("I thirst"). He seeks closure with his enemies ("Father, forgive them, for they know not what they do") and for himself ("It is finished"). Though the Book of Genesis proclaims that "there is none other than the House of God, and this is the gate of Heaven," for Jesus, as for all of us, at times of death the House of God is first and foremost a house of sorrow. No matter how fervently priest and congregant alike may believe that their dearly departed has departed to a better residence, funeral masses and memorial services are not happy occasions. The promise of Heaven may glimmer through death's gate, but God brings us first through a vale of shadows.

By the same token, to be at home with life we must make our peace with death. Death is one of two hinges on which life turns; without death, life as we know it could not be. Each individual is the unique combination of gametes, not a copy replicated by division. For this reason, every time a woman gives birth she gives death. Or, to put it more gently, death is our birthright, life's only guarantee. At birth we receive a life sentence that is also a death sentence. The particulars of our sentencing will differ, some aspects being mandatory (fated by the accidents of birth), others subject to parole for good, often courageous, behavior. Yet, immortality notwithstanding, though we may receive pardon and forgiveness during the course of our lifetime, the death sentence we receive at birth cannot be lifted.

To the extent that religion is above all a death-defying act—offering heavenly insurance policies or extended-life warranties—our reverence for life itself can only be diminished. Remember, we were immortal once. We were immortal before we became interesting. To recall our most ancient ancestors (single-celled organisms, replicated in each succeeding generation), early in the history of our evolution death did not exist for us. Death came into the picture only when we evolved into complex sexual beings that reproduce their kind but not themselves.

It's not that I *disbelieve* in an afterlife; I simply have no experience of an afterlife and therefore have little to say concerning one. I do know this, however. First, nothing (including any imaginable afterlife) could possibly be more amazing than life itself is. Second, life as we know it is impossible without death. Finally, theology may begin at the tomb's door—the specter of death prompting reflection on what life means—but surely no revelation is more compelling or worth pondering than that of a newborn infant emerging from its mother's womb. When "doing theology" I try to remind myself that theologians are wise to close their learned tomes at times and reopen the book of nature. Theology's heartbeat is the miracle of our own existence. This miracle encompasses both birth and death.

One contemporary spiritual guide who appears to have reconciled himself to death is Frederick Buechner. "Ten years ago if somebody had offered me a vigorous, healthy life that would never end, I would have said yes," he admits. "Today I think I would say no. I love my life as much as I ever did and will cling on to it for as long as I can, but life without death has become as unthinkable to me as day without night or waking without sleep." By making peace with death, we awaken to a song reminding us that life is not a given but a gift. That this gift will be taken away as suddenly as it was first bequeathed is not only the one condition that is placed upon our lives but also a token of their preciousness. To Buechner, "The secret of the universe is a room where life is reborn out of death. A room where you are commissioned in darkness. A room where the white wicker rocker ticks and morning after morning you are given back the world. . . . This room where you are now, crowded with angels."

When they sing to us of death, rarely do we welcome the angels' song. At the strike of midnight, the natural tendency is to forget our kinship with mortality and suffering, imagining ourselves as somehow unfairly set apart, unlike all others shouldered with a unique and unbearable burden. It is hard to answer the why of death or illness with a simple *because*. We have difficulty accepting that, in the main, someone we love died because death is natural, not the exception but the rule. We resist conceding that she contracted a rare disease because some small percentage of us simply will. Few of us reconcile ourselves completely to the haphazard laws that pertain to human suffering. In fact, we gladly try to escape reminders that, being human, like Jacob in the Bible we must suffer, wrestle with angels in the darkness, and be wounded.

Having sent his family to safety across the Jabbok River, Jacob is alone. When darkness falls, he finds himself locked in mortal combat with a stranger. In yet another midnight passage, they wrestle until daybreak, neither one the victor. Jacob is wounded in the groin but keeps on fighting. His adversary begs, "Let me go. It is almost morning."

Wounded, his night spent in unrelenting struggle, Jacob replies, "I will not let you go, unless you bless me."

The stranger asks, "What is your name?"

"My name is Jacob."

"Then no longer shall your name be Jacob, but Israel, for you have struggled with God and with man and have prevailed."

"What then is your name?" Jacob Israel responds.

"Why do you ask after my name?" his mysterious adversary replies.

Jacob doesn't receive an answer to life's ultimate question, but he does wrest meaning from what otherwise might be viewed as a night spent in utmost futility. Rising to the full height of his humanity, he struggles and prevails, not begging divine sufferance but demanding to be blessed. And he is blessed. Jacob shows the mark of his struggle for the remainder of his days, but he emerges born again, a new man.

Religion is a peculiarly human enterprise, because we humans are driven to explore the mysterious ground of our own being. We may not be the only creatures who know they are going to die, but I wager we are the only ones who wonder why we live. Many religions give final answers to these questions. Like Jacob's angel, mine does not. In either case, in the face of death, by not giving up in our struggle for meaning and by demanding to be blessed no matter what the cost, we too can be born again.

⁂

Many of the same guides who teach us how to live teach us also how to die. They may even do both at once. As her therapist told Anne Lamott just before Lamott's best friend died, "Watch her carefully right now, because she's teaching you how to live." Lamott herself reflects, "To live as if we are dying gives us a chance to experience some real presence. Time is so full for people who are dying in a conscious way, full in the way that life is for children. They spend big round hours. So instead of staring miserably at the computer screen trying to will my way into having a breakthrough, I say to myself, 'Okay, hmmmm, let's see. Dying tomorrow. What should I do today?' "

The great teachers of religion and philosophy tend to take

their own advice and therefore die quite well. Untroubled on the eve of his death, the Buddha comforts his disciples by reminding them that they don't need him in order to find peace. "Be ye lamps unto yourselves," he preaches in his farewell sermon. "Hold to the truth within yourselves as the only lamp." Socrates accepts his own death sentence with equal equanimity. "The difficulty, my friends, is not to avoid death, but to avoid evil; for it runs faster than death. . . . Those who believe death to be a calamity are in error." And (following the example of Jesus) while mounting the scaffold Sir Thomas More forgivingly assures his tearful executioner, "Quiet yourself, good Master Pope, and be not discomforted; for I trust that we shall, once in Heaven, see each other full merrily where we shall be sure to live and love together, in joyful bliss eternally." Though the Buddha, Socrates, and Sir Thomas More held contrasting views of the afterlife, all were equally at peace with death.

My father blessed life as he was dying. So have many of the parishioners who have enhanced my understanding of life by sharing their deaths with me. In this regard, ministers are particularly graced. People teach us how to die, and therefore how to live, almost every day. I have found that one can never have too many instructions in this regard. Even ministers are tempted to run from death and thereby run from God.

~ ~ ~

I knew only this about the young couple who were driving me to the airport. Just before Thanksgiving, they had lost their eight-week-old daughter. No one knows why she stopped breathing.

Their minister told me the story. When he arrived at the

emergency room, the baby was barely alive, having been revived and placed on a respirator. The doctors held out no hope. As minister and father stood helplessly by, the child's mother sang her baby lullabies. Sweetly and softly, she sang her favorite hymns: "For the Beauty of the Earth." "Transience." "Morning Has Broken." My colleague, the late Irving Murray, who had served in the ministry for nearly fifty years, said he'd never seen anything like it. The following day, she requested that these same hymns be sung at her daughter's funeral.

As this couple and I traveled together toward the airport exchanging pleasantries, I tried to summon forth the courage to acknowledge their loss. This shouldn't have been difficult. I do it all the time. Yet for some reason—perhaps rationalizing that they weren't my parishioners and therefore not my "responsibility"—I couldn't muster the necessary presumption to shift our conversation away from the weather and the morning news. But then Cathy and Stewart asked me about my family. "Do you have children?"

"Yes, I do."

"How old?"

I couldn't go on. Just as I was about to tell them how sorry I was about their baby's death, Stewart said matter-of-factly, "You should know that we lost our daughter this fall."

"I do know," I replied. "Irving told me. Nothing is more tragic than the death of a child."

Cathy commented from the backseat, "Sometimes I get the feeling that other people have a harder time dealing with it than we do. It's so real to us. We know what we've lost. But other people can't face it. They can't talk about it. They're frightened."

"They're frightened of us too," Stewart added, "as if we

had some kind of disease that they might catch if they got too close."

"You're absolutely right," I said, too knowingly. "The only taboo left, the only subject almost no one dares to talk about in polite company, is not politics or sex or religion but death."

"We're doing pretty well," he continued. "Cathy's right about that, but we sure could use some help, and not just from the therapist we're going to. On any given day, one of us may need to work on the past, just as the other is trying to break free from it and focus on the present or make future plans. Yet with the whole world, our family and friends, tiptoeing around us, we are left almost wholly dependent upon each other. Sometimes the resources just aren't there."

"It's funny," Cathy added. "Though most people can't seem to handle talking about Sally's death and are awkward around us, when we are together with them, laughing or chatting about some silly thing, I get this odd feeling that we're being judged, as if our behavior were somehow inappropriate."

"Perhaps we should wear black and not speak to anybody," Stewart said and laughed. "That would take them off the hook."

We went on chatting, now easily. About the conspiracy of silence concerning death. About how the most natural thing in the world has been turned into a monster that people are frightened even to name. About Sally. About their decision to try to have another child.

Just before we reached the gate, I said, "You know, in God's eye, Sally's life is just as precious as your life or mine. Whether eight weeks in duration or eighty years, viewed in the light of eternity the length of one life is indistinguishable from that of any other. What really matters is that she taught you something about how fragile life is, and how much we need one another. Even in her dying, Sally touched and changed her little corner of the universe."

"You may be right," Sally's father said to me softly.

"I know one thing," her mother added in a bright, clear voice. "Now, when someone I know loses a loved one, I'll be there with a casserole and all the time in the world."

When anyone says that we learn more from our failures than we do from our successes or that the most important experience in his or her life was a scrape with death, it is not that failure is to be preferred to success or suffering to an absence of pain. That simply is not true. What is true is that deep feeling and profound caring put sleepwalking through life to shame. A child or sage will be as awake to joy as to sorrow, but most of us fully awaken to the beauty of life only when what we love is placed in jeopardy.

Love is a self-replenishing resource. The more we love, the more love we have to give to others. When loss enhances our human sympathies rather than estranging us from the ground of being, our love proves itself to be authentic.

Until it ends, the book of life is open for revision. The Roman poet Ovid observed that we should therefore never judge a person's life until the moment of his or her death. I'm not sure that we should waste much of our lives judging other people's at all, but the truth of this adage is borne out daily. One such story stands out in memory, a parable rich with reminders that, when time is running short, one still can accomplish so very much.

The old man was dying. He summoned his children to his bedside to tell them good-bye. Dutifully they assembled. His was not a happy family. With its members related to one another by bonds of mutual estrangement as much as by blood, feelings had been strained for years, muted by pretense, insulated by formality.

In times past, whenever the old man had engaged members of his family in serious conversation, he somehow managed to direct the subject to his will. He seemed to think of his children and grandchildren principally as beneficiaries. They addressed him as Sir. Always proper, he was one of those people for whom it would have been much easier to write an obituary than a eulogy. His accomplishments were many but all in the public domain: a brilliant business career, success in government service, renown as a philanthropist. Respected by all who knew him, feared by many, and loved by none, he served humanity through his industry and generosity, yet apparently had no inclination to establish intimacy with anyone. None of those who remember his late, stately wife recall ever having seen the two of them touch, even accidentally. But now he was dying, and one by one he called his children to him.

"Andrew, I have not given you the respect or shown you the love that you deserve. I know how much this hurt you, though you never seem to show it. In that way, you are just like your father. But in other ways, you've far outstripped me. Please know that I am prouder of you, and all the things you have done, than I am of my own accomplishments.

"Elizabeth, when your mother died, a part of me died with her. The pain was so great that I retreated from everyone, especially from the people I loved best. Probably because you are so like her, I retreated from you most of all. I never had the strength to tell you this. If only Mother and I had given you a glimpse of how deeply we loved one another, so many of your problems might have been avoided. I'm sorry. I love you.

"Billy, I know you have rejected all the things I seem to value—position, money, status in society. You won't believe this, but I almost did the same thing myself when I was your age. But I didn't have the courage. Please don't let anyone force you to be someone you are not. To me you will always be the man I might have been. I love you, Billy."

Then the dying man took out a thick book of clippings and letters, filled with his grandchildren's accomplishments, their wedding pictures, academic awards, and stories recounting triumphs on the athletic field. Who could have imagined how deeply he cared? Leafing page by page through their adult lives, he told his sons and daughter how proud they should be of themselves and of their own children.

As the evening wore on, they began to exchange stories, laughing together, and crying a bit too, in relief as much as pain. He told them tales of his youth, especially of his passion for and devotion to their mother. Then he kissed them each good-bye. He died a short time later. At his funeral, a mutual friend told me, "The old man finally accomplished in death something that eluded him in life. He brought his family together." In a real (if not the Christian) sense, this man was born again before he died.

One can be born again in Jesus. In Paul's words, one can "throw off the old man and put on the new." Yet, to adopt William James's terminology, others among the "twice-born" find different paths to the gates of redemption. Not that everyone has or develops a disposition for rebirth. Some individuals (in James's term, the "once-born") may live their entire lives happily without God or dwell with the God of their childhood until the day they die. None among the once-born seems to feel the need to be born again. But many of us do. At some point along the way we hunger to begin our lives anew. This is certainly my experience. Though not born again in Jesus, I list myself gratefully among the "twice-born."

So understood, being born again follows a familiar script. At birth we come unconscious into the world, which, if not our oyster, is our teat. When we move from the womb into our earthly residence, we perceive everything around us as nothing more than an extension of our own being. From our first breath and well before, we accept the life force that animates and sustains us as a given. Then, as we grow through the pains of separation and personal development—having to compete for affection, shelter, and sustenance—the complexities of the human condition become more manifest. Yet we may continue taking life for granted. Lacking some kind of second birth, in half-conscious flight from death we follow the path we set out on all the way to the grave. If our first birth is an unconscious passage during which the gift of life is bestowed without our knowing, to be born again is to receive the same gift consciously, with humility and thanksgiving. In return for the gift, we understand that the world doesn't owe us a living. It is we who owe the world a living: our own.

When it issues in our hearts, the summons to be born again is sometimes but a passing fancy, a trifle to amuse us between pockets of emptiness. So long as the search continues on this level, no matter what novelty we seize upon with which to freshen up, we remain in bondage. The fundamental, almost unmentionable fact remains: we are wandering aimlessly toward death. Distracted by amusements (our daily tasks, little lusts, and self-consuming fears), we walk through the valley of the shadow of death and God is not with us; God's rod and staff do not comfort us. We don't even recognize that this is where we are, for the valley is lit up like a gaudy, half-alluring, half-appalling Broadway marquee. The irony is, we live in hiding from death yet know that we will be caught. Deep within we sense that, when all is said and done, our lives will turn out to have been nothing more than a shell game, in which we squandered all we had for the barker's amusement.

There are certain advantages to keeping our windows closed to the song of the angels. If at the price of a diminished humanity, by paying death as little mind as possible we protect our illusions of invulnerability. We construct attractive prisons for ourselves, places to hide where our illusions will be safe. Yet, however safe we feel, we remain in Limbo, lacking only the presence of a guard to remind us we are living out our sentence on death row.

At the opposite extreme, one can desire the extinguishing of desire so deeply that death itself becomes a kind of passion. As sung and storied by nineteenth-century Romantic poets, death represents the consummation of the heart's unrequited longing. John Keats—though a young man—fell "half in love with easeful Death." And so he sang his song to death, consecrated in the perfect voice of a nightingale.

> *Now more than ever seems it rich to die,*
> *To cease upon the midnight with no pain,*
> *While thou art pouring forth thy soul abroad*
> *In such an ecstasy!*

Having prepared the way so eloquently, when Keats died at the age of twenty-five he became a symbol for his fellow Romantics. Clearly he was at peace with death, more so than he was with life itself perhaps.

In my own adolescence, I often boasted that I would die before the age of twenty-five. At this same age my father had been given six months to live. I was a baby then. Though he survived his first bout with cancer, I seem somehow to have interiorized it. Perhaps—melodramatically and self-importantly—I viewed my own impending death as a sacrifice due the gods in exchange for my father's life. More likely, I merely enjoyed basking in the pathos of my mortality. Besides, since I was going to die before turning twenty-five, I could live a life of abandon in the meantime, untethered to future responsibility. Abetting my fantasy of death was the late Romantic composer Gustav Mahler. I remember once imagining that I could hear my casket being lowered into the ground during the first movement of Mahler's Resurrection Symphony. It was so beautiful, I almost cried.

Nowhere is this Romantic obsession with death captured more tellingly than by Richard Wagner in the "Liebestod" (love death) from his opera *Tristan und Isolde,* with Isolde expiring in ecstasy on Tristan's corpse. Anticipating Freud, Wagner saw death not as the final frustration of desire but as desire's fulfillment. Given that, short of death, our desires can never be fully satisfied, in the Romantic mythos death alone promises redemption—in Wagner's words, "the highest bliss, . . . the bliss of quitting life, of being no more, of last redemption into that wondrous realm from which we stray the furthest when we strive to enter it by fiercest force." Interpreting his own text, Wagner rhetorically asks, "Shall we call it death? Or is it not night's wonder world, whence—as the story says—an ivy and a vine sprang up in locked embrace o'er Tristan and Isolde's grave?"

Once we survive adolescence, to make peace with our mortality is not to celebrate death as Keats or Wagner did but rather to accept it as the fated end of every earthly journey, coupling such acceptance with a further sense, not of desire's fulfillment, but of life's completion. We shouldn't forget the story of Jacob, however. Not only does the angel of death wait by our sickbeds to transport us to our eternal rest. The angel also wrestles with us when we need blessing, reminding us how vulnerable we are and how precious the honor of vulnerability is. Once we survive the crisis of such an awakening, we remember, as if for the first time, that all our earthly cares are nothing when measured against the privilege of having them—that any day in which we do not acknowledge how blessed we are in our loved ones, in the tasks we are called to do, even in the burdens we bear and trials we face, is a day squandered. Though nothing we remember could be more important, there are few things in life we so easily forget.

When we receive life's gift with gratitude, awakening to the angel's song we stand at Heaven's door: not a Heaven beyond but Heaven within; not an eternity of time but eternity in time, expressive of life's abundance. Because eternity is not a length of time but instead the very depth of time, this Heaven can be entered as easily through doors that swing open and closed as through doors that are open forever. One who sat at William Blake's bedside when Blake was dying reported that, "just before he died, his countenance became fair, his eyes brightened, and he burst into singing of the things he saw in Heaven." But this same poet also saw the trees outside his window filled with angels when he was but a boy of seven.

Does that mean angels really exist? Not in the sense you might imagine. In fact, it is impossible to prove the existence of angels without leaving their realm. Like God, angels are beyond proof. Once we start arguing about whether or not angels exist, we have already missed the point. I will venture this, however. When angels dance on the head of a pin, they don't concern themselves with how many can fit, as if they were crowding into a phone booth. Their full attention is devoted to the joy of the dance.

Numbering is a grown-up game. But, if we follow Jesus' counsel and become again as children, we will be able to dance in the ring of eternity. At the very least, by remembering that "Swing Low, Sweet Chariot" will play for us one last time and then the earthly strains will cease, we will join the dance of life with more exuberance. How much finer it will be, when our band is struck, if we have loved the music while it lasted and not forgotten to dance.

The music will end regardless. Having frittered away so many dances, I take some consolation in knowing—whether we bless life as we live it or not—death will bring us peace. We will join our departed loved ones. We will be with Jesus. God will carry us home.

12 *At Home in the Universe*

I am a man: little do I last
and the night is enormous.
But I look up:
the stars write.
Unknowing I understand:
I too am written,
and at this very moment
someone spells me out.

Octavio Paz, "Brotherhood"

When we are at home within ourselves, we are at home everywhere. Yet to be at home within myself, I found I needed God's company. When God dwells in my heart, I abide in God's presence. I live in an apartment of the creation furnished by the Creator. However humble—and its occupant but animated dust—when I make my home there the whole universe is my dwelling place. God's dominion is my domicile.

The nineteenth-century Transcendentalist Margaret Fuller once proclaimed, "I accept the universe." Thomas Carlyle responded, "Gad, she'd better." He was thinking of the universe as housing for our bodies; Fuller accepted it as her soul's true residence. When our soul is at home in the universe, the universe makes its home in our soul. In the strangest way, God and we *are* mates. We pay the bills, but God subsidizes the rent. We buy the food, but God makes it grow. Being human, at times we falter, but God grants forgiveness to a forgiving heart. And though fear and anger have their way with us at times, when tempered and redeemed by love, our lives are now and then quite lovely.

"He walks with me and he talks with me," the old hymn sings of Jesus. This is easier to imagine than walking and talking with God. By proclaiming Jesus fully God and fully man, ancient Christian theologians make intimacy to God a little more conceivable. My experience of God is personal also; not that God is a person but that I am. As a "personified" part of the creation, I best relate to that aspect of the Creator that encompasses personality. The Trinity works nicely for me this way: God above us, God within us, God among us. Unitarianism being a nondoctrinal faith, I am one Unitarian who finds the Trinity more suggestive of God's possible nature than is undifferentiated oneness. This particular aspect of the orthodox Christian mythos liberates my mind to explore the creation more poetically.

I am well aware that myth makes people nervous. How eagerly it is abjured by biblical literalist and logical positivist alike. There is a fundamentalism of the left as well as one of the right. If grounded in radically different sets of principles, their approaches are similar. Positivists and fundamentalists share a penchant for thoroughgoing rationalism.

Take the Bible. Both true believer and hard-core atheist test it for its facts. To the former the facts are absolutely convincing. Following the logic of one fundamentalist leader—"I believe that Jonah was a literal man who was swallowed by a literal fish and vomited up on a literal beach"—the scriptural record is an exact transcript of events as they actually occurred. The skeptic finds this incredible and loses his or her faith. Both forget that the Bible is a religious storybook, not a historical record that will stand or fall only upon its facts. It is a storybook rich with mythic overtones and parabolic undertones, helping us to set humanity in divine, and divinity in humane, perspective. As for its stories, like that of every story their truth depends entirely upon their listeners. They will prove as true as love and hope are true, but only if they awaken us to possibilities for love and hope within our lives.

We are back in the fields surrounding Bethlehem. Suddenly, the sky shines with a great light, an angel of God. We are terrified, but the angel says, "Be not afraid; for behold, I bring you glad tidings of great joy, which will be to all people." What could be simpler or more startling? A child is born: the spark of cosmic consciousness planted in animal flesh; the miracle of human birth fixed at the cross point of the vertical axis, which is God's axis, and the horizontal axis, which is the axis of temporal as opposed to eternal things. Here birth, death, and eternity link inextricably in a mythic pattern expressed within a parable. As Emerson reminds us, "Infancy is the perpetual Messiah, which comes into the arms of fallen men and pleads with them to return to paradise." With every birth something of eternity is made incarnate in time. In this sense, not only does Jesus' birth prefigure our own but also, in the bloom of its promise, the birth of the baby Jesus witnesses to the limitless nature of our own possibilities. Placed within our arms, Jesus reawakens us to the miracle of our own existence.

The creation itself inspires awe and beckons exploration. But the vastness of the universe also makes it difficult for us to feel at home there. In the face of infinitude, we sense ourselves shrinking into infinitesimal insignificance. To strike up a personal relationship with the Creator, especially the God of the scientists, caricatured by some as a "great oblong blur," is inconceivable at times. Pascal (who kept abreast of the science of his day) confessed, "The eternal silence of these infinite spaces terrifies me." Yet I can't help but think of the words my father put on his tombstone.

Looking to the heavens when composing the text for his own grave marker, Conrad Aiken spiced my father's humility with a dash of humor. As the story goes, on a visit to Savannah, Georgia, Aiken was struck by the name of a boat he saw in the harbor: *Cosmic Mariner.* Curious as to her next port of call, he consulted "The Shipping News." The posted itinerary read, "Destination unknown." Inspired by this serendipitous juxtaposition, he fashioned the following epitaph:

Conrad Aiken
Cosmic Mariner
Destination Unknown

In the true poetic spirit, Aiken is right. Our spiritual journey from birth to death and beyond is a cosmic pilgrimage as well as an earthly one. This understanding requires a new religious model, its nature suggested by that stunning image of the blue-green earth as seen from space, marbled with clouds, rising over the moon's horizon. "Think of how we spoke of things under the old model," Joseph Campbell reminds us:

> Everything was seen from earthbound eyes. The sun rose and set. Joshua stopped both the sun and the moon to have time to finish a slaughter. With the moonwalk, the religious myth that sustained these notions could no longer be held. With our view of earthrise, we could see that the earth and the heavens were no longer divided but that the earth is in the heavens. . . . There is a unity in the universe.

We can resist this perspective. When Neil Armstrong walked on the moon, many in the Islamic world were scandalized. The moon had been desecrated; there would be hell to pay. I was working that summer in Washington, D.C., as a groundskeeper for the Park Service. The moonwalk scandalized my African-American co-workers for a different reason. They didn't believe that it had happened. A Hollywood production, they said, whipped up to take people's minds off real problems—racism, the plight of the poor—our own idolatrous proof of Marx's characterization of religion (here civic religion) as the opiate of the masses.

Other religious overtones spring to mind, such as the astronauts' reading of Genesis 1, broadcast back to earth from the spacecraft on its return flight from the heavens. "Then God said, 'Let us make man in our image, after our likeness; and let them have dominion over the fish of the sea, and over the birds of the air, and over the cattle, and over all the earth.' " From today's perspective these are ominous words, in stark contrast to those of the Psalmist, "The earth is the Lord's and the fullness thereof."

Ancient theologians understood hubris and nemesis—presumption and fall—in the context of a divided ground of spiritual being, ours and God's. Unsolicited trespass beyond our appointed territory invited swift destruction. Today two major shifts alter our perspective. First, we are no longer the center of the universe. Not only does the sun not revolve around the earth but the sun itself is a lesser sun in the great scheme of things, a peripheral star. The other shift is that, while we recognize ourselves to have receded in cosmic importance, we continue to augment our mastery to such an extent that powers once considered the unique prerogatives of God (creation and apocalypse) are now within human grasp. No longer are we responsible only for our personal salvation; we are responsible also for the cultivation and preservation of life itself. Having arrogated God's prerogative, we inherit certain essential responsibilities once thought to be exclusively part of the heavenly domain. This presents an ethical challenge. John Kennedy framed it clearly in his inaugural address: "Here on earth God's work has truly become our own."

In addition to deepening our ethical obligations, such an understanding can fire our theological imaginations as well. Being made of the very matter that composes our home invests our earthly journey with metaphysical moment. We move within and beyond ourselves into a new realm of encounter and discovery. Russell Hoban alludes to this promise in his novel *Pilgermann*: "As far as I could see, the will of God was simply that everything possible would indeed be possible. Within that limitation the choice was ours, the reckoning God's. And God was in us, that was the Fire of it, that was the Garden of it, at the center of every soul and contiguous with infinity."

Ancient cartographers would illustrate seas beyond the limit of the known world with monsters: "Here there be dragons." Yet travelers who venture to map the human soul can return through the gates of the unknown with a profound sense that—at the limits of their vision—they may catch within themselves a glimpse of God's inner sanctum.

Henry David Thoreau did precisely that, describing his own spiritual science as "home-cosmography." Seeking evidence of the divine within the ordinary and God's residence within his own mind, he traveled within himself on a cosmic mission.

I hear beyond the range of sound,
I see beyond the verge of sight,
New earths—and skies—and seas—around,
And in my day the sun doth pale his light.

For Thoreau, to discover ourselves within the cosmos is to discern the cosmos within ourselves.

⁂

At the outset of my ministry, within my own Unitarian tradition, I found confirmation for my beliefs more in Jefferson's rational than in Thoreau's and Emerson's mystical approach to faith. I believed only in what I could comprehend. The ethics of Jesus moved me; home cosmography did not. I approached the creation as a taxidermist, not a worshiper. Even the most fragile and beautiful manifestations of the creation I examined as a blindered lepidopterist might a butterfly. I netted, chloroformed, and mounted them for observation. After long study of my favorite specimens, I could only conclude that butterflies don't fly.

Over the years to follow, I attempted much the same thing in response to my life's monsters. I muzzled as many as I could, all the while doing everything possible to keep those that eluded me from hiding under my bed and haunting my sleep. Unfortunately, I accomplished this only by deepening my sleep, by medicating against consciousness and thereby muting my conscience. Keeping my fears at bay, not only was I not at home in the universe—I was not at home in myself.

Well before I faced down my demons, my theology took a transcendental turn. Several funerals after I began my work in the parish, I began to discover that the self-confident posture of Enlightenment philosophy did not serve me as well as it appears to have served Thomas Jefferson. Jefferson and the French *philosophes* who inspired him brought God home by clipping God's wings, by domesticating mystery and caging it. I know that there are many possible ways to interpret God (or to interpret the creation without benefit of God); the ones that finally worked for me are not for everyone. But early in my ministry I needed to make room in my theology for a more capacious, unfathomable power. I had to clear a place for mystery on the altar of my hearth, which before I had crowded with icons to knowledge. As for the walls of my study, the eighteenth-century classical lithographs of architectural drawings that I favored while at divinity school could no longer divert my awareness from the cracking plaster behind them and between. I needed something more arresting and humbling, something like Vincent van Gogh's *Starry Night*.

I still try to approach the world with as clear a mind as possible. As surely you have heard or said, God wouldn't have given us minds and not intended for us to use them. But, ever since the Renaissance and Reformation, modern critics of the traditional worldview have been conducting a theological search-and-destroy mission, its purpose to strip away the trappings of religion in an attempt to restore to faith its intellectual and ethical integrity. This endeavor is a little like trying to find the seed of an onion by peeling away its layers. Eventually, nothing is left but our tears. If wary of superstition, I am not at all convinced that by dint of sheer rationality we can come close to apprehending the mystery of being alive and having to die. *Life is a miracle that can't be explained without explaining it away.* Our most profound encounters lead inexorably from the rational to what might be called the transrational realm.

This doesn't mean that the search for truth or knowledge is in vain. Discoveries such as the Heisenberg uncertainty principle—pointing out that the experimenter affects the data—are breakthroughs in knowledge. Nor does it suggest that all truths are relative (and therefore functionally interchangeable), only that no truth within the compass of human knowledge is absolute or final. That ultimate Truth is not privileged to any one particular religious, philosophical, or scientific system in no way rules out the possible existence of such a Truth (or God). Reflecting the best of postmodern thinking, it simply underscores the intrinsic limitations of every human truth claim.

Many leading scientists are far ahead of us in this regard. From subatomic "strings" to cosmic "inflation" and "dark energy," recent metaphors in physics and cosmology make little sense according to known canons of rationality. Probing the mysteries of the universe and the mind, researchers on the cutting edge of knowledge find themselves moving freely between the rational and transrational realms. Where does that leave the poor camp followers, who believe in science but don't embrace mystery? Having traded God for truth, they are left with neither.

Reason and rationality are entirely different things. Drawing from experience, reason dares us to imagine beyond what mere rationality excludes. Rationality excludes only the irrational. There is gain in this exclusion, for much religion today continues to be irrational. That is to say, it bases its truth claims on the evidence of a privileged revelation. No matter by what faith, claims of scriptural inerrancy (with the scriptures, not the cosmos, as primary evidence) limit rational activity to so closed a circle as to be indeed irrational. But an equally serious charge can be leveled at rational religion and irreligion both. In a principled flight from irrationality, rationalists betray reason by losing sight of the transrational realm (the world of myth and parable, of poetry and paradox), where rationalism is not rejected but transcended.

The danger of excluding the transrational realm from our field of contemplation is that, when we sophisticate our minds against mystery, each irrational straw man we kill may clear a place for an equally insidious self-delusion. Presuming to understand, even to control, powers so beyond our control and understanding as to be in fact unimaginable, we lose our sense of humility and awe. We take the creation for granted rather than receiving it with fitting gratitude as an undeserved, unfathomable gift. When rationalism supplants mystery, our imagination and sense of wonder are just as likely to die as are the gods we pride ourselves for having killed.

Today my theology might best be described as a form of Christian universalism—universalism modified by Christianity, not the other way around. Universalism can be perverted in two ways. One is to elevate one truth into a universal truth ("My church is the one true church"); the other is to reduce distinctive truths to a lowest common denominator ("All religion is merely a set of variations upon the golden rule"). The universalism I embrace does neither. It holds that the same Light shines through all our windows, but each window is different. The windows modify the Light—refracting it in myriad ways, shaping it in different patterns, suggesting various meanings—even as Christianity does my universalism.

One can be a Buddhist universalist, a Pagan universalist, a Humanist universalist, a Jewish universalist. But one cannot in any meaningful sense be a Universalist universalist; it is impossible to look out every window. Neither can one be, say, a Universalist Christian. When the modifier of one's faith becomes its nominative, primary allegiance is relegated to but one part of the whole that encompasses it.

⁂

Plato's most memorable image is his metaphor of the cave from the *Republic.* We are sitting, facing a wall, our legs and necks chained so that we cannot turn and see what is going on behind us. Through the opening of the cave, the light shines. Between it and us there is a ramp along which figures walk, carrying vessels and statues. Their images play in shadow form before us on the wall of the cave. What would happen, Socrates asks, if we were to be freed from our bondage and invited to leave our prison and walk toward the light? At first we would be blinded. But even once our eyes became accustomed to the brightness, if an instructor were to point out the figures and objects along the ramp and name them for us, would we recognize them?

Socrates suggests that initially we would not, for they would be far less familiar to us than the shadows they cast. If eventually we were enlightened as to the true nature of things and then returned to share our newfound knowledge with our fellow prisoners (those who had never loosed themselves from their straitjackets), they would surely shake their heads and say that we had returned from up above "without our eyes; and that it was better not even to think of ascending; and if any one tried to loose another and lead him up to the light, let them only catch the offender, and they would put him to death."

This parable addresses the question of appearance and reality. We are under tremendous pressure to conform to the mores, opinions, practices, and prejudices of our time. Often we do so without question, because we know no better. We too see more clearly—or think we do—in the darkness than in the light. There is even a strange kind of solidarity in the darkness, grounded in our common fear of the unknown. Yet to explore the unknown pays great dividends, especially within our souls.

To expand Plato's metaphor, imagine the world as a vast cathedral. This cathedral is as ancient as is humankind. Its cornerstone is the first altar, marked with the tincture of blood and blessed by tears. Search for a lifetime—which is all we are surely given—and we shall never know its limits, visit all its transepts, worship at its myriad shrines, nor span its celestial ceiling with our gaze.

The builders have labored in this cathedral from time immemorial. Daily, work begins that shall not be finished in the lifetime of the architects who planned it, the patrons who paid for it, the builders who construct it, or the expectant worshipers. Nonetheless, throughout human history one generation after another has labored lovingly, sometimes fearfully, crafting memorials and consecrating shrines. Untold numbers of these today collect dust in long-undisturbed chambers; others (cast centuries or millennia ago from their once respected places) lie shattered in shards on the cathedral floor. Not a moment passes without the dreams of long-dead dreamers being outstripped, crushed, or abandoned, giving way to new visions, each immortal in reach, ephemeral in grasp.

Above all else, contemplate the windows. In the Cathedral of the World there are windows beyond number, some long forgotten, covered with many patinas of dust, others revered by millions, the most sacred of shrines. Each in its own way is beautiful. Some are abstract, others representational, some dark and meditative, others bright and dazzling. Each tells a story about the creation of the world, the meaning of history, the purpose of life, the nature of humankind, the mystery of death. The windows of the cathedral are where the Light shines through.

As with all extended metaphors, this one is imperfect. The Light of God (or Truth or Being Itself) shines not only upon us but out from within us as well. Together with the windows, we are *part of* the cathedral, not *apart from* it. We constitute an interdependent web of being. The cathedral is constructed out of star stuff, and so are we. We are that part of the creation that contemplates itself.

Because the cathedral is so vast, our life so short and vision so dim, we are able to contemplate only a tiny part of the whole creation. We can explore but a handful of its many chambers. Our allotted span permits us to reflect on the play of darkness and light through remarkably few of its myriad windows. Yet, since the whole is contained in each of its parts, as we ponder and act on insights derived from even a single reflection, we may experience self-illumination. We also discover or invent meanings that invest both the creation and our lives with coherence and meaning.

A twenty-first-century theology based on the concept of one Light and many windows promises to its adherents both breadth and focus. Honoring many different religious approaches, it excludes only the truth claims of absolutists. This is because fundamentalists—whether on the right or on the left—claim that the Light shines through their window only. Skeptics draw the opposite conclusion. Seeing the bewildering variety of windows and observing the folly of the worshipers, they conclude that there is no Light. But the windows are not the Light, they are only where the light shines through.

Not that we need reminders, but religion can be deadly, especially on a shrinking globe where, with discrete backyards things of the past, conflicting faith positions contest one another in almost every human precinct. Yet every generation has had its holy warriors, hard-bitten zealots, terrorists for "Truth" and "God," for whom the world is large enough for only one true faith. Not only have they been taught to worship at a single window but they also incite one another to demonstrate their faith by throwing stones through other people's windows. Tightly drawn, their logic makes a demonic kind of sense:

1. Religious answers respond to life and death questions, which happen to be the most important questions of all.
2. You and I may come up with different answers.
3. If you are right, I must be wrong.
4. But I can't be wrong, because my salvation hinges on being right.
5. Therefore, short of abandoning my faith and embracing yours, in order to secure my salvation I am driven to ignore, convert, or destroy you.

Aristotle coined something called the law of the excluded middle. As a logical certainty, he asserted that A and not-A cannot both be true at once. By the light of my cathedral metaphor (and also by that of quantum uncertainty), Aristotle is wrong, at least with respect to theology. His logical certitude oversteps the law of experience. Contrast one stained-glass window (its dark center bordered by more translucent panes) with another (configured in the opposite fashion). Though the one Light shines through both, they will cast diametrically opposite shadow images on the cathedral floor (A and not-A, if you will). Even as we cannot gaze directly at the sun, we cannot stare directly into the Light of God. All the great world scriptures make this point. No one can look God in the eye. Truth therefore emerges only indirectly, as refracted through the windows of tradition and experience. "Tell me all the truth, but tell it slant," Emily Dickinson wrote. "Slant" is the only way in which truth *can* be told. Similarly, since the same light can be refracted in decidedly different ways (even A and not-A), the only religious truth claims we can dismiss completely are those that discount all other views for failing to conform to their own understanding of the creation.

One presumably impartial response to the war of conflicting theological passions is to reject religion entirely, to distance ourselves from those who attempt—always imperfectly—to interpret the Light's meaning. There are two problems with this perspective. The first is that such a rejection deprives us of a potentially deep encounter with the mysterious forces that impel our being, thereby limiting our ability to invent and discover meaning. The second is that none of us is actually able to resist interpreting the Light. Whether we choose the windows that enlighten existence for us or inherit them, for each individual the light and darkness mingle more or less persuasively as refracted through one set of windows or another. Attracted to the partial clarification of reality that emerges in patterns of light and the playing of shadows, even people who reject religion are worshipers of truth as they perceive it. Their windows too become shrines.

Because none of us is able fully to comprehend the truth that shines through another person's window, nor to apprehend the falsehood that we ourselves may perceive as truth, we can easily mistake another's good for evil, and our own evil for good. A twenty-first-century universalism tempers the consequences of inevitable ignorance and meets the need for focus, while addressing the overarching crisis of our times:

dogmatic division in an ever more intimate, fractious, yet interdependent world. It posits the following fundamental principles:

1. There is one Power, one Truth, one God, one Light.
2. This Light shines through every window in the cathedral.
3. No one can perceive it directly, the mystery being forever veiled.
4. Yet on the cathedral floor and in the eyes of each beholder, refracted and reflected through different windows in differing ways, it plays in patterns that suggest meanings, challenging us to interpret and live by these meanings as best we can.
5. Each window illumines Truth (with a capital *T*) in a unique way, leading to various truths (with a lowercase *t*), and these in differing measure according to the insight, receptivity, and behavior of the beholder.

Though set in a modern frame, my cathedral metaphor recalls certain of the old theologies and employs traditional religious language. It embraces the faith expressed by St. Paul in the Acts of the Apostles, when he preaches to the Greeks that we are here "to seek God, and, it might be, touch and find him; though indeed he is not far from each one of us, for in him we live and move, in him we find our being." So understood, mythic exploration of our cosmic home becomes itself a parable. We gaze into the universe with God's eyes.

~ ~ ~

If I were to single out two guides among the many who help me bring God home, they would be Ralph Waldo Emerson and the Sufi mystic Rumi, both poets schooled in paradox and gifted with an eye for God's presence. Before closing, I should like to express my profound gratitude to each of them. When I had reached the point that, unless God was everywhere, I could never have hoped to find God within the narrow and forbidding walls I had constructed around my life, Emerson and Rumi reminded me that God might indeed be everywhere, even in my dark chambers. Then they helped me knock down the walls of my prison, letting the Light shine in.

Like Margaret Fuller, Emerson was a Transcendentalist. For years I slighted Emerson. Today he is among my favorite guides. To the cosmic voyager Emerson cautions, "Thou seek'st in globe and galaxy, He hides in pure transparency." Rather than losing himself in the cosmos, Emerson perceives God's tracings in the most intimate created object. For him, "the fresh rose . . . gives back the bending heavens in dew." He views his own life through the same cosmic microscope. When he finds a fresh rhodora on one of his many walks through the woods neighboring Concord, a recognition of divine kinship tempers his solitude. Of this beauty ("its own excuse for being") Emerson ponders,

I never thought to ask, I never knew;
But, in my simple ignorance, suppose
The self-same Power that brought me there brought you.

One of Emerson's tough-minded critics, the philosopher George Santayana, dismissed the sentimentality of Transcendentalism while admiring Emerson's ability to entrance an audience. "They flocked to him and listened to his word, not so much for the sake of its absolute meaning as for the atmosphere of candour, purity, and serenity that hung about it, as about a sort of sacred music." With a tin ear for sacred music, Santayana truly puzzled over Emerson's appeal. The man had no doctrine. The deeper he got into something, the vaguer and more metaphorical Emerson became. "Did he know what he meant by Spirit or the 'Over-Soul'?" Santayana asks. "Could he say what he understood by the terms, so constantly on his lips, Nature, Law, God, Benefit, or Beauty? He could not." Santayana is right. The old language is imprecise. All Emerson could do was to mirror his awe and humility in childlike reverence for the creation and his small yet consciousness-charged place in it. Santayana was at home in his books and nothing if not confident in his aesthetic doctrine; Emerson, with Fuller, was at home in the universe, because the universal God dwelled in his mind and heart.

Emerson would have understood Santayana's criticism, having cautioned, "Heaven walks among us ordinarily muffled in such triple or tenfold disguises that the wisest are deceived and no one suspects the days to be gods." He resisted codifying his experience of life and God into doctrine for another reason as well. He had no interest in having others see through his eyes. For Emerson, a true disciple would be one who would greet each dawn in a new way, one unique to his or her particular insight and vision. For this same reason, he called on American artists and philosophers to liberate themselves from bondage to the received old world models—not that these were false or bad in and of themselves, only that what was authentic to the experience of others would prove itself inauthentic for a different time and place. Not only is derived experience certain to leave the creation muffled in multifold disguises but also there are as many gates to perception as exist travelers who would venture to enter them. Since no doctrine can possibly encompass our collective intuition or experience of God, neither can one individual walk for another down the road that leads to God. Each of us defines the road we take, and our heart determines its destination.

Thomas Merton compared the great religious traditions to spokes of a wheel, all of which lead to one and the same hub. Emerson instead saw each of us at the hub, following out one spoke or another toward the same rim and beyond, with the entire wheel turning by divine motion. One can play with this metaphor in many ways. In his first sermon the Buddha spoke of "the wheel of truth," with its eight spokes representing our eightfold path to right conduct and our "constant mindfulness the hub on which the axle of truth is borne." For him, this wheel would take us home by guiding our conduct in such a way that we might find liberation from the misdirection of self by untutored desire. Emerson took a more cosmic view, echoing that of the seventeenth-century Metaphysical poet Thomas Traherne, whose childlike sense of God and self is that both are of the same spirit, with each soul

Being Simple like the Deity
In its own Center is a Sphere
Not shut up here, but everywhere.

Transcendentalism appears in many of the world's religions. The Sufi mystic Mansur al-Hallaj writes, "I saw my Lord with the eye of the Heart. I said: 'Who are you?' He answered: 'You.' " In such expressions Transcendentalist mysticism affirms not that we are God (for we are but a tiny part of the creation), only that God—greater than all and yet present in each—dwells within us.

Like Emerson, Rumi too imposes no doctrine. His enthusiasm for life inspires us to look for God with new eyes, yet our own. Interpreting one passage of the Qu'ran, Rumi writes,

> Lo, I am with you always *means when you look for God,*
> *God is in the look of your eyes,*
> *In the thought of looking, nearer to you than to your self,*
> *Or things that have happened to you*
> *There's no need to go outside.*

Rumi was born in Afghanistan in the early thirteenth century. His father was a theologian and jurist, a combination common to Muslim tradition. When he was a boy, Rumi's family emigrated to Turkey. When his father died Rumi inherited his father's position as a sheikh among the dervishes, an ecstatic yet orthodox Muslim sect. In his late thirties Rumi had an experience that would change his life. He met a wandering dervish, Shams of Tabriz, and almost at once became his disciple and closest friend. According to legend, Shams won his new apostle's heart when a professor asked the question "Who is greater, Muhammad or Bestami?"—noting that the teacher Bestami had proclaimed of himself, "How great is my glory!" whereas in his prayers Muhammad confessed to Allah, "We do not know You as we should." (In the Islamic tradition, the prophet Muhammad is not himself God but fully man.) Shams replied that Muhammad was the greater of the two. Whereas Bestami celebrated his possession of divine knowledge, Muhammad confessed the limits of his and was therefore ever searching to extend them. Unlike his most fanatical modern-day adherents, for Muhammad the way was always unfolding. With newfound humility Rumi reopened his own search, seeking manifestations of the divine presence ever more deeply within himself and widely within the creation. With Emerson, Rumi too recognized, "Mystery glows in the rose bed, the secret is hidden in the rose."

Legend tells that, jealous of his brotherly discipleship to Shams, Rumi's friends killed Shams. All we know for certain is that, when Shams disappeared, Rumi traveled far and wide in search for him. For years, bereft and lost, Rumi was spiritually homeless. Finally, one day when in Damascus, Rumi experienced a revelation, which he records in these simple words:

Why should I seek? I am the same as
He. His essence speaks through me.
I have been looking for myself.

Thus began the years of Rumi's triumphant artistry. No body of spiritual poetry compares in immediacy and power with the words in which Rumi invested God's mystic yet palpable—and almost always paradoxically received—presence.

Though he put his unique spin on the wheel metaphor, Rumi, too, believed that there are numberless paths, each leading to the same destination. "Every prophet, every saint has his path, but as they return to God, all are one." God can be discovered anywhere or nowhere depending on our own receptivity. Rumi tells the story of two pilgrims arguing as to whether God is in the fire or in the fountain. At the conclusion of their discussion, he suggests that the answer is neither and both: "The voice of the fire tells the truth saying, 'I am not fire. I am fountainhead. Come into me and don't mind the sparks.' "

Sarah York followed her heart to the Himalayas, venturing high into the mountains of the Annapurna range. From this lofty perch at first she felt homeless, alone in the cosmos. Later, camping in the village of Larjung, she went out one evening after dinner into the middle of the Kali Gandaki riverbed in order to get a sweeping, 360-degree view of the surrounding peaks, including the colossus, Daulaghiri. Reflecting on this experience in her book *Pilgrim Heart*, Sarah, a Unitarian Universalist minister, writes: "In that moonlit Himalayan bowl of astounding beauty, I felt much as I had before—lost, alone, and homeless. I also felt connected and at home."

To experience paradox is not to resolve but to embrace it. On the mountain crest, Sarah experienced the depth of despair; down in the valley she had, in the psychologist Abraham Maslow's term, a peak experience. As she describes this: "It occurred to me that I had come this far from home in order to feel lost in strangeness; to remove the structures of home and feel, bone-deep, an inner ache for the home I could neither describe nor remember. Now, however, I knew I was not lost or alien in the infinite universe, but rather immersed in it—a part of its immense grandeur." Alone in the riverbed, yet at home in the universe, Sarah York belted out the old hymn "How Great Thou Art." More than thirty years had passed since she had heard or sung this hymn, but the words came flooding back. She sang with such gusto that villagers came out of their homes to see what the fuss was all about.

Oh Lord my God, when I in awesome wonder,
Consider all the worlds thy hands have made,
I see the stars, I hear the rolling thunder,
Thy power throughout the universe displayed.

Then sings my soul, my savior God to thee,
How great thou art, how great thou art.
Then sings my soul, my savior God to thee,
How great thou art, how great thou art.

Today my soul sings much the same song. Not that God is always with me. I continue to jam the doors I try to open and shutter my windows against the Light. I run away sometimes, if less frequently than before, and on occasion I find myself lost at sea. More sadly, especially for those who love me, I return to the comforts of my prison house now and then to dwell in mock safety from my feelings. I still am sometimes frightened by the dark. The home fires may flicker. Pride crowds out humility more often than I would wish. My life is not always as open and therefore as hospitable as it should be. I have not yet made my peace with death. And I am numb to the universe as often as it floods my being with humility and awe. Nonetheless, on my good days, I too lift my voice and sing, "How great thou art, how great thou art."

Whether we bring God home or not is up to us. It depends solely on the breadth of our imaginations. The story is told of a Zen sage who sought enlightenment. Before practicing Zen, he said he saw mountains and rivers. When he was engaged in his pursuit of enlightenment, he did not see mountains and rivers. Upon attaining enlightenment, he saw mountains and rivers again. Awakening is like returning after a long journey and seeing the world—our loved ones, cherished possessions, and the tasks that are ours to perform—with new eyes. The question is not where to look for God in the universe but how. How, when we look upon the sun, to see, as William Blake did, "an Innumerable company of the Heavenly host crying, 'Holy, Holy, Holy is the Lord God Almighty.' "

Testifying to this, witnesses abound.

Vincent van Gogh opened the door of the asylum at St.-Rémy, beheld the firmament, "the Starry Night," and saw a masterpiece: nature trembling, dancing with energy; maker swirling, pulsating; star stuff; an orange crescent moon; the sensuous purple hills; and a simple village church, its steeple reaching tentatively into the vivid sky.

Admiral Richard Byrd gazed out upon an Antarctic sunset near the Bay of Whales, the day dying, the night being born, and heard the music of the spheres: "It was enough to catch that rhythm, momentarily, to be myself a part of it. In that instant I could feel no doubt our oneness with the universe. . . . It was a feeling that transcended reason, that went to the heart of our despair and found it groundless. The universe was a cosmos, not a chaos."

And the Hungarian author Hans Habe, interned by the Nazis during the war, arrived in America and ventured out one silvery evening, the sky gleaming like a frozen lake, to greet "the passersby . . . the houses on the road, the cows in the pastures, butterflies in the air, the earth that was fragrant and the heavens that were so close to me. I tried to find someone whom I could help. Never was anyone in rags so rich."

Three nights, just like every other night. Three epiphanies of Light, shining through the windows of the creation.

Homecoming

I was sitting with my wife, Carolyn, late one evening, the two of us in a hospital reception area, awaiting word from the doctor concerning whether the surgery to remove a rare cancerous tumor from our son Jacob's leg had been successful. Jacob spent the better part of sixth through eighth grade in either a wheelchair or a body cast. This was his fourth operation in half as many years. Three times the tumor had returned.

The operation went on longer than we anticipated. The last attendant had left the waiting room. Carolyn and I were alone. There was nothing more to say to each other that we hadn't said a hundred times before, so we sat in silence as the minutes passed. Then Carolyn reached out her hand to me. "We're so lucky," she said. "Life is such a gift."

Whenever someone asks me, or I ask myself, "What have I done to deserve this?" the larger answer is always "Nothing." We did nothing to deserve being born. We did nothing to earn life's privileges of joy and pain. And on the day we die, we will still know almost nothing about what life was all about.

Life on this planet is billions of years old. Our span of three score years and ten (give or take a score or two) is barely time enough to get our minds wet.

By cosmologists' latest reckoning, there are some 100 billion stars in our galaxy, and ours is one of perhaps 100 billion galaxies. And that is only our cosmos. There could be others. Divide the stars among us, and in our galaxy alone every individual alive on earth today would be the proud possessor of sixteen personal stars. If you choose to name yours (actually a fun thing to do), you can't start too soon. Naming one's own stars is more than a lifelong project. By my reckoning, the cosmic star-to-person ratio is 1.6 trillion to one.

So what do we do? Do we name our stars and shake our heads in humility and wonder? No. We sit on a single grain of sand on this vast cosmic beach and argue over who has the goods on God. Is it the atheist or the theist? The Hindu or the Buddhist? The Catholic or the Protestant? The Muslim or the Jew? We duel (sometimes to the death) over which religious teacher has the best insider information on God and the afterlife. Is it Jesus? The Buddha? Muhammad? How about Nietzsche, Gandhi, or Freud? Billions of accidents conspired to give each of these compelling teachers the opportunity even to teach. Knowing this—pondering numbers beyond reckoning—doesn't strip me of my faith. It inspires my faith. It makes me humble. It fills me with awe.

If our religion doesn't inspire in us a humble affection for one another and a profound sense of awe at the wonder of being, one of two things has happened. It has failed us, or we it. Should either be the case, we must go back to the beginning and start all over again. We must reboot our lives until the wonder we experience proves itself authentic by the quality of our response to it. I may not believe as Jesus did, but I should dearly hope to love as Jesus did, to forgive and embrace others as unconditionally as he. The principal challenge of theology today is to provide symbols and metaphors that will bring us, in all our glorious diversity, into closer and more celebratory kinship with one another as sons and daughters of life and death.

Jacob is fine. His tumor is in full remission. He even placed third in his weight class in his high school wrestling tournament. This aside—in fact, everything aside—Carolyn is still right. We are so very lucky. Life *is* a gift.

So where do we go from here? Coming full circle, I take my cue from T. S. Eliot:

> *What we call the beginning is often the end*
> *And to make an end is to make a beginning.*
> *The end is where we start from.*

ACKNOWLEDGMENTS

Authors customarily free the people who helped them write their books from all responsibility. I can't do that. Without the assistance of my family, friends, colleagues, and editors, not only would this book be poorer but it would not have been possible. To write a traveler's guide for others, I needed my own set of directions home. More than anyone my wife, Carolyn, with love and remarkable patience, has led me to recognize and follow the Light. Two dear friends, George Dorsey and Bill Thompson, also supported me with their wisdom and companionship, helping to make the past two years the most rewarding of my life. To all three I dedicate this book. It is truly theirs.

Many others have assisted me along the way. My splendid personal assistant, Megan Martin (who is family to me), worked magic on my first draft, turning it into something readable. Tim Bent, my editor at St. Martin's Press, is simply the finest editor with whom I have had the pleasure to work. His passion, knowledge, and insight complement a fine eye and sharp pencil. With the able aid of his assistant, Julia Pastore,

Tim devoted heart and soul to this book. I am deeply grateful to him.

Among the many at All Souls who have encouraged me in this project, I wish particularly to thank Mary-Ella Holst, who read several drafts and kept me from wandering too far off track. Karen Tse, Alison Miller, and Kenneth Orliff (three of the Forrest Church Scholarship recipients at Harvard Divinity School) each reciprocated with thoughtful criticism and support. For their kind assistance, I also thank my ministerial colleagues Stephen Kendrick and Stephen Bauman; Kelly Murphy Mason, a student at Union Theological Seminary; and the All Souls staff members Annie Gorycki, Suzanne May, Candice Thompson, and Scott Will. Finally, I wish to thank my research assistant, Adrien Smith of Wellesley College, who ably helped me tie up loose ends in preparing the manuscript for publication.

For acknowledgments of a different order, I should mention how this book fits into my body of published work. To illustrate my life and also to support my narrative, I have recast several stories here from my early books, *Father & Son, The Devil & Dr. Church, Entertaining Angels, The Seven Deadly Virtues,* and *Everyday Miracles.* My definitions of God and religion also date to my earliest published writings. Should anyone trouble to trace my theological development from my writings, he or she will therefore discover more continuity than discontinuity. In one respect that is correct. Since I emerged from the rational aridity of my school days and earliest ministry, the intellectual underpinnings of my universalism have remained quite constant. I tentatively began moving from the letter toward the spirit of my own beliefs in *A Chosen Faith,* my introduction to Unitarian Universalism. With respect to the awakening I chronicle here, the gradual unfolding of a more personal dimension to my religious thought developed over the past decade, hinted at in *God and Other Famous Liberals* and embodied more expressively in *Life Lines* and *Lifecraft*. As I travel onward in my quest to bring God home, I have no quarrel with my earlier statements of belief—beyond my tendency then to intellectualize what now I feel. Yet what a world of difference: to feel, not merely know, what one believes.

One final word. I completed this book on Labor Day, one week before the terrorist attack on America. In the wake of this tragedy, my beliefs stand as written. If anything—charged with new moment—they carry me forward on stronger wings.

All Souls Unitarian Church
New York City
Thanksgiving 2001

GUIDES AND COMPANIONS

Should you wish to delve further into the pilgrimage literature cited here, I can think of no better starting place than the first ten chapters of St. Augustine's *Confessions.* There are many editions; I cite Maria Boulder's translation (Vintage Spiritual Classics, 1997). I remain fond of two of the older translations of Dante's *Divine Comedy,* Laurence Binyon's verse translation in *The Portable Dante* (Viking, 1947) and Dorothy Sayers's prose version (Penguin, 1988). John Bunyan's *Pilgrim's Progress* (Oxford University Press, 1998) might be read in conjunction with Nathaniel Hawthorne's "The Celestial Rail-road" (in *Nathaniel Hawthorne: Tales and Sketches,* Library of America, 1982). Homer's *Odyssey* always repays a visit. For a verse translation, I suggest that of Robert Fitzgerald (Farrar, Straus & Giroux, 1998); here I quote the prose translation by E. V. Rieu (Penguin, 1991).

For a more open-ended search, you might begin with the anthology *Pilgrim Souls* (Touchstone, 1999). The editors Amy Mandelker and Elizabeth Powers have gathered pivotal passages from a number of spiritual autobiographies, including selections from Petrarch, Tolstoy, Johannes Jøgensen, Charles Colson, Eldridge Cleaver, and Madeleine L'Engle (who also wrote the introduction). Itself illuminating, this collection will likely entice you to read further in its sources.

Among the many contemporary spiritual autobiographies, my own touchstones include Anne Lamott's *Traveling Mercies* (Anchor Books, 1999); Frederick Buechner's *Sacred Journey* (Harper & Row, 1982), *Now and Then* (Harper & Row, 1982), and *A Room Called Remember* (Harper & Row, 1984); Dan Wakefield's *Returning* (Beacon Press, 1997); and Sarah York's *Pilgrim Heart* (Jossey-Bass, 2001). I also recommend anything by Annie Dillard (beginning with *Pilgrim at Tinker Creek*) and, of slightly earlier vintage, C. S. Lewis's *Surprised by Joy* (Harcourt Brace Jovanovich, 1955); Thomas Merton's *Seven Storey Mountain* (McFarland & Company, 1998); and Dag Hammarskjöld's *Markings* (Ballantine, 1983).

As for the poets, William Wordsworth's pilgrimage poem, *The Prelude*, is excerpted in many anthologies; you will find all its redactions in *The Prelude: Four Texts* (Penguin, 1996). Samuel Taylor Coleridge's "Rime of the Ancient Mariner" appears in two versions in *Coleridge: The Complete Poems* (Penguin Classics, 1997). T. S. Eliot's "Four Quartets" is included in *T. S. Eliot: The Complete Poems and Plays* (Harcourt Brace & Company, 1967). Should you wish to explore the English Metaphysical poets (George Herbert, Richard Crashaw, Henry Vaughan, and Thomas Traherne), their best-known poems are conveniently collected in *George Herbert and the Seventeenth-Century Religious Poets* (Norton, 1978). Rumi's output is vast and may be sampled in any number of translators' collections. A good place to begin is Coleman Barks's translations in *The Essential Rumi* (HarperCollins, 1995). Walt Whitman's *Leaves of Grass* and other poems are nicely presented in a recent Modern Library Classics edition (2000). For Ralph Waldo Emerson, among several good anthologies *The Essential Writings of Ralph Waldo Emerson* (Modern Library Paperbacks, 2000) contains a representative selection of essays and verse.

Finally, if you are not superstitious, open your Bible to the thirteenth chapters of Genesis, Deuteronomy, First Chronicles, and First Corinthians. Together they offer a road map for bringing God home.

Forrest Church lives with his wife, Carolyn, in New York City. They have four children, Frank, Nina, Jacob, and Nathan. For twenty-four years he has served as Senior Minister of All Souls Unitarian Church in Manhattan. He is the author of several books, most recently Life Lines *and* Lifecraft.

(*Continued from page iv*)